MENTAL DISORDER AND THE LAW

MENTAL DISORDER AND THE LAW:

A Primer for Legal and Mental Health Professionals

Hy Bloom, LL.B., M.D., F.R.C.P.(C.)

Hon. Richard D. Schneider, PH.D, LL.M., C.PSYCH.

IRWIN
LAW

Mental Disorder and the Law: A Primer for Legal and Mental Health Professionals
© Hy Bloom & Richard D. Schneider, 2006

Published in 2006 by

Irwin Law
14 Duncan Street
Suite 206
Toronto, Ontario
M5H 3G8

www.irwinlaw.com

Design: Heather Raven

ISBN-10: 1-55221-121-5   ISBN-13: 978-155221-121-2

Library and Archives Canada Cataloguing in Publication

Bloom, Hy
    Mental disorder and the law : a primer for legal and mental health professionals / Hy Bloom, Richard D. Schneider.

Includes bibliographical references and index.
ISBN 1-55221-121-5

1. Mentally ill offenders—Legal status, laws, etc. 2. Insanity—Jurisprudence—Canada. 3. Criminal procedure—Canada. I. Schneider, Richard D. II. Title.

KE514.B565 2006   345.71'050874   C2006-904547-X

The publisher acknowledges the financial support of the Government of Canada through the Book Publishing Industry Development Program (BPIDP) for its publishing activities.

We acknowledge the assistance of the OMDC Book Fund, an initiative of Ontario Media Development Corporation.

Printed and bound in Canada.

1 2 3 4 5   10 09 08 07 06

Summary Table of Contents

Detailed Table of Contents

CHAPTER TEN

DANGEROUS AND LONG-TERM OFFENDERS *237*

Acknowledgments

The original work upon which this book is based — *The Mentally Disordered Offender: An Electronic Bench Book* (National Judicial Institute, 2005) — would not have been possible without the conceptual, editorial, and technical assistance of the National Judicial Institute (NJI) staff: Susan Lightstone, Christine Woodrow, Benjamin Gianni, and Charles Nezan. We are also indebted to George M. Thomson, Senior Director, NJI, and to the Honourable Douglas H. Carruthers, Chair of the Ontario Review Board, for their foresight in recognizing the need for judicial education in this area, and for their encouragement throughout.

A work of this scope and depth is either made difficult or rendered impossible without a "point person" — a hands-on administrative and organization task master. In this regard, we express our gratitude to Saena Cha, who tirelessly oversaw this project, added her creative touch, and insured its unwavering course to press.

Hy Bloom dedicates this book to his family: Resa, Samuel, Wilbur, and Nellie-Belle. Richard Schneider dedicates this book to his children: Heidi, Erik, and Nils.

Introduction

Over the past decade or so, Canada's criminal courts have had to deal with escalating numbers of mentally disordered accused. The swelling numbers of "criminalized" mentally disordered accused has neither been an anticipated nor welcomed state of affairs, and there does not appear to be any reason to believe that the situation will reverse itself soon. Nevertheless, the criminal justice system has had to respond.

The Attorneys General in a number of provinces have implemented "diversion" programs for mentally disordered accused as a vehicle for reconnecting these unfortunate individuals with the civil mental health care systems from which they have become disconnected. In Toronto, in addition to the diversion program, a specialized court has been set up to deal exclusively with this group. The court's mandate is to expedite the resolution of preliminary mental health issues and reduce the probability of reoffending. Apart from dealing with scores of accused whose fitness to stand trial has come to be questioned, the court also attends to bail hearings, disposition hearings, sentencing, and trials of criminal responsibility. The court runs every day and is staffed by psychiatrists and social workers. A court based upon the U.S. drug court model has been set up in St. John, New Brunswick, to deal with mentally disordered accused on a voluntary basis.

With the proclamation of Bill C-30 in 1992 we now have a "mini-code'" contained in Part XX.1 of the *Criminal Code*,[1] specifically dedicated to the mentally disordered accused. Since the proclamation of Bill C-30, there have been a number of important decisions rendered by the Supreme Court of Canada. The first such decision, and perhaps the most important in terms of colouring the new statutory landscape, is *Winko v. British Columbia (Forensic*

---

1   R.S.C. 1985, c. C-46.

Psychiatric Institute).[2] Madame Justice McLachlin (as she then was) sets the stage as follows:

> In response to Swain, Parliament introduced sweeping changes by enacting Part XX.1 of the *Criminal Code* in 1991: *An Act to amend the Criminal Code (mental disorder) and to amend the National Defence Act and the Young Offenders Act in consequence thereof*, S.C. 1991, c. 43. Part XX.1 reflected an entirely new approach to the problem of the mentally ill offender, based on a growing appreciation that treating mentally ill offenders like other offenders failed to address properly the interests of either the offenders or the public. The mentally ill offender who is imprisoned and denied treatment is ill-served by being punished for an offence for which he or she should not in fairness be held morally responsible. At the same time, the public facing the unconditional release of the untreated mentally ill offender was equally ill-served. To achieve the twin goals of fair treatment and public safety, a new approach was required.[3]

Part XX.1 rejects the notion that the only alternatives for mentally ill people charged with an offence are conviction or acquittal; it proposes a third alternative. Under the new scheme, once an accused person is found to have committed a crime while suffering from a mental disorder that deprived the accused of the ability to understand the nature of the act or know that it was wrong, that individual is diverted into a special stream. Thereafter, the court or a review board conducts a hearing to decide whether the person should be kept in a secure institution, released on conditions, or unconditionally discharged. The emphasis is on achieving the twin goals of protecting the public and treating the mentally ill offender fairly and appropriately. Justice McLachlin's words poignantly describe the core of Part XX.1: the recognition of mentally disordered accused as a unique group with special needs, and the protection of the public from the harm they might perpetrate.

An earlier version of this work, entitled *The Mentally Disordered Offender*, was written specifically for the National Judicial Institute's Electronic Bench Book series as an overview of the key subjects judges were likely to encounter in their day-to-day work with mentally disordered offenders. The premise was to meld psychiatric/clinical information with key legal principles, case law, and applicable statutory provisions. The design of the work allowed judges to quickly access relevant theoretical and practical information from

---

2   *Winko v. British Columbia (Forensic Psychiatric Institute)*, [1999] 2 S.C.R. 625.

3   *Ibid.* at para. 20.

both disciplines (psychiatry and law) and their interface at the press of a key or roll of a mouse. That same practical approach has been preserved in this work, although it was necessarily restructured and adapted to suit the needs of a wider readership, and to include information in print that was previously only available through a hyperlink.

The subjects we chose to include in this volume were selected from our experience straddling both disciplines. The chapters, for the most part, follow the logical sequence of addressing the issues a mentally disordered accused is likely to encounter along a temporal continuum from arrest to sentencing, or, in the case of an accused found not criminally responsible (NCR), until that point when he is absolutely discharged by a provincial or territorial review board.

We hope that this book is informative, promotes understanding, and demystifies an area of which both mental health providers and lawyers have been wary historically. Collaboration between the two disciplines will undoubtedly play a pivotal role in facilitating the provision of service to this afflicted and invariably underserviced population.

CHAPTER ONE

Basic Psychiatric Terms and Concepts

The purpose of this chapter is to introduce the reader to basic terms and concepts within the discipline of psychiatry, as they arise in the course of dealing with mentally disordered accused. The list of definitions for mental disorders, symptoms, treatments, psychological tests, and other investigative procedures and laboratory tests contained in this chapter is far from exhaustive; it covers the terms legal practitioners are most likely to encounter when working in this field.

A. *DIAGNOSTIC AND STATISTICAL MANUAL OF MENTAL DISORDERS (DSM IV-TR)*

Analogous to the case with almost all medical disorders, classification of psychiatric conditions and setting out the clinical criteria that define the condition is an evolving process. Whether a proposed condition has sufficiently definable features to achieve a threshold for consideration as a syndrome or diagnosis generally results from the collection, synthesis, and critical appraisal of substantial amounts of information derived from reviews of published literature, analyses and re-analyses of collected data, and field trials. Work groups that collect this data ultimately report to a task force which submits its recommendations for approval to the American Psychiatric Association's Committee on Psychiatric Diagnosis and Assessment.

What constitutes a mental disorder is never fixed and unchangeable, and, in fact, can change with the course of time to not only reflect new science in the field, but also changes in the social landscape. Homosexuality is the most frequently cited example of this. It was considered a psychiatric disorder over the tenure of an earlier edition of the *Diagnostic and Statistical*

Manual of Mental Disorders[1] (DSM), but was delisted as a mental disorder in a subsequent edition of the DSM following an American Psychiatric Association plebiscite on the subject in 1973, which was inspired by several years of demonstrations by gay activists at annual meetings of the American Psychiatric Association.

The *Diagnostic and Statistical Manual of Mental Disorders* has gone through six revisions—some minor and some major—since the first edition was published in 1952.[2] DSM I and DSM II, both of which predate a virtual explosion of research into the biological basis of psychiatric conditions, were very psychodynamic in their approach. The etiology (or origin) of psychiatric disorders was thought more likely to have its roots in upbringing and environmental events than in neurochemical dysfunction. Cruder distinctions, for example, between psychosis and neurosis dominated these earlier editions of the DSM, although, again, both were seen as problems emanating from the person's upbringing and psychology, and not as disturbances in their biology. *Psychoses* were breaks in realities frequently associated with hallucinations and delusions, whereas *neuroses* were thought of as milder mental disorders, typically characterized by depression and anxiety, which, at the most, involved minor distortions of reality.

In the third edition of the DSM,[3] the psychodynamic model was supplanted by the biopsychosocial model. Seven years later, DSM III-R[4] revised a number of the criteria for mental disorders listed in DSM III.

DSM IV-TR is the acronym for the *Diagnostic and Statistical Manual of Mental Disorders*, 4th edition, Text Revision.[5] The DSM was created to establish a uniform and common language amongst psychiatrists. Setting the specific criteria for a mental disorder would facilitate communication, and clarity would foster research into mental disorders. DSM IV-TR is fundamentally similar to its predecessor, the fourth edition of the *Diagnostic and*

---

1   American Psychiatric Association, *Diagnostic and Statistical Manual of Mental Disorders*, 2d ed. (Washington, DC: American Psychiatric Association, 1968) [DSM II].

2   American Psychiatric Association, *Diagnostic and Statistical Manual of Mental Disorders* (Washington, DC: American Psychiatric Association, 1952) [DSM I].

3   American Psychiatric Association, *Diagnostic and Statistical Manual of Mental Disorders*, 3d ed. (Washington, DC: American Psychiatric Association, 1980) [DSM III].

4   American Psychiatric Association, *Diagnostic and Statistical Manual of Mental Disorders*, 3d ed., Revised (Washington, DC: American Psychiatric Association, 1987) [DSM III-R].

5   American Psychiatric Association, *Diagnostic and Statistical Manual of Mental Disorders*, 4th ed., Text Revision (Washington, DC: American Psychiatric Association, 2000) [DSM IV-TR].

Statistical Manual of Mental Disorders.[6] The clinical descriptions and diagnostic criteria for mental disorders most frequently implicated in criminal proceedings have not undergone any significant changes between those two editions. DSM IV-TR categorizes psychiatric disorders, and lists their diagnostic criteria. DSM IV-TR serves the following purposes:

- it fosters uniformity and clarity in its diagnostic approach to a patient;
- it creates a common language and operational criteria to ensure inter-rater consistency amongst clinicians;
- it provides, to the extent possible, research-based inclusion criteria for the various psychiatric conditions;
- it serves as an educational tool, providing descriptive narratives that precede the diagnostic criteria for any condition as well as reviewing the condition, its course, prevalence, associated features, familial pattern, and differential diagnosis; and
- it provides a multiaxial coding system that describes the interrelationships amongst conditions (mental, physical, characterological) that have impacted the individual's current and longitudinal functioning; considers current stressors that have implications for diagnosis, treatment and prognosis; and allows for the rating of the individual's current level of functioning. Relying on a multiaxial system provides a convenient format for organizing and communicating relevant information about a patient derived from a comprehensive and systematic evaluation that relies on a biopsychosocial model. A description of what is coded or described on each of the five axes in a multiaxial diagnosis system is provided below:

  ▷ *Axis I* describes clinical disorders and other conditions that may be a focus of clinical attention; for example, acquired major mental disorders such as schizophrenia, mood disorders, substance abuse disorders, learning disorders, or developmental disorders.

  ▷ *Axis II* describes conditions more intrinsic to the person which endure over a lifetime such as personality disorders and intellectual limitations.

  ▷ *Axis III* includes general medical conditions such as diabetes, positive HIV, or Hepatitis C status.

---

6   American Psychiatric Association, *Diagnostic and Statistical Manual of Mental Disorders,* 4th ed. (Washington, DC: American Psychiatric Association, 1994) [DSM IV].

> *Axis IV* rates the impact of psychosocial and environmental stressors.
> *Axis V* is the clinician's rating of the patient's global assessment of functioning (GAF). The GAF Scale, commonly referred to as Axis V of the DSM IV-TR multiaxial assessment and diagnosis system, is used to report the clinician's appraisal of an individual's overall level of functioning. The GAF scale may be useful especially in following an individual's clinical progress over time. It is reported numerically, using a range of 1–100. For example, a GAF of 100 would represent superlative functioning, whereas a very low GAF would indicate a risk of self-harm or harm to others, ongoing marked impairment in reality testing, etc.[7]

B. DEFINITIONS OF MENTAL DISORDER[8]

1) Definition in Psychiatry (per DSM IV-TR)

A mental disorder, in psychiatry, is defined as a clinically significant behavioural or psychological syndrome often associated with distress (a painful symptom), disability (impairment in functioning), or with a significantly increased risk of suffering death, pain, disability, or important loss of freedom.

2) Definition at Law

"A disease of the mind" is a legal concept which "... embraces any illness, disorder or abnormal condition which impairs the human mind and its functioning, excluding however self-induced states caused by alcohol or drugs, as well as transitory states, such as hysteria or concussion. Thus personality disorders may constitute disease of the mind.[9]

---

7   DSM IV-TR, above note 5 at 27–34.
8   All definitions that follow in this section are drawn from standard psychiatric, psychological and medical dictionaries, and the glossary section of the DSM IV-TR. The definitions are adapted, wherever necessary, to suit the requirements of the non-medical reader. In-depth descriptions of syndromes, conditions, symptoms, and concepts described in this work may be obtained from the primary sources cited under Bibliography. A full and precise description of the diagnostic criteria for any condition posited to be implicated in an accused's behaviour, exonerating or mitigating the accused's culpability, is likely to be necessary, in any event, before the psychiatric evidence is admitted by the court.
9   *R. v. Cooper*, [1980] 1 S.C.R. 1149 at 1159.

C. DEFINITIONS

1) Key Diagnoses

Adjustment Disorder: A condition of clinically significant emotional and/or behavioural symptoms caused by an identifiable psychosocial stressor of any severity that has occurred within three months of the stressor event. The distress experienced by the individual is generally in excess of what might be expected given the nature of the stressor, or the stressor causes impairment in social and occupational functioning that is exaggerated relative to the nature and severity of the stressor.

Amnestic Disorder: A condition characterized by memory impairment, generally caused by a known organic factor such as substance abuse, a medical condition, or, more specifically, a brain disorder.

Attention-Deficit/Hyperactivity Disorder: A disorder of children, with onset usually before the age of seven. It is characterized by persistent difficulties in sustaining attention; an inability to listen, concentrate, or persist at day-to-day tasks and activities; and by hyperactivity-impulsivity. The hyperactive child is constantly in motion, fidgets, and cannot seem to sit still. The disorder may persist into adulthood, generally in attenuated form. The adult form is referred to as residual attention-deficit or hyperactivity disorder.

Bipolar Mood Disorder: In this condition (formerly known as manic-depressive disorder), the individual experiences either depression or elation as the predominant mood. There may be no evidence whatsoever of the disorder during disease-free intervals (remission).

Conduct Disorder: According to DSM IV-TR's diagnostic criteria, a repetitive and persistent pattern of behaviour in which the basic rights of others or major age-appropriate societal norms or rules are violated, as manifested by the presence of three (or more) of the following criteria in the past twelve months, with at least one criterion present in the past six months:

- Aggression to people and animals (often bullies, threatens, or intimidates others):
  - often initiates physical fights
  - has used a weapon that can cause serious physical harm to others (for example, a bat, a brick, a broken bottle, a knife, a gun)
  - has been physically cruel to people
  - has been physically cruel to animals

  ▹ has stolen while confronting a victim (for example, mugging, purse snatching, extortion, armed robbery)
  ▹ has forced someone into sexual activity
- Destruction of Property:
  ▹ has deliberately engaged in fire setting with the intention of causing serious damage
  ▹ has deliberately destroyed others' property (other than by fire setting)
- Deceitfulness or theft:
  ▹ has broken into someone else's house, building, or car
  ▹ often lies to obtain goods or favours or to avoid obligations (that is, "cons" others)
  ▹ has stolen items of non-trivial value without confronting a victim (for example, shoplifting, but without breaking and entering; forgery)
- Serious violations of rules:
  ▹ often stays out at night despite parental prohibitions, beginning before age thirteen
  ▹ has run away from home overnight at least twice while living in parental or parental surrogate home (or once without returning for a lengthy period)
  ▹ is often truant from school, beginning before age thirteen[10]

Delirium: A state characterized by clouded consciousness; an inability to maintain or focus attention on external stimuli and to shift attention where necessary; disorganized thought and speech; disorientation; memory impairment; increased or decreased psychomotor activity; perceptual disturbances; and derangement of the normal sleep-wake cycle. Delirium is almost invariably attributable to a definable organic disturbance; for example, a toxin, intoxication or withdrawal from a substance, a general medical condition, or some other cerebral or metabolic insult.

Delirium Tremens: A severe alcohol withdrawal syndrome occurring in individuals who have been consuming substantial amounts of alcohol on a daily basis for a prolonged period of time (colloquially known as the DTs or "rum fits"). Within 48–72 hours of abrupt cessation, patients generally experience varying (but increasing) degrees of anxiety, confusion, disorientation, hallucinations, and agitation, accompanied by signs of physiological instability (elevated blood pressure, elevated temperature, and increased pulse rate).

---

10   DSM IV-TR, above note 5 at 98–99.

Delusional (Paranoid) Disorder: A mental disorder essentially characterized by one of a number of different types of delusions. While a delusion is the central feature of the disorder, other psychotic phenomena such as auditory hallucinations may be present, but are not likely to be prominent. Behaviour is usually not bizarre and thought processes are generally intact. Often, delusional patients do not appear conspicuously mentally ill. Occupational and social functioning may appear entirely unaffected until something in the environment—a stressor, or other event—brings the patient's delusions to the fore, or until the subject matter of the delusion(s) comes up in discussion (although patients with delusional disorder will often conceal their delusion, and more generally, what they are thinking and feeling). There are five subtypes:

- Somatic Type: The predominant theme is the delusional belief that the patient has some form of illness, disease, or physical defect.
- Persecutory Type: The patient believes that she is the victim of a conspiracy, or that she is otherwise being treated unfairly or will be harmed or thwarted by others.
- Grandiose Type: The patient conveys an unrealistic picture of greatness, importance, intelligence, ability, or power, or an affiliation with powerful and famous individuals, even with a deity.
- Erotomanic Type: The patient believes that a person (usually a person of higher social station) is in love with him.
- Jealous Type: The patient is convinced of her partner's infidelity.

Dementia: Alzheimer's is the best known type of dementia, which is generally characterized by multiple cognitive deficits, including impaired memory. Dementia may be classified according to its presumed cause.

Depressive Episode: A mood disorder characterized by a prevalently depressed mood and/or loss of interest in previously sustaining activities. These symptoms persist for more than two weeks and are accompanied by a number of (neurovegetative) symptoms that demonstrate disrupted body and/or mental functioning. Common symptoms of depression include changes in appetite, weight, sleep, energy, concentration, libido, future outlook, and self-esteem, as well as feelings of hopelessness and helplessness. Depression is also associated with a high risk for suicide.

Dissociative Disorders: A group of disorders in which the essential feature is an alteration of the normal integrative functions of consciousness, memory, and identity. Dissociated mental processes may be segregated from the remainder of mental processes. More common dissociative disorders include the following:

- Dissociative Identity Disorder (formerly known as Multiple Personality Disorder): A disturbance in identity where two or more distinct personalities or personality states exist within the same person.
- Dissociative Fugue (formerly known as Psychogenic Fugue): A disturbance in memory and identity in which the individual suddenly and unexpectedly travels to a new location and is unable to recall his past. He assumes a new identity, either in whole or in part.
- Dissociative Amnesia (formerly known as Psychogenic Amnesia): A sudden inability to recall important personal information.
- Depersonalization Disorder: A disturbance in consciousness where the individual feels detached from her body or mental processes.

Dysthymic Disorder: A condition within the spectrum of mood disorders. Its essential feature is a chronically depressed mood that lasts throughout most of the day and occurs on an almost daily basis for at least two years. Dysthymic disorder can otherwise be characterized as a chronic form of lower-grade depression. DSM IV-TR requires that in addition to the core depressive symptom, the individual should have experienced at least two of six symptoms associated with depression (see above).

Fetal Alcohol Syndrome/Effect: In more recent years, the original diagnostic entity, fetal alcohol syndrome, has progressively been replaced by the broader term "fetal alcohol spectrum disorder" (FASD). This subsumes a wide range of adverse effects on the fetus caused by alcohol consumption by the mother. In 1996, the Institute of Medicine defined several categories of pathology related to maternal alcohol abuse. The range of presentations includes cases with characteristics typical of the now-antiquated term fetal alcohol syndrome (FAS). These characteristics include growth retardation, typical facial changes and brain dysfunction, and neurodevelopmental abnormalities without the presence of the characteristic physical and facial changes. Children with fetal alcohol spectrum disorder[11] can suffer from a wide variety of cognitive and behavioural limitations as well as other problems including:

- attention deficit-hyperactivity disorder;
- poor judgment and inability to weigh consequences;
- inability to learn from previous experience;
- inappropriate or immature behaviour;
- lack of organization;

---

11   For a detailed review, see G. Koren & I. Nulman, *The Motherisk Guide to Diagnosing Fetal Alcohol Spectrum Disorder* (Toronto: The Hospital for Sick Children, 1992).

- learning problems;
- poor abstract reasoning;
- poor impulse control;
- poor adaptability; and
- speech, language, and other communication problems.

Huntington's Disease (or Huntington's Chorea): An inherited deteriorating neurological disease characterized by involuntary movements and dementia. Average age of onset is thirty-five years. The movement disorder is often heralded by a marked personality change. The condition is associated with a high risk of suicide. The disease has come to be colloquially referred to as "Woody Guthrie's Disease," after the folk legend who suffered from it.

Hypomania: Reflects a distinct period of mood alteration, lasting at least four days, which is characterized by a sense of exhilaration, euphoria, and optimism, as well as tireless activity, incessant loquacity, effervescence, uninhibited behaviour, reckless spending, and preoccupation with unrealistic schemes and solutions to problems. It is also called hypomanic state. Hypomania is not merely a milder form of mania. Although it shares a number of symptoms in common with mania, the degree of impairment characteristic of manic episodes is not nearly so severe in hypomania. The mood disturbance in hypomania is by definition not severe enough to cause marked impairment in social or occupational functioning, or to require hospitalization. Hypomania is not associated with psychotic features.

Impulse Control Disorders: Includes five disorders that are recognized by DSM IV-TR as representing a disturbance in the patient's ability to control a particular impulse: intermittent explosive disorder, kleptomania, pyromania, pathological gambling, and trichotillomania (compulsive hair pulling). DSM IV-TR distinguishes these conditions from other disorders associated with impulse control such as substance abuse disorders, paraphilias, and antisocial personality disorder.[12]

Malingering: The deliberate feigning of an illness or condition, or, the exaggeration of symptoms or disability, which is motivated by obvious external incentives or the prospect of (usually financial) gain. Examples include faking illness to avoid military conscription, to evade criminal responsibility, to avoid work, and to win financial compensation in a civil suit or disability claim, etc. Malingering must be suspected in any medico-legal context.

---

12   DSM IV-TR, above note 5 at 663.

Manic Episode: A mood disorder characterized by a distinct period of elevated, expansive, or irritable mood which lasts at least a week and during which at least three of the following symptoms are present: an increase in goal-directed activity or in level of restlessness; an acceleration of thought processes; pressured speech; grandiosity; a decreased need for sleep; distractibility; and involvement in potentially foolish and high-risk activities that show poor judgment (for example, poorly thought-out business ventures, spending sprees, sexual acting out, or substance abuse). Unlike the milder version of the condition, hypomania, mania may be accompanied by psychotic features. By definition, the mood disturbance is severe enough to cause marked impairment in occupational functioning, usual relationships, or social activities, or, severe enough to require hospitalization to prevent harm to others or to self.[13]

Mental Retardation: A condition characterized by intellectual functioning that is significantly sub-average as measured by well-accepted and standardized tests of intelligence.[14] Mild mental retardation can be further classified in terms of degree of severity:

- Mild: I.Q. between 50–55 and 70
- Moderate: I.Q. between 35–40 and 50–55
- Severe: I.Q. between 20–25 and 35–40
- Profound: I.Q. below 20 or 25

Mild mental retardation is the commonest form of the disorder, occurring in about 85 percent of those individuals classified as suffering from mental retardation.

Obsessive-Compulsive Disorder: An anxiety disorder in which persistent obsessions and/or compulsions are a significant source of distress and interfere with the individual's educational, vocational, recreational, and social functioning (see Section C.2, below).

Organic Mental Syndrome/Disorder: A group of mental disorders producing a wide variety of behavioural, perceptual, and emotional disturbances which share the common characteristic of being attributable to a particular organic factor. When the factor is known (as in alcohol withdrawal delirium), the illness is referred to as a "disorder." The use of the word "syndrome" refers to a cluster of behavioural signs and symptoms without reference to the presumed or known causative agent. The following are subsumed under the heading organic mental syndromes:

---

13 DSM IV-TR, above note 5 at 362.
14 For example, D. Wechsler, *Wechsler Intelligence Scale for Children — Revised*, 3d. ed. (San Antonio: Psychological Corp., 1991).

- delirium;
- dementia of unspecified origin;
- amnestic syndrome;
- organic hallucinosis;
- organic delusional syndrome;
- organic mood syndrome;
- organic anxiety syndrome;
- organic personality syndrome; and
- intoxication and withdrawal.

The following are subsumed under the heading organic mental disorders:

- primary degenerative (Alzheimer's) and multi-infarct dementia; and
- psychoactive substance-induced organic mental disorders: the mental disorder is caused by either intoxication with, or withdrawal from, a number of substances, including alcohol, amphetamines, cannabis, caffeine, cocaine, hallucinogens, nicotine, opioids, phencyclidine, sedatives, hypnotics, or anxiolytics.

Paraphilias: The essential feature of this group of psychosexual disorders is the necessity of unusual, deviant, or bizarre images, urges, or behaviours for sexual arousal. The arousing fantasies or activities involve either non-human objects (fetishism); the use of children or adult non-consenting individuals (pedophilia, exhibitionism, voyeurism, frotteurism, or toucheurism); or causing one's partner or one's self to experience either suffering or humiliation (rape, sadism, or masochism). The following are subsumed under the heading paraphilias: ephebophilia, exhibitionism, fetishism, frotteurism, hebephilia, pedophilia, sexual sadism, voyeurism, and zoophilia. See definitions for the various paraphilias in Chapter 7.

Personality Disorder: A pervasive and inflexible pattern of maladaptive personality functioning that generally begins in adolescence and continues throughout life, especially if untreated. Personality disorder denotes dysfunction severe enough to cause either subjective distress or significant impairment in social, occupational, and interpersonal functioning. DSM IV-TR lists ten personality disorders in three "clusters":[15]

CLUSTER A (COLLOQUIALLY REFERRED TO AS THE "MAD"):
Paranoid Personality Disorder: A personality disorder characterized by pervasive suspiciousness and distrust of others. Individuals with this personality

---

15   DSM IV-TR, above note 5 at 685.

pathology tend to be suspicious of the good intentions of others and tend to perceive innocuous actions as threatening. They are litigious, unforgiving, and ever-doubtful of the loyalty and trustworthiness of friends or associates. They are often very reactive to perceived slights and may respond angrily and retributively. They are frequently suspicious, without justification, of the fidelity of a spouse or sexual partner. As such, these individuals tend to be distant and aloof, and are often, if not characteristically, humourless.

Schizoid Personality Disorder: A personality disorder characterized by a pervasive pattern of detachment from social relationships, a restriction in the expression of emotionality in interpersonal settings, and a lack of interest in developing intimate or close interpersonal relationships. Individuals with this personality pathology are characteristically "loners," reflected in the solitary types of vocational interests or recreational activities they pursue. These individuals take very little pleasure, if any, in activities that others usually find interesting or sustaining. They may appear to be aloof, cold, detached, and indifferent to the commentary of others, be it praise or criticism.

Schizotypal Personality Disorder: This personality pathology is similar to schizoid personality disorder in that the two are characterized by restricted emotionality and social detachment. Schizotypal personality disorder is distinguishable, however, by the presence of cognitive and/or perceptual distortions and by eccentricities of behaviour. Patients with schizotypal personality disorder may experience ideas of reference; odd beliefs or magical thinking; and unusual perceptual experiences. In addition, their thinking and speech may be odd. They are often markedly constricted in their social interactions and lack close friends, confidantes, or lovers.

CLUSTER B (COLLOQUIALLY REFERRED TO AS THE "BAD"):
Antisocial Personality Disorder: A personality disorder characterized by chronic antisocial behaviour, usually beginning before age fifteen and established by age eighteen. Evidence of a conduct disorder before age fifteen is a prerequisite. A diagnosis can be made when a number of criteria are met, including poor employment record; significant history of unlawful behaviour; aggressivity; irresponsibility; failure to plan and have meaningful goals; recklessness; substance abuse; impulsivity; lack of capacity for remorse; disregard for the truth; and an inability to maintain a monogamous relationship. The terms psychopath, sociopath, and habitual criminal are often used synonymously with antisocial personality disorder. Psychopathy, however, has taken on a more precise and specific meaning in more recent times.

Borderline Personality Disorder: A personality disorder characterized by long-standing difficulties in interpersonal relationships, affective instability, and severe self-image problems. The disorder begins by late adolescence/early adulthood. It manifests itself in virtually every aspect of the individual's life. Borderline patients are particularly prone to depressive feelings, angry outbursts, acting out behaviour, self-damaging acts, and manipulation. In particular, borderline patients act out in an aggressive, or, more characteristically, a self-destructive manner, in response to either threatened or *de facto* abandonment, or, when an interpersonal scenario induces strong feelings of badness (and ensuing self-loathing) or guilt. Borderline patients can experience transient stress-induced paranoid ideation or severe dissociative symptoms.

Histrionic Personality Disorder: Histrionic patients are defined by their irrepressible need to be the centre of attention and they will often attempt to achieve that role by dramatic and theatrical displays as well as exaggerated, albeit shallow and rapidly shifting, expressions of emotion. These patients are often impressionistic in their speech and they are notably suggestible. They falsely perceive the quality of their relationships, often imbuing their interpersonal relationships with more depth and intimacy than is actually the case. These patients can be provocative and seductive.

Narcissistic Personality Disorder: As a symptom or condition, narcissism refers to self-preoccupation and an idealized and grandiose image of oneself that one presents to the world. Narcissists tend to be exploitative in interpersonal relations. They are preoccupied with their own sense of self-importance and their brilliance. They are vain and shallow, and they crave the constant attention and admiration of others. Narcissists are highly reactive to criticism and feelings of shame or humiliation, but they lack empathy and concern for the feelings of others. Narcissism is considered by many as the reciprocal of, and a defence to, feelings of low self-esteem and little personal worth. A grandiose image is presumably generated to counteract feelings of worthlessness.

CLUSTER C (COLLOQUIALLY REFERRED TO AS THE "SAD"):
Avoidant Personality Disorder: The defining feature of this personality disorder is a pervasive and long-standing pattern of feelings of social inadequacy, fear of rejection, and avoidance of vocational and social interactions that could lead to criticism, disapproval, or rejection. These patients have great difficulty taking personal risks that involve new relationships or new challenges for fear of failure. They invariably feel inadequate.

Dependent Personality Disorder: This personality disorder is defined by a pervasive pattern of shunning responsibility for even everyday decisions and relying heavily on another individual for guidance, direction, and support. These patients have difficulty asserting their needs. Their fear of being alone often has an exaggerated, and at times frantic, quality such that they will do most anything to secure another relationship that provides them with the support and comfort they desperately crave.

Obsessive-Compulsive Personality Disorder: A personality disorder characterized by a pervasive pattern of focus on orderliness, perfection, and control. Obsessive-compulsive personalities are overly attentive to detail to the extent that a view of the bigger picture is often lost. Perfectionism interferes with the completion of task. Extreme focus on industriousness and productivity lead to the exclusion of friendships and leisure activities. Obsessive-compulsive personalities hold onto possessions and objects that others would have discarded. They are reluctant to delegate tasks to others. Their undue attention to detail can disable them from making decisions and/or completing tasks. Obsessive-compulsive disorder (see definition above) and obsessive-compulsive personality disorder can co-exist.

Passive-aggressive personality disorder was listed as a discrete personality disorder in DSM IV's predecessor edition, DSM III, but subsequently de-listed in DSM IV due to lack of clarity about the validity of this diagnostic entity and imprecision about its criteria. The construct is useful, however, and clinicians still refer to passive-aggressive personalities or passive-aggressive personality pathology. The designation describes an individual who conveys their displeasure and anger through passive and symbolic means, rather than directly and adaptively. Their characteristic tendency is to resist, thwart, undermine, and protest in more of an obstructionist manner than as an attempt to resolve an issue. Other defining features of a passive-aggressive personality are listed below:

- procrastinates so that she fails to meet deadlines;
- is prone to becoming irritable and argumentative, or sulks when asked to do something she does not want to do;
- appears to work deliberately slowly or performs poorly, particularly with respect to tasks she wishes to resist doing;
- feels that others make unreasonable demands of her and protests accordingly;
- avoids obligations by claiming to have "forgotten";
- believes she is performing well, when that is clearly not the objective reality;

- resents suggestions from others concerning how she could be more productive; and
- is critical and perhaps hateful of people in positions of authority.

Personality Disorder Not Otherwise Specified (NOS) (also known as Mixed Personality Disorder): This category is reserved for personality pathology or a personality disorder that does not meet the full criteria for any one personality disorder and often incorporates the characteristics of a number of personality disorders into a cluster of symptoms and signs that cause clinically significant distress or impairment in one or more important areas of functioning.

Pervasive Developmental Disorder: This category includes a number of conditions usually first diagnosed in infancy, childhood, or adolescence. Two conditions under this heading that are relevant to forensic scenarios are autistic disorder and Asperger's disorder, both of which are defined below:

- Autistic Disorder: The essential features of this condition include the presence of a significantly abnormal development in communication skills and social interaction and a notably restricted inventory of interests and activities. The condition, by definition, onsets prior to the age of three. Only a small percentage of patients go on to live and work independently, although about a third can live partially independently. Even the highest functioning adults with autistic disorder continue to exhibit problems in communication and social interaction. Relatively infrequent instances of behavioural acting out, including impulsive and aggressive behaviour, may result in criminal charges and entry into the forensic system.
- Asperger's Disorder: This condition resembles autistic disorder in terms of impaired communication and social interaction (albeit not to the degree as autism), and in the development of restricted and repetitive activities, patterns of interest, or behaviour. Unlike autistic disorder, mental retardation is not usually a feature of Asperger's disorder; when present, it is invariably mild. Also, unlike autistic disorder, early language and cognitive skills are within normal limits. The social and communication defects in Asperger's disorder are often subtle and go unnoticed until some specific difficulty or situation brings the person affected to attention. Although very little work has been carried out on the relationship between Asperger's disorder and violence, criminality, and sexually anomalous behaviour, there is some evidence to suggest that Asperger's disorder is overrepresented in juvenile forensic settings, hence, it has become a condition of increasing interest to both forensic clinicians and researchers.

Post-traumatic Stress Disorder: An anxiety disorder induced by a severe stress (assault, rape, torture, accident, or natural disaster) that the person has experienced or witnessed, involving actual or threatened death, serious injury, or harm to the physical integrity of the individual or to others to which the person responds with horror, intense fear, or helplessness. The event is out of keeping with everyday experience. The syndrome is characterized by intrusive recollections and re-experiencing of the event, emotional numbing, detachment from others, disinterest in previously meaningful activities, symptoms associated with central nervous system arousal (irritability, difficulty concentrating, anger, hypervigilence, and increased startle response), and avoidance of activities reminiscent of the traumatic event.

Psychopathy: The designation psychopath defines a personality construct that has frequently been considered as synonymous with sociopath, habitual criminal, and antisocial personality. Psychopathic personalities frequently subsume the unempathic, aloof, grandiose, and interpersonally exploitative style of narcissistic personalities and the behavioural, impulsive, and lifelong criminal lifestyle characteristics of antisocial personalities. Clinicians and researchers frequently rely on the *Hare Psychopathy Checklist — Revised* (PCL-R)[16] as a means of defining the extent to which an individual qualifies for the clinical construct "psychopath."

Schizoaffective Disorder: A major mental disorder that represents a clinical hybrid of the signs and symptoms of schizophrenia and a mood disorder. Patients with the condition, in fact, concurrently meet the criteria for a mood disorder and schizophrenia. The individual exhibits the behavioural manifestations and experiences the symptoms of both disorders in varying degrees. Mood symptoms and psychotic symptoms may occur independently of each other, or together.

Schizophrenia: A major mental disorder characterized by delusions; hallucinations; disordered thinking; blunted and inappropriate affect; and a deterioration in social, occupational, and educational functioning. Schizophrenia has a strong genetic component. Predisposed males often develop the disorder in their late teens/early twenties. Females tend to develop the disorder in their early to mid-twenties.

Schizophrenia is generally considered to be an incurable condition. Its more florid symptoms (hallucinations, delusions, and disordered thinking—often referred to as the "positive symptoms" of schizophrenia) can be significantly ameliorated through the use of several classes of anti-psychotic (neuroleptic) drugs.

---

16   R. Hare, *The Hare Psychopathy Checklist — Revised* (Toronto: Multi-Health Systems, Inc., 1991) [PCL-R]. For further discussion, see below, Chapter 1, Section C.4.

In some instances, psychopharmacologic intervention can help the individual to achieve a fairly good recovery (with little or no evidence of the usual signs and symptoms of schizophrenia) and promote a return to reasonable psychosocial functioning. While psychopharmacologic treatment is the mainstay of treatment for this condition, a more comprehensive program includes social rehabilitation, a psychoeducational family approach, stress management, etc. Schizophrenia is a common condition, affecting one percent of the population. Sufferers often lack insight into the depth and scope of their illness and the need for psychiatric supervision and medications. Medication compliance is therefore a significant issue.

Somatization Disorder: The patient with somatization disorder, from prior to age thirty, has suffered from numerous physical complaints over a protracted period of time that have brought about significant impairment in a number of spheres of functioning. To meet the diagnostic criteria,[17] the individual must have suffered, at any point of the disturbance, from at least four pain symptoms; two gastrointestinal symptoms; one sexual symptom; and one pseudo-neurological symptom (other than pain) such as tingling, difficulty swallowing, imbalance, hallucinations, double vision, deafness, seizures, or dissociative symptoms (such as amnesia). The final criterion for the diagnosis is that the symptoms that the individual experiences either cannot be entirely explained by a known organic condition, or, where there is an underlying medical condition, the symptoms are either in excess of or out of keeping with what might be expected in regard to that condition. The symptoms experienced by the patient are not intentionally feigned or produced as might occur in malingering or factitious disorder.

2) Key Signs/Symptoms

Affect: A person's apparent emotional state, as judged by others.

Compulsion: A persistent and often uncontrollable need to repetitively perform a frequently irrational act, such as washing one's hands twenty-five times a day.

Delusion: A fixed false belief arising from an incorrect understanding or inference about external reality. The belief is fastidiously held in spite of its irrationality and incontrovertible evidence to the contrary. The belief is inconsistent with the individual's culture. There are numerous types of delusions. *Somatic delusions* involve the belief that the person has some form of illness or physical defect. In *persecutory delusions*, the individual feels that she is the subject of a conspiracy or that others are out to harm, thwart, or unfairly treat her. Individ-

---

17   DSM IV-TR, above note 5 at 490.

uals with persecutory delusions see sinister motives behind fairly innocuous behaviours. In *grandiose delusions*, the individual believes she is an important, powerful, and/or unusually intelligent person. An *erotomanic delusion* involves the belief that another person (usually a person socially out-of-reach for that patient) is in love with her. A *jealous delusion* involves the belief that one's partner is being unfaithful. Other well-known delusions include the following:

- Thought Insertion: The belief that thoughts can be inserted into one's mind by outside persons, agencies, or influences.
- Thought Withdrawal: The belief that thoughts can be magically extracted from one's head by outside persons, agencies, or influences.
- Thought Broadcasting: The belief that others can hear the patient's thoughts being broadcast aloud.
- Delusion of Reference: The interpretation of innocuous events and matters in a self-referential manner. Most commonly, the schizophrenic patient believes that the radio or television are talking about him, or that the subject matter of the broadcast pertains to him in a unique fashion. Any printed or other media may be involved (for example, newspapers, billboards, street signs, books, and magazines).

Dissociation: An interruption in the usually integrated functions of consciousness, often associated with a subjective feeling of lapsed awareness or of being out of touch with one's environment.

Hallucination: A disturbance in one or more of the five sensory modalities. The individual falsely perceives a stimulus related to seeing, hearing, smelling, touching, or tasting for which there is no basis in reality. Auditory hallucinations are the most common hallucination and usually involve voices communicating directly with the subject, or talking between or amongst themselves, frequently about the subject and/or the subject's actions. Command auditory hallucinations, instructing the patient to harm herself or another, are the most ominous auditory hallucinations, and, when present, require careful evaluation by a physician. Hallucinations involving taste or smell justify a hypothesis of a neurological disorder.

Obsession: An unwanted, intrusive, and persistent thought, impulse, or image that may dominate a person's consciousness and interfere with work, social, or family life. Sometimes referred to as rumination.

Paranoia: A psychological symptom involving suspiciousness or the belief that one is being persecuted, harassed, or treated unjustly. As a symptom, paranoia can be seen in a number of mental disorders, including mood disorders, schizophrenia, delusional disorder, and organic states. In milder forms, paranoia may be experienced as a symptom or facet of personality (paranoid personality traits or personality disorder). In more severe mental conditions (schizophrenia, delusional disorder, and mania) paranoia often reaches delusional proportions.

Thought Disorder: A disturbance of thought processes that affects the individual's ability to think clearly and communicate with others. Examples of manifestations of thought disorder include the following:

- Thought Blocking: Thoughts are blocked and speech interrupted, often due to distraction, difficulty concentrating, or because the patient experiences the thought as being magically removed from his head (see thought withdrawal).
- Circumstantiality: A term used to describe speech that is circuitous and digressive. The patient provides irrelevant detail in the process of discussing a topic or answering a question, but generally remains within the realm of the topic.
- Concrete Thought: The inability to see the whole picture or understand an abstract concept. Often seen in schizophrenia, delusional disorder, and depression.
- Loosening of Associations: The most characteristic thought disturbance in schizophrenia, loosening of associations refers to thought and speech in which ideas shift from one subject to another in an unrelated or oblique fashion. There is no meaningful relationship between one thought and a successive thought. A number of seemingly unrelated and irrelevant subjects are often grouped together within a stream of thought or sentence. When loosening of associations is very severe—that is, when words and phrases are grouped together with no logical coherence—the phenomenon is referred to as "word salad."
- Tangentiality: A symptom or manifestation of disordered thought and speech. The tangential individual responds to a question or provides an account that contains irrelevant detail. The point is never made and the question is never answered.
- Flight of Ideas: A rapid shifting from one idea or flow of thought to another. There is often an abundance of thought. This symptom is seen most commonly in mania.
- Neologism: This is a word created by a patient. It may be entirely invented and bear no likeness to a known word, or it may be an adaptation/adulteration of a known word, or a combination of two or more words. Neologisms may be seen in both schizophrenia and mania.

- Pressured Speech: Speech that is conspicuously rapid in flow. This form of speech is often associated with flight of ideas.
- Word Salad: A severe disorder of thought seen most often in schizophrenia. Words and phrases are mixed together with no apparent meaning or logic. The patient may be incomprehensible.

3) Diagnostic/Investigative Tests & Procedures

Alcohol Tolerance Test: The patient is given a measured amount of alcohol at regular intervals, during which time blood alcohol levels are obtained; behavioural observations are noted and recorded; and clinical observations of the patient's thought patterns, reasoning, and speech are noted. The patient may or may not be under brainwave monitoring (EEG) throughout the test. The test is particularly useful in assessing the possibility of an alcohol idiosyncratic intoxication problem.

Amytal Interview (Sodium Amytal): An interview using the barbiturate drug sodium amytal, commonly but erroneously referred to as "truth serum." It may help to uncover repressed memories. While it may be clinically useful, it has never been established as efficacious in terms of what it purports to do (that is, elicit repressed memories and facilitate access to "the truth"), and, to many, the test is, in a legal context, relegated to the category of "junk science."

Computerized Tomography Scan (CT Scan): A technique for imaging anatomical structures using X-rays. A computer reconstructs and interprets the X-ray beam absorption data and generates an image of the structure scanned. It is used for detecting changes in anatomical structure as may often occur when the patient has suffered a stroke, has a tumor, and has experienced atrophy of the brain.

Electroencephalograph (EEG): A recording of the brain's electrical activity. Electrodes are placed around the scalp and measurements are recorded on graph paper from various locations in the brain. EEG is a means of determining whether or not a person has a predisposition to seizure activity.

Hematologic Evaluation: Blood is drawn to determine the hemoglobin level as well as the numbers of individual types of red and white blood cell lines. A blood smear detects any abnormality in cell morphology.

Hypothalamic-Pituitary-Gonadal Axis: The interactive system of glands that regulates the synthesis and action of testosterone, the male hormone responsible for sex drive. Some evidence indicates that over-activity in this system—in particular, an excessive amount of testosterone or a greater sensitivity to a normal amount of testosterone—is associated with a high sex drive, sexual deviancy, and aggression. There is similarly evidence that reduction of serum testosterone—or interference with its action—reduces sex drive, deviant fantasy, and impulses, and, therefore, reduces the propensity to act out sexually.

Liver Function Tests: These include a variety of blood tests used to determine the liver's physiologic functioning; that is, the extent to which it is serving as a filter for waste products and toxins, and whether it has been obstructed, or otherwise compromised, by a pathological process. Liver damage is often seen in individuals who abuse alcohol and/or street drugs. Hepatitis is a generic term that means that the liver is inflamed. This can be the result of any pathological process (infection or toxin) that impacts on the liver.

Magnetic Resonance Imaging (MRI): A specialized imaging technique that relies on radiowaves and powerful magnets to construct images of the body. In the context of a forensic psychiatric evolution, an MRI provides a very high degree of structural detail in determining evidence of organic brain disorder.

Phallometric Testing: Phallometric testing, otherwise referred to as penile plethysmography, is a physiologic test of sexual arousal. It measures an individual's arousal by looking at even minute changes in penile responses to a number of visual and/or auditory stimuli presented in the test procedure. Phallometric testing evaluates an individual's sexual preferences in hierarchy.

Polysomnography (Sleep Studies): The individual is attached to an EEG machine recording brain wave patterns throughout the night. Those recordings are then compared to established norms for brain waves during sleep to determine whether or not there is evidence of a sleep disorder.

Psychological Testing: The use of objective, norm-referenced (that is, empirically based) standardized tests to measure a number of mental functions and capacities, including overall intellectual functioning, scholastic aptitude, attitudes, values, and personality traits. Psychological testing is occasionally used as an adjunct to a psychiatric evaluation. In this context, the psychiatrist will ask a psychologist colleague to carry out testing, either of a general nature (intelligence and personality) or to evaluate particular aspects of brain function (for example, memory). Neuropsychological testing is a series of specialized psychological tests designed to determine whether or not there is impairment in particular functional networks within the brain. These are usually undertaken by a specially trained psychologist known as a neuropsychologist. Neuropsychological testing is particularly useful in establishing the presence of brain damage due to specific structural changes in the brain resulting from a head injury or due to a variety of conditions, including multiple sclerosis, drug abuse, and alcohol abuse. Hypotheses of brain damage generated by specific deficits noted in neuropsychological testing may be confirmed by brain imaging techniques; for example, magnetic resonance imaging. Some of the more commonly used psychological and neuropsychological tests are described below:

- Alcohol Dependence Scale (ADS):[18] A test that evaluates recent alcohol use/abuse.
- Aphasia Screening Test (AST):[19] A test that evaluates possible disruptions in language functioning.
- Beck Anxiety Inventory (BAI):[20] A self-report measure of current symptoms of anxiety.
- Beck Depression Inventory (BDI):[21] A self-report measure of current depressive symptoms.
- Buss-Durkee Hostility Inventory (BDHI):[22] A measure of hostile attitudes and behaviour.
- Buss-Perry Aggression Questionnaire (BPAQ):[23] A measure of various aspects of aggressive behaviour.
- Clock Drawing Test (CDT):[24] A screening test for visuospatial and constructional impairment.
- Drug Use Questionnaire (DAST-20):[25] A questionnaire which evaluates patterns of drug use over the past year.
- Gudjonsson Suggestibility Scale (GSS):[26] A measure of the personal inclination to accept as true suggestions offered by an interrogator.

---

18   H.A. Skinner & J.L. Horn, *Alcohol Dependence Scale* (Toronto, ON: Centre for Addiction and Mental Health, 1984).

19   R. Whurr, *Aphasia Screening Test*, 2d ed. (London: Whurr Publishing, 1996).

20   A.T. Beck & R.A. Steer, *Beck Anxiety Inventory* (San Antonio: PsychCorp, 1993).

21   A.T. Beck, R.A. Steer *et al.*, *Beck Depression Inventory-II* (San Antonio: PsychCorp, 1996).

22   A.H. Buss & A. Durkee, A. "An Inventory for Assessing Different Kinds of Hostility" (1957) 21 Journal of Consulting Psychology 343.

23   A.H. Buss & M. Perry "The Aggression Questionnaire" (1992) 63 Journal of Personality and Social Psychology 452.

24   M.I. Freedman, L. Leach, *et al.*, *Clock Drawing: A Neuropsychological Analysis* (Oxford: Oxford University Press, 1994).

25   H.A. Skinner, *Drug Abuse Screening Test* (Toronto, ON: Centre for Addiction and Mental Health, 1982).

26   G.H. Gudjonsson, *Gudjonsson Suggestibility Scales Manual* (Hove, UK: Psychology Press, 1997).

- Hooper Visual Organization Test (HVOT):[27] A test of perceptual differentiation and the ability to reorganize visual information.
- Michigan Alcohol Screening Test (MAST):[28] A questionnaire which assesses alcohol abuse and dependence over the evaluee's lifetime.
- Millon Clinical Multiaxial Inventory-III (MCMI-III):[29] A widely-used self-report inventory for diagnostic screening and assessment of clinical populations. The MCMI-III's particular focus is defining personality pathology, personality disorder, and psychological distress.
- Minnesota Multiphasic Personality Inventory-2 (MMPI-2):[30] A self-reporting paper-and-pencil psychological test in which the individual answers true or false to a variety of questions which are then analyzed statistically to provide a profile of the individual's personality and screen for the presence of emotional disorder. In addition to the ten primary clinical scales, the MMPI-2 has five validity scales to evaluate a patient's approach to testing (for example, fake bad, fake good). It is one of the most common psychological tests undertaken.
- Novaco Anger Scale (NAS):[31] A measure that requests the respondent to indicate the degree of anger they would experience in specific situations or circumstances.
- Paulhus Deception Scales (PDS):[32] The PDS measures both self-deception, the tendency to give sincere but overly favourable self-descriptions, and impression management, defined as an attempt to either deliberately or unconsciously present oneself in the most favourable light. It is a common test used to detect response bias in individuals undergoing a psychological assessment.
- Peabody Individual Achievement Test—Revised (PIAT):[33] A test of reading comprehension.

---

27   H.E. Hooper, *Hooper Visual Organization Test* (Los Angeles: Western Psychological Services, 1983).

28   M. L., Selzer, "The Michigan Alcoholism Screening Test: The quest for a new diagnostic instrument" (1971) 127 American Journal of Psychiatry 1653.

29   T. Millon, R. Davis *et al.*, *Millon Clinical Multiaxial Inventory-III* (Bloomington, MN: National Computer Systems, 1994).

30   J.N. Butcher, L. Dohlstrom *et al.*, *Minnesota Multiphasic Personality Inventory-2* (Minneapolis: University of Minnesota Press, 1989).

31   R.W. Novaco, *The Novaco Anger Scale and Provocation Inventory* (Los Angeles: Western Psychological Services, 2003).

32   D.L. Paulhus, "Two-Component Models of Socially Desirable Responding" (1984) 46 Journal of Personality and Social Psychology 598.

33   F.C. Markwardt, Jr., *Peabody Individual Achievement Test — Revised* (Circle Pines, MN: AGS Publishing, 1998).

- Personal Reaction Inventory (PRI):[34] This is a measure of socially desirable responding. The PRI measures both self-deception, the tendency to provide sincere but overly favourable self-descriptions, and impression management; that is, a deliberate attempt to present oneself in a favourable light.
- Personality Assessment Inventory (PAI):[35] The PAI is a measure of personal attitudes, beliefs, and experiences. Apart from screening for psychopathology, it is designed to provide information that assists in clinical diagnosis and treatment planning.
- Post-traumatic Stress Diagnostic Scale (PSDS):[36] This is a self-report measure of post-traumatic stress disorder symptoms corresponding to DSM IV-TR criteria.
- Post-traumatic Stress Disorder Symptom Scale (PSS):[37] A formal measure of post-traumatic symptoms.
- Rorschach Inkblots Test:[38] The Rorschach test is one of a number of projective tests, so called because the subject projects what is in his mind in order to supply meaning to the otherwise ambiguous stimuli. This is a projective test in which the subject is presented with ten ink blots. The test is then scored (most commonly using the Exner system) to interpret the subject's personality structure with respect to such variables as cognitive style, creativity, propensity towards psychosis, defence patterns, and level of emotionality. The test is helpful for developing hypotheses about personality and cognitive style to further gains in therapy. The usefulness of conclusions based on Rorschach testing for forensic purposes is considered questionable.
- Shipley Institute of Living Scale (SILS):[39] A self-administered test that provides an estimate of intellectual functioning.
- State-Trait Anger Expression Inventory (STAXI):[40] A self-report measure of subjective anger and patterns of anger expression.

---

34 J. Hall, *Personal Reaction Index* (Waco, TX: Teleometrics International, 1971).

35 L.C. Morey, *Personality Assessment Inventory* (Lutz, FL: Psychological Assessment Resouces, Inc., 1991).

36 E.B. Foa, *Post-traumatic Stress Diagnostic Scale* (Bloomington, MN: Pearson Assessments, 1995).

37 E.B. Foa, D.S. Riggs *et al.*, "Reliability and Validity of a Brief Instrument Assessing Post-Traumatic Stress Disorder" (1993) 4 Journal of Traumatic Stress 459.

38 J.E. Exner, *The Rorschach: A Comprehensive System*, 2d ed., vol. 1 (New York: Wiley, 1986).

39 W.C. Shipley & R.A. Zachary, *Shipley Institute of Living Scale: Revised Manual* (Los Angeles: Western Psychological Services, 1988).

40 C.D. Spielberger, *State-Trait Anger Expression Inventory-2* (Lutz, FL: Psychological Assessment Resources, Inc., 1999).

- Structured Clinical Interview for DSM IV (SCID-IV):[41] The SCID-IV is a semi-structured interview, the various modules of which provide specific questions crafted to define whether the explicit criteria of a DSM IV diagnosis are met. The imposed structure minimizes diagnostic errors.
- Structured Interview of Reported Symptoms (SIRS):[42] Evaluates systematic distortions in self-report of symptoms and response styles that not only have implications for diagnosis and treatment, but assist in evaluating the authenticity of the evaluee's presentation, particularly as regards psychotic symptoms.
- Test of Malingered Memory (TOMM):[43] A test that evaluates the authenticity of cognitive symptoms, particularly memory.
- Trail Making Test: A & B (TMT):[44] A test of visual search and sequencing ability.
- Wechsler Adult Intelligence Scale—Revised (WAIS-R):[45] The WAIS-R is one of the more commonly used tests of intellectual functioning. When the test is scored, a full scale IQ (intelligence quotient) is derived from the verbal IQ and performance IQ. The examiner evaluates any discrepancy between the verbal and performance measures and offers an overall score of where the individual falls relative to the general population. Significant inter-scale discrepancies suggest acquired brain impairment. The latter can be clarified and quantified by neuropsychological testing. There is also a Wechsler Intelligence Scale for Children—Revised (WISC-R)[46] which has been standardized for children in the age range of five to fifteen.
- Wechsler Memory Scale—Edition III (WMS-III):[47] A test designed to assess key domains of memory function and learning capacity.
- Wide Range Achievement Test—Revision 3 (WRAT-3):[48] A measure of academic achievement.

---

41   M.B. First, R.L. Spitzer *et al.*, *Structured Clinical Interview for DSM IV Axis I Personality Disorders* (Washington, DC: American Psychiatric Publishing, Inc., 1997); M.B. First, M. Gibbon *et al.*, *Structured Clinical Interview for DSM IV Axis II Personality Disorders* (Washington, DC: American Psychiatric Publishing, Inc., 1997).

42   R. Rogers, R. Bagby *et al.*, *Structured Interview of Reported Symptoms* (Lutz, FL: Psychological Assessment Resources, Inc., 1992).

43   T.N. Tombaugh, Test of Memory Malingering (Toronto, ON: Multi-Health Systems, 1996).

44   *Trail Making Test* (Army Individual Test Battery, 1944).

45   D. Wechsler, *Wechsler Adult Intelligence Scale—Revised* (San Antonio, TX: PsychCorp., 1981).

46   Above note 14.

47   D. Wechsler, *Wechsler Memory Scale III* (San Antonio, TX: PsychCorp., 1997).

48   G.S. Wilkinson, *Wide Range Achievement Test 3* (Wilmington, DE: Wide Range, Inc., 1993).

- Wisconsin Card Sort Test (WCST):[49] A test that measures higher executive functioning.

Single Photon Emission Computerized Tomography Scan (SPECT): Brain SPECT imaging provides information about metabolic activity patterns of the brain by imaging underlying cerebral blood flow. It is useful for identifying specific areas of the brain implicated in specific problems.

Thyroid Function Tests: These are blood tests used to determine the functional state of the thyroid gland, which, if abnormal, can, amongst other things, lead to altered mood and behaviour.

4) Violence and Criminal Recidivism Risk Assessment Tools

Hare Psychopathy Checklist — Revised (PCL-R): An empirically validated measure of the clinical construct of psychopathy shown to be associated with the risk of antisocial or criminal behaviour. PCL-R scores have been significantly related to recidivism in numerous studies and while they are less effective predictors of violent recidivism, they provide the bulk of predictive validity of the more commonly used violence risk assessment schemes. The twenty characteristics scored by the PCL-R are:

- glibness/superficial charm;
- grandiose sense of self-worth;
- need for stimulation/proneness to boredom;
- pathological lying;
- conning/manipulative;
- lack of remorse or guilt;
- shallow affect;
- callous/lack of empathy;
- parasitic lifestyle;
- poor behavioural controls;
- promiscuous sexual behaviour;
- early behavioural problems;
- lack of realistic, long-term goals;
- impulsivity;
- irresponsibility;
- failure to accept responsibility for own actions;

---

49   R.K. Heaton, G. Chelune *et al.*, Wisconsin Card Sorting Test (Lutz, FL: Psychological Assessment Resouces, Inc., 1993).

- many short-term marital relationships;
- juvenile delinquency;
- revocation of conditional release; and
- criminal versatility.[50]

HCR-20:[51] The HCR-20 is a risk assessment scheme comprised of twenty items. The items include historical (H), clinical (C), and risk management (R) items. Use of the scheme involves melding historical and dynamic risk factors in order to come up with a crude estimation of risk, expressed as low, moderate, or high risk for violent recidivism.

Level of Service Inventory—Revised (LSI-R):[52] The LSI-R evaluates minor and major risk factors for antisocial behaviour, and the interventions necessary to reduce that risk. The instrument is fairly unique in that the score produced evaluates not only risk but also the interventions necessary to manage that risk concurrently.

Sexual Offender Risk Appraisal Guide (SORAG):[53] The SORAG is an actuarial instrument specifically designed to predict sexual recidivism. The SORAG emphasizes historical risk factors in arriving at a probability for violent (sexual) recidivism.

Sexual Violence Risk-20 (SVR-20):[54] The SVR-20 is a checklist of the key historic and dynamic risk factors for sexual recidivism. The SVR-20 considers the nature of the offence, the frequency of offending behaviour, and the severity and likelihood of sexual violence in the future.

Spousal Assault Risk Assessment Guide (SARA):[55] The Spousal Assault Risk Assessment Guide—SARA (second edition) is a twenty-item clinical checklist of risk factors for spousal assault, developed by Kropp, Hart, Webster and

---

50   PCL-R, above note 16 at 1.

51   C.D. Webster, D. Eaves *et al.*, *The HCR-20 Scheme: The Assessment of Dangerousness and Risk* (Vancouver: Simon Fraser University and Forensic Psychiatric Services Commission of British Columbia, 1995); C.D. Webster, K.S. Douglas *et al.*, *The HCR-20: Assessing the Risk for Violence, Version 2.* (Burnaby, BC: Mental Health, Law, and Policy Institute, Simon Fraser University, 1997).

52   D.A. Andrews & J.L. Bonta, *The Level of Service Inventory — Revised* (Toronto: Multi-Heatlh Systems, Inc., 1995).

53   V.L. Quinsey, G.T. Harris *et al.*, *Violent Offenders: Appraising and Managing Risk.* (Washington, DC: American Psychological Association, 1998).

54   H.S. Boer, P.R. Kropp, & C. Webster, *Sexual Violence Risk-20* (Burnaby, BC: Mental Health, Law and Policy Institute, Simon Fraser University, 1997).

55   P.R. Kropp, S.D. Hart *et al.*, *Manual for the Spousal Assault Risk Assessment Guide* (Toronto: Multi-Health Systems, Inc., 1999).

Eaves for the British Columbia Institute on Family Violence. The SARA is not a test or scale in the usual sense in that it does not provide an absolute or relative measure of risk using established norms. It is best seen as a structured inventory of pertinent information that should be weighed and considered in assessing an individual's risk for spousal assault. The SARA includes twenty items (under four headings) that touch on the individual's criminal history, psychosocial adjustment, and history of previous spousal assault. Three items focus on evaluating the gravity of the offence.

Violence Risk Appraisal Guide (VRAG):[56] The VRAG is an actuarial tool drawing on historical or static risk factors alone in order to forecast the evaluee's risk of violent recidivism within a circumscribed period of time.

5) Treatment

a) Psychopharmacology

Psychopharmacotherapy is the treatment of a mental illness by the administration of drugs, as opposed to other forms of treatment such as electroconvulsive therapy or psychotherapy. Pharmacotherapy is the mainstay of treatment for a number of psychiatric disorders. A drug's anticipated effectiveness flows from the biological dysfunction presumed to be the cause of the particular disorder. A number of classes of drugs are typically used for various psychiatric conditions most likely to be seen in a forensic context:

Antiandrogens: A group of drugs directed at reducing the level and/or action of male sex hormones. This group includes female sex hormones, such as medroxy-progesterone acetate (Provera®) or drugs that interfere with the action of the male hormone, testosterone, such as cyporterone acetate (Androcur®), or a fairly new agent, leuprolide acetate (Lupron®) which acts at the level of the brain. It inhibits the action of brain chemicals that signal the gonads to synthesize testosterone.

Antidepressants: This group of drugs includes several classes of drugs used to treat depressive disorders. They are postulated to exert their action on brain chemicals (neurotransmitters) by either blocking the reuptake of the neurotransmitter and/or by making the receptors for that neurotransmitter more sensitive to it. The net effect is to increase the deficient neurotransmitter and/or enhance its effect.

There are several classes of antidepressants. A class called serotonin-specific reuptake inhibitors (SSRIs) (for example, Prozac®, Luvox®, Zoloft®, Cel-

---

56   V.L. Quinsey, G.T. Harris *et al.*, above note 53.

exa®, Paxil®) contains the most widely prescribed antidepressants. Aside from alleviating depression in 85–90 percent of patients, SSRIs have also been used for obsessive-compulsive disorder, panic disorder, social phobia, and eating disorders. They are emphasized here as a group because of their use in forensic contexts to reduce impulsivity, aggression, and anger dysregulation.

Mood Stabilizers: There are essentially three classes of drugs within this group: lithium, anticonvulsants, and antipsychotics. The oldest and best-known mood stabilizer to treat bipolar disorder is lithium carbonate. Anticonvulsants such as carbamazepine (Tegretol®); valproic acid (Epival®); lamotrigine (Lamictal®); gabapentin (Neurontin®); and topiramate (Topamax®) have become increasingly useful in recent times. Even more recently, newer generation antipsychotic medications, such as olanzapine (Zyprexa®); risperidone (Risperdal®); and quetiapine (Seroquel®) have proven to be particularly helpful in first settling the symptoms of mania, and then promoting stability of mood. The primary use of both of these groups of drugs is to keep mood from elevating towards mania or from declining into depression.

Antipsychotics/Neuroleptics: This large group consists of various classes of drugs that are principally used to treat acute and chronic psychoses, as commonly seen in schizophrenia and schizoaffective disorder. Each class of drugs is associated with particular risks and side effects. The exact pharmacological actions of these drugs is still a matter of some controversy. Their principal action is to bind to dopamine (D2) receptors in order to block excessive dopamine activity, which is presumed to be the principal neurotransmitter anomaly in psychotic disorders such as schizophrenia.

There are several other classes of drugs used fairly commonly in psychiatry to manage offenders, particularly in correctional settings. A brief description of each class of these drugs follows:

Anxiolytics: A group of several classes of drugs, of which benzodiazepines are best known, that reduce severe anxiety or tension. Some of the best-known benzodiazepine drugs include:

  • Alprazolam (Xanax®);
  • Diazepam (Valium®);
  • Lorazepam (Ativan®);
  • Flurazepam (Dalmane®);
  • Oxazepam (Serax®); and
  • Chlorodiazepoxide (Librium®).

Perhaps the best known of the non-benzodiazepines anxiolytics is bus-pirone (Buspar®). Buspar®, which may take up to two weeks for onset of action, is useful in generalized anxiety disorder. It augments the antidepressant treatment of major depressive disorder and may be the drug of choice in symptomatically anxious patients for whom a benzodiazepine anxiolytic is unsuitable because of a past history of benzodiazepine addiction.

Hypnotics: A group of drugs that induce sleep. Up until the 1970s, barbiturates (secobarbital and pentobarbital) were the most commonly prescribed sedative hypnotics. By the middle of the 1970s, they were replaced by the benzodiazepines and related groups of hypnotic drugs (flurazepa (Dalmane®); temazepam (Restoril®); and triazolam (Halcion®)). Barbiturates and benzodiazepines are highly addictive. Zopiclone (Imovane®) is perhaps best known of the non-benzodiazepine hypnotics.

Psychostimulants: A class of central nervous system activating drugs used to treat attention-deficit/hyperactivity disorder, narcolepsy (a sleep disorder), and rarely, depression. They were previously used (abused) to induce weight loss, and abused on the street as "speed." The class of drugs includes:

- Amphetamine (Benzedrine®);
- Methylphenidate (Ritalin®, Ritalin SR®, Concerta®). An amphetamine-like substance used in the treatment of attention-deficit disorder with hyperactivity and narcolepsy;
- Dextroamphetamine (Dexedrine®); and
- Atomoxetin (Strattera®).

Substance Dependence Management and Withdrawal: A number of drugs used either to promote abstinence or to manage withdrawal:

- Antabuse®: Otherwise known by its chemical name, disulfiram, Antabuse® is a drug prescribed to promote abstinence in alcohol abusers. Its mechanism is to induce a severe reaction in an individual who consumes alcohol while on this drug (the alcohol-Antabuse® reaction). The person becomes quite ill. Knowing about the likelihood of this reaction serves as a strong deterrent for some alcohol abusers. Antabuse® is best used in conjunction with other therapeutic measures to reduce alcohol abuse.
- Clonidine (Catapres®): By its nature it is an antihypertensive agent, but it is commonly used in managing opioid and methadone withdrawal in that it reduces the central nervous system's signs and symptoms of withdrawal. It does not have an affect of craving.

- Methadone: Methadone is synthetic opioid used firstly to detoxify opioid addicts and then to maintain them on (hopefully) decreasing amounts of methadone to avoid a relapse of opioid use. Physicians and clinics that prescribe methadone require special licenses for that purpose.
- Naltrexone (ReVia®): Naltrexone blocks the pleasurable effects of opioids, as well as alcohol, in the brain. Used acutely for suspected opioid toxicity, it can induce potentially severe withdrawal symptoms in patients who are severely physically dependent on opioids. In a maintenance context, Naltrexone is helpful in reducing cravings in opioid addicts. Its ability to reduce those cravings in alcohol dependent patients is a current subject of study.

b) Electroconvulsive Therapy

Electroconvulsive Therapy (ECT) is also known as "shock treatment." It is used for the treatment of mania; schizophrenia; and, particularly, depression. The technique involves administering electric current to the brain to induce a grand mal seizure. The exact mechanism by which ECT is thought to exert its therapeutic effects has not been fully elucidated. It has been postulated that the seizure either increases the release of brain chemicals (neurotransmitters) that are believed to be deficient in depression, and/or resynchronizes brain rhythms which have become desynchronized.

The treatment disposition provisions of PART XX.1 of the *Criminal Code*[57] (section 672.58 and following) do not contemplate the use of electroconvulsive therapy in order to render an accused fit to stand trial. That modality (as well as psychosurgery) is specifically excluded by virtue of subsection 672.61(1). The specific provisions relevant to this discussion have been reproduced in Chapter 3, Section K.

c) Psychotherapy

Psychotherapy is a treatment modality that uses psychological means to treat mental, emotional, and behavioural disorders. In psychotherapy, a trained individual (the psychotherapist) sets out to ameliorate or remove a patient's symptoms, modify maladaptive thought and behaviour, and promote personality growth. The various forms of psychotherapy include individual psychotherapy (insight-oriented, supportive, cognitive-behavioural), couple therapy, family therapy, and group therapy.

---

57   R.S.C. 1985, c. C-46.

CHAPTER TWO

Psychiatric Consultation and Evidence

A. DEFINITION OF FORENSIC PSYCHIATRY

Forensic psychiatry is that area of psychiatric sub-specialization that focuses on mental state and psychological issues that might arise in the course of any legal, administrative, or professional regulatory body proceeding.

1) Correctional Psychiatry

The interface of law and psychiatry further includes psychiatric consultation and treatment carried out within penal facilities. This particular area is commonly referred to as correctional psychiatry.

B. ROLE OF THE PSYCHIATRIC CONSULTANT

1) Duty of Care Owed by the Forensic Psychiatrist

The forensic psychiatric expert serves as a consultant to the party retaining him, and it is to that party the mental health care expert operating in a forensic context owes a primary duty of care.

2) Task of the Expert

Behavioural sciences experts are often in a position to provide their legal colleagues and the criminal justice system with a unique perspective. The primary task of the expert is to serve as a consultant; that is, to diagnose a mental disorder; to define psychological variables that may be at play in a case; and, above all, to educate the court (and lawyers and retaining agencies) about matters the court knows little about.

3) Qualifications Required of Experts

There are no specific professional qualifications in Canada necessary in order to offer an expert opinion in court. A psychiatrist will be expected to hold a medical license and higher qualifications in psychiatry. Other mental health professionals will require corresponding credentials. There is no designated expertise (that is, a Royal College of Physicians and Surgeons of Canada specialty designation) in forensic psychiatry. Forensic psychiatrists obtain their expertise in that area either by having taken a special course of training during or after their residency programs (for example, a fellowship in forensic psychiatry, or accumulating expertise through experience). Expertise in specific areas (for example, domestic violence or sexual deviation) in which there are also no formal qualifications, will be assessed by the court on a case-by-case basis, drawing on criteria such as professional experience, publications, etc.

4) Biased Experts and Hired Guns

A psychiatric expert involved in a medico-legal matter is presumed to be neutral, regardless of whether he or she was retained by the accused or the prosecution. Most experienced experts are likely to concede that complete impartiality and objectivity are close to impossible. Impartiality is not itself the pivotal consideration. Rather, the key concern, absent marked bias, is whether the expert is able to recognize problems with her impartiality that could impinge upon, or potentially even contaminate, the evaluation and her participation in the process. Firmly entrenching herself in the role of consultant/educator is generally the safest and most comfortable way for an expert to avoid the suggestion of bias. The term "hired gun" is a pejorative term that refers to a clinician who is prepared to contour the results of her assessments and testimony to meet the needs of the party paying her fees, regardless of what the data in the case actually determines. Lawyers should know—but it is otherwise incumbent on psychiatrists to make clear—that clinicians/experts are not a part of either the defence or the prosecution team, as much as spirited involvement and camaraderie can sometimes motivate that degree of participation.

a) "Forensic Identification"

Zusman and Simon have hypothesized the role of a concept called "forensic identification"[1] to designate the unintentional process whereby clinicians

---

1   M.D. Zusman & J. Simon, "Differences in Repeated Psychiatric Examinations of Litigants to a Lawsuit" (1983) 140 American Journal of Psychiatry 1300.

adopt the perspective of the lawyers who retained them. Some lawyers either knowingly or unwittingly foster this "forensic identification" by developing a personal relationship with the expert. The expert becomes more inclined, as a result of this relationship, to bring his opinions in line with the legal strategy of the lawyer who has retained him.[2]

5) Psychiatric Experts vs. Treating Clinicians

Whether court-appointed or party-appointed, psychiatric experts do not ordinarily have a doctor/patient relationship, in the usual sense, with the evaluees they assess. Treating clinicians (that is, the accused's own physicians) should generally avoid being conscripted into the expert role as it requires them to compromise their treatment alliance with the patient/accused. Treating physicians are by definition supposed to advocate for the interests of their patients. That role is generally incompatible with being an expert in a legal proceeding. The expert role necessarily involves participating in a truth-finding process to which the treating physician has not dedicated himself. At a minimum, a treating physician should acknowledge that his primary involvement with the accused was as the latter's treating physician. In this way, it is the clinician who preemptively raises the appropriateness of his participation, and of testifying qua expert. There are, of course, circumstances where treating clinicians cannot avoid—nor should they avoid—testifying on behalf of their patients. In those instances, it is important that the reality of the doctor/patient relationship is brought to the court's attention. The clinician involved in a court proceeding in this way may well be functioning more as a material witness, even though his evidence derives from the realm of medical expertise.

C. THE SCOPE OF PSYCHOPATHOLOGY THAT ARISES IN FORENSIC PSYCHIATRIC CASES

The field of forensic psychiatry is quite diverse. Cases may, and often do, require an understanding of other areas of sub-specialization within psychiatry such as child and adolescent psychiatry, adult, and geriatric psychiatry, as well as fluency in biologic, phenomenologic, dynamic, and transcultural psychiatry. Any number of psychiatric disorders or conditions may be relevant,

---

2   See S. Hucker, "The Expert Witness" in H. Bloom & M. Bay, eds., *A Practical Guide to Mental Health, Capacity, and Consent Law of Ontario* (Toronto: Carswell, 1996).

or of central importance, in a criminal or civil proceeding. A non-exhaustive
list of conditions (refer to Chapter 1, Section C(1) for a full definition of each
condition) includes:

- schizophrenia;
- delusional disorder;
- organic mental disorders;
- depressive episode;
- bipolar disorder (a hypomanic or manic episode);
- post-traumatic stress disorder;
- panic disorder;
- mental retardation;
- fetal alcohol effect;
- conduct disorder;
- attention deficit hyperactivity disorder;
- personality disorders;
- psychopathy;
- impulse control disorders;
- substance abuse and dependence;
- dissociative disorders;
- paraphilias; and
- conversion disorder, somatization disorder, and chronic pain disorder.

D. THE PSYCHIATRIST-LAWYER RELATIONSHIP

The sometimes ill-assorted relationship between the lawyer and mental
health expert can potentially be fraught with suspicion, misapprehension of
one another's functions, and language problems, on either side.[3]

It is important for psychiatrists to take the time to educate lawyers about
the psychiatric aspects of their client's case. Lawyers are sometimes (understandably) very uninformed about how mental disorder could operate to either exonerate their clients, or mitigate the consequences of an encounter
with the criminal justice system. Psychiatrists should neither overstate nor
understate their abilities in a particular area, and should be forthcoming
about any limitations, biases, or other baggage they might bring to a case
that could jeopardize either the accused's or the prosecution's interests. The

---

3   H. Bloom & B.T. Butler, *Defending Mentally Disordered Persons* (Toronto: Carswell, 1995) at 15.

psychiatrist must be prepared to communicate with counsel on an ongoing basis. She must avoid acting without instruction or direction as that could compromise the position of the party who retained her.

1) Keeping the Expert Informed

Lawyers should be extremely careful about either intentionally or unintentionally withholding relevant or critical information from an expert because that information is likely to influence the expert's opinion in an unfavourable way. Not only is this an unethical practice, but it is at high risk for backfiring if the opposing lawyer brings the information up during cross-examination in an attempt to impugn the expert's credibility.

Lawyers and referring agencies should carefully appraise the nature and scope of the information provided to the expert. Reading or reviewing superfluous information is not only cost ineffective, but may provide excessive information that obfuscates, rather than clarifies. At a minimum, in a criminal prosecution the expert should be provided with relevant Crown disclosure documentation, including witness statements; inculpatory or exculpatory statements by the accused; audios and videos; and medical, psychiatric, probation and parole, and other documentation relevant to the accused's criminal history. Some cases, both civil and criminal, require expanding the inquiry to include the interviewing of previous or current teachers, previous or current employers, family members, and current and previous romantic partners. In addition, obtaining documentation such as school records, work records, and military records may be required. The general rule is that an expert needs to be provided with a sufficient fund of information to support the opinion she provides. The greater the reliability of the facts underpinning the opinion, the greater the weight to be attached to that opinion.[4]

E. THE USES OF PSYCHIATRIC EVIDENCE IN CRIMINAL PROCEEDINGS

Psychiatric consultation and evidence may be of use in a wide variety of scenarios. The need for psychiatric expertise can arise in any instance where a mental health, psychological, or behavioural issue becomes a focus of concern or interest in a proceeding before a criminal court. There is a great deal of room for the creative use of psychiatry, provided it meets the threshold test

---

4   *R. v. Abbey* (1982), 68 C.C.C. (2d) 394 (S.C.C.); *R. v. Lavallee* (1990), 55 C.C.C. (3d) 97 (S.C.C.).

of relevance and reliability.[5] The DSM IV-TR includes an explicit caution to clinicians about the uncritical application of the manual and its diagnostic criteria to forensic settings:

> When the DSM IV categories, criteria, and textual descriptions are employed for forensic purposes, there are significant risks that diagnostic information will be misused or misunderstood. These dangers arise because of the imperfect fit between the questions of ultimate concern to the law and the information contained in a clinical diagnosis. In most situations, the clinical diagnosis of a DSM IV mental disorder is not sufficient to establish the existence for legal purposes of a "mental disorder," "mental disability," "mental disease," or "mental defect." In determining whether an individual meets a specified legal standard (e.g., for competence, criminal responsibility, or disability), additional information is usually required beyond that contained in the DSM IV diagnosis. ...
>
> ... the fact that an individual's presentation meets the criteria for a DSM IV diagnosis does not carry any necessary implication regarding the individual's degree of control over the behaviors that may be associated with the disorder. Even when diminished control over one's behavior is a feature of the disorder, having the diagnosis in itself does not demonstrate that a particular individual is (or was) unable to control his or her behavior at a particular time.[6]

Examples of the various issues that can arise in a criminal proceeding for which psychiatric expertise may be of assistance are provided in this section.

1) Mental Illness, Confessions, Voluntariness & Inculpatory Statements

See Chapter 4, Section F.1.

a) False Confessions

See Chapter 4, Section F.2.

2) Psychiatric Aspects of Bailworthiness

See Chapter 4, Section A.1.

---

5   See *R. v. Mohan*, [1994] 2 S.C.R. 9; *R. v. Olscamp*, [1994] O.J. No. 2926 (Ct. J.).

6   American Psychiatric Association, *Diagnostic and Statistical Manual of the American Psychiatric Association*, 4th ed., Text Revision (Arlington, VA: American Psychiatric Association, 2000) at 32–33 [DSM IV-TR]. Reprinted with the permission of the American Psychiatric Association. © 2000.

3) Fitness to Stand Trial

See Chapter 3.

4) Testimonial Capacity

See Chapter 4, Section F.3.

5) Criminal Responsibility

See Chapters 5 and 6.

6) Automatism

See Chapter 5, Section H.

7) Diminished Responsibility—Intoxication and Intent

See Chapter 6.

8) Provocation, Self-Defence, and Duress

While any two accused may be alike, no two accused are psychologically the same. What is provocative to one—based on his or her personality and life experience (for example, previous sensitization to trauma), or stressors—may be inconsequential to another.

The same holds true, from a psychiatric perspective, for self-defence and duress.

A psychiatric assessment and report could elucidate psychiatric conditions, symptoms, and psychological factors that have a bearing on why the accused acted or reacted in the manner implicated in his or her charge.

9) Dangerousness & Risk Assessment

See Chapter 8 for an overview of risk assessment and Chapter 10 for an examination of dangerous and long-term offenders.

10) Sentencing—Subgroups of Offenders

See Chapter 9, Section C for a more in-depth look at sentencing considerations with mentally disordered offenders.

a) Violent Offenders

See Chapters 8 and 10.

b) Domestic Abusers

A psychiatric evaluation may be useful for the purpose of assisting the court in sentencing a domestic abuser or perpetrator of other family violence. Apart from focusing on the accused's treatability, the psychiatric assessment may assist by elucidating the basis for the offender's behaviour, and, importantly, describing his risk for recidivism (see Chapter 9).

c) Mentally Disordered Offenders

It has been known for some time that the concepts of specific and general deterrence have little or no applicability when sentencing mentally disordered offenders. In the case of offenders of this kind, the objectives of the maintenance of the integrity of the justice system and the security of society can be met best by careful attention to those variables that will reduce a mentally disordered offender's risk for relapse and consequent recidivism.[7]

d) Sex Offenders

The psychiatric contribution to sentencing sex offenders focuses on defining the basis of the offender's behaviour (for example, due to pedophilia), defining his risk for recidivism, and setting out a treatment plan that addresses every component of his risk (see Chapter 8).

e) Substance Abusers

There are now specialized courts in Toronto and elsewhere in North America that deal with issues unique to substance abusers. These courts and their personnel generally have greater intrinsic expertise to draw on to assist them in fashioning a rehabilitation-oriented sentence for an offender whose primary problem is substance abuse. These courts are otherwise connected to various community resources that specialize in alcohol and drug abuse rehabilitation.[8]

---

7   For a detailed discussion of issues that have to do with sentencing mentally disordered accused, see R.D. Schneider, "Sentencing Mentally Ill Offenders" in J.V. Roberts & D.P. Cole, eds., *Making Sense of Sentencing* (Toronto: University of Toronto Press, 1999).

8   For a detailed discussion of the workings of "Drug Courts," see P. Bentley, *Canada's First Drug Treatment Court* (2000), 31 C.R. (3d) 257.

f) Arsonists

Psychiatric experts can provide the court with an in-depth understanding of the motivation behind arson and address the fire-setter's risk for recidivism. Fire-setters engage in behaviour leading to arson for a number of reasons. At times, the behaviour is utilitarian and designed for material gain or for some other criminal purpose. A number of other fire-setters engage in this behaviour due to their psychopathology. Some are psychotic and are driven by voices and delusions to set the fire for a psychotic purpose, some are depressed and suicidal, and others set fires due to personality pathology (for example, borderline personality disorder patients). There are small subsets of fire-setters who have an impulse control disorder (pyromania), or, even more rarely, fire-setters who set fires for the purpose of sexual gratification.

g) Shoplifters

A significant number of shoplifters engage in this behaviour for purposes other than material gain. Often, the design and purpose of the act is not within the conscious awareness of the perpetrator. She may engage in the behaviour as a plea for help, as a symbolic act to replace an actual or impending loss, or because she feels deserving of punishment.[9]

h) Fraud Perpetrators

Psychiatric evaluation is useful in the case of some individuals who commit fraud where the behaviour is prompted by psychological conflicts and motivations that are not truly criminal in nature, but rather more likely have to do with dynamics similar to those touched on above with respect to shoplifters.

Psychodynamic Explanations for Criminal Behaviour: Many quirks of behaviour and flaws in character do not meet diagnostic thresholds for either major mental illness or personality disorders. A number of individuals who find themselves before the courts have come to behave in the manner that prompted the charge(s) due to psychological conflicts or sub-threshold emotional issues (that is, not major depression). Many are influenced by psychological forces (fantasies, wishes, impulses, and conflicts) of which they themselves are unaware (that is, unconscious motivation). It is invariably challenging for a clinician to explain the complex psychodynamic factors that might have motivated an accused at an unconscious level in a manner that makes the behaviour understandable to the court. Courts may nevertheless

---

9   Note that a number of shoplifters are clinically depressed.

receive psychodynamic explanations about an accused from a clinician as the best means for understanding what motivated his behaviour.

F. USE OF PSYCHIATRIC CONSULTATION AND EVIDENCE IN CIVIL PROCEEDINGS

While the focus of this module is criminal proceedings, it is worthwhile noting the various purposes for which psychiatric participation may be of value in civil proceedings as listed in the table below.

The Various Uses of Psychiatric Consultation and Evidence in Civil Proceedings	
Mental health & capacity • Civil commitment • Capacity to consent to treatment • Testamentary capacity • Capacity to contract • Financial competency	*Family law* • Suitability of mother or father for custody or access • Alleged sexual impropriety/impact of incest • Child welfare—abuse and neglect • Adoption • Matrimonial—claims of mental damages by a divorcing spouse

Civil liability
• Motor vehicle—damages for psychiatric injury
• Sexual victimization—post-traumatic stress disorder
• Sexual harassment—psychological impact
	Professional regulatory body
	• Professional misconduct
	  ▷ sexual abuse of patient or client
	  ▷ financial irregularities
	  ▷ disruptive and unprofessional behaviour
	• Fitness to practice

Worker's compensation • Psychiatric disability • Workplace stress claim	*Employment law* • Incapacitated employee • Sexual harassment in the workplace • Workplace threats, aggression, and violence • Fitness for duty and disability • Stress claims
Medical (psychiatric) malpractice • Liability for suicide • Liability for harm to third parties • Liability for medication side effects—tardive dyskinesia	*Immigration* • Mental disorder preventing entry into Canada • Impact of torture/mistreatment and claim to refugee status • Too dangerous to remain in Canada • Psychological impact of deportation

G. PSYCHIATRIC OPINION EVIDENCE

1) Generally

The ability of an expert opinion to meet the standard of acceptance depends, amongst other things, on the quality, integrity, and durability of the underlying facts upon which the opinion rests. Trainees in forensic psychiatry do well to bear in mind the analogy of a pyramid (see the figure below). The opinion (at the pyramid's summit), whether it concerns fitness to stand trial, criminal responsibility, diminished responsibility, or dangerousness, rests on a number of supportive structural components. Each structural component represents a reliable block of relevant information that both forms the factual foundation for the opinion and supports the opinion. Insufficiency in any one block may weaken the foundation of the opinion; a succession of weak structural elements (for example, unproven fact, unsupportable inferences, and poor reasoning) cannot but topple the opinion.

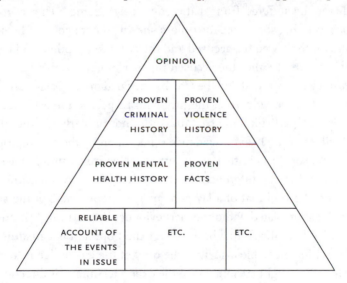

Expert Psychiatric Opinion

2) *R. v. Abbey*

In *R. v. Abbey,*[10] an accused charged with importing cocaine relied on a defence of insanity at trial. Both defence psychiatrists as well as the crown psychiatrist opined that he was suffering from hypomania (see Chapter 1, Section C), but differed in their views as to whether the accused was able to appreciate the

---

10   *R. v. Abbey*, [1982] 2 S.C.R. 24 [*Abbey*].

nature and quality of his acts at the time. A defence psychiatrist's opinion that the accused was suffering from hypomania at the time of the offence derived from interviews with the accused, the accused's mother, and other psychiatric reports. No other evidence was adduced that independently corroborated the facts upon which the opinion was based. The Supreme Court (per Dickson J.) ruled that "before any weight can be given to an expert's opinion, the facts upon which the opinion is based must be found to exist."[11] There was no admissible evidence before the Court with respect to the delusions the accused reportedly experienced (which, if proven, would have potentially exonerated him).

3) *R. v. Lavallee*

In *R. v. Lavallee*,[12] the accused shot and killed her common-law husband after he had assaulted her. She was charged with murder and relied on a defence of self-defence. In support of the accused's defence, a psychiatrist testified that she suffered from "battered-wife syndrome." The accused evidently believed that she would die unless she killed her spouse. The defence psychiatrist interviewed the accused and the accused's mother, and had read the police reports. Neither the accused nor her mother testified at the trial. The accused was acquitted and the Crown appealed on the basis that the trial judge did not properly instruct the jury with respect to the evidence of the psychiatrist,; in particular, the trial judge did not properly instruct the jury as to the effect of the hearsay evidence relied upon by the psychiatrist. The court (per Wilson J.) held that an expert could be called upon to assist the trier of fact in drawing inferences in areas where the expert has knowledge or experience beyond that of a lay person. The mental state of the accused could not be appreciated without expert evidence concerning "battered-wife syndrome." Where the factual basis of an expert opinion is a mixture of admissible and inadmissible evidence, the duty of the trial judge is to caution the jury that the weight attributable to the expert testimony is directly related to the amount and quality of admissible evidence on which it relies.

4) *R. v. Mohan*: The Four Criteria for the Admissibility of Expert Evidence

In *R. v. Mohan*,[13] the accused, a physician, was charged with four counts of sexual assault. The defence sought to call evidence that the perpetrator was

---

11   *Ibid.* at 46.

12   *R. v. Lavallee* (1990), 55 C.C.C. (3d) 97 (S.C.C.) [*Lavallee*].

13   *R. v. Mohan*, [1994] 2 S.C.R. 9 [*Mohan*].

a member of a limited and unusual class of perpetrators (from a psychiatric perspective), that the accused did not belong to that class, and that, consequently, he could not have committed the crimes. The trial judge had found that to have committed the acts in question, the perpetrator did not need to belong to a sufficiently distinctive class. It was not behaviour that could only be committed by a unique class of offenders. The issue was whether the opinion evidence the defence sought to adduce was admissible. The court (per Sopinka J.) reviewed and then restated the law regarding the admissibility of expert psychiatric evidence. His Lordship set out the following four criteria to be considered in establishing whether or not expert evidence is admissible.[14]

a) Factor 1: Probative Value Must Exceed Prejudicial Effect

To assist in determining legal relevance one can look at the benefits of the evidence; for example, the materiality, weight, and reliability of the evidence compared to its cost. Note that here "cost" not only means the practical ability of the trier of fact to receive the evidence, but also the cost of its prejudicial effect. The reliability requirement tests the scientific method or theory behind the evidence tendered. Appropriate questions here include can the underlying hypotheses behind the method be falsified?; have the expert's peers reviewed the expertise or test?; and has it received general acceptance in the relevant academic or scientific community?

In order for relevant evidence to be admissible, its probative value must exceed its prejudicial effect.

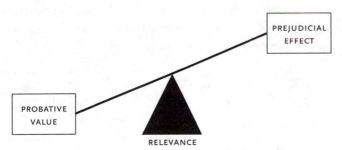

b) Factor 2: Evidence Must Be Necessary for the Trier of Fact

The evidence must be necessary in the sense that it provides information which is likely to be outside the experience and knowledge of the trier of fact. The test of necessity, sometimes referred to as the "test of helpfulness," is intended to prevent superfluous or redundant expert evidence from be-

---

14   *Ibid.* at para. 17.

ing presented. As Justice Dickson stated in *Abbey*,[15] experts provide judges and juries with "ready-made inference[s] which the judge and jury, due to the technical nature of the facts, are unable to formulate." If triers of fact can form their own opinions and conclusions without the purported expert evidence, then the expert's opinion is unnecessary.

Expert evidence is necessary when without it, triers of fact are at risk of coming to the wrong conclusion.

c) Factor 3: Evidence Must Not Be Subject to an Exclusionary Rule

Compliance with the three other Mohan criteria of relevance, necessity, and a properly qualified expert does not guarantee that expert evidence will be admissible if that evidence is at odds with an exclusionary rule. The most important and commonly encountered exclusionary rule, as regards the expert evidence of psychiatrists and psychologists, is the exclusionary rule for hearsay evidence. The case of *Abbey*[16] stands for the proposition that an expert's opinion must be based on a proven foundation of evidence and not on hearsay. In other words, the weight attached to relevant expert evidence is correlated with the strength of its factual foundation.

---

15   Above note 10.
16   *Ibid.*

In *Lavallee*,[17] the Supreme Court relaxed a previously stated rule in *Abbey* which required that psychiatric opinions be based only on proven facts if they were to be admitted into evidence. *Lavallee* allowed opinion evidence to be admitted if it was based on any admissible evidence; that is, a mixture of admissible and otherwise inadmissible evidence. If the factual foundation for the expert's opinion was rife with hearsay, however, it would likely be accorded little weight.

d) Factor 4: Psychiatric Evidence Must Be Given by a Properly Qualified Expert with Accepted Expertise

Psychiatric evidence must be put forward by a properly qualified expert. Evidence must be presented that establishes that the witness has acquired special or peculiar knowledge through education and/or experience with respect to the subject upon which he proposes to testify. The properly qualified expert concept extends to the requirement that the evidence tendered be properly qualified expertise. In this regard, a special caution was issued by Justice Sopinka in the *Mohan* case:

> ... expert evidence which advances a novel scientific theory or technique is subjected to special scrutiny to determine whether it meets a basic threshold of reliability and whether it is essential in the sense that the trier of fact will be unable to come to a satisfactory conclusion without the assistance of the expert. The closer the evidence approaches an opinion on an ultimate issue, the stricter the application of this principle.[18]

This consideration has arisen in relation to expert tests or methods over the last number of years and it is the reason that tests and methods, such as the polygraph test, sodium amytal interviews, and, most recently, phallometric testing, have yet to be accepted as admissible scientific evidence. In a recent case

LACK OF EXPERTISE

UNPROVEN TEST OR METHOD

RECOGNIZED EXPERTISE

PEER-ACCEPTED METHOD

PROPERLY QUALIFIED EXPERTISE

---

17   Above note 12.
18   Above note 13 at 25.

involving phallometric testing (an investigative procedure that has been around for thirty-five or forty years), Justice Binnie, writing the decision for a unanimous court, said of phallometric testing, that there is a very real possibility that "such evidence—cloaked under the mystique of science—would distort the fact-finding process ..."[19] In that case, a qualified psychiatrist/sexological expert intended to use the accused's phallometric testing results to provide the court with an opinion that the accused was not likely to have committed a series of sexual assaults against a three-year-old and a five-year-old boy.

H. GROUNDING THE EXPERT EVIDENCE IN SCIENCE

Many aspects of psychiatry (for example, motivation for behaviours, feelings, and thoughts) are not directly visible; instead, such psychopathological processes are inferred by creating an overall picture from signs and symptoms (overt behaviour, non-verbal communication, and speech) apparent to the examiner. A symptom is suggestive of disorder, but is not diagnostic in and of itself. A cluster of symptoms (that is, a syndrome) historically associated with a mental illness, and verified through research as being associated with that mental illness, meets with greater acceptance within the scientific world and in the courts.

Most judges recognize that psychiatry and psychology are not exact sciences. Courts cannot expect scientific precision when dealing with human behaviour; thus, courts are often in the position of making weighty decisions without any scientific accuracy. Gold,[20] however, implores psychiatric (and other) experts to hold dear "the primacy of the scientific method." He goes on to describe his concern that "faced with an expert's impressive credentials and mastery of scientific jargon, which lay jurors do not easily understand, jurors are likely to overvalue the evidence, giving it more weight than it really deserves, or even to abdicate their role as fact-finders and simply attorn, or defer, to the opinion of the expert in their desire to reach a just result." In a paper based on a talk presented at a joint conference of the Canadian Society of Forensic Science and Canadian Bar Association, Gold sets out a series of principles, propositions, and suggested areas of study that clinicians should know in order to be effective expert witnesses:

+ the concept of experimental design and the principles underlying the importance of blind and double-blind studies as an important aspect thereof;

---

19   *R. v. J-L. J.*, [2000] 2 S.C.R. 600 at para. 55.
20   A.D. Gold, *Expert Evidence in Criminal Law: The Scientific Approach* (Toronto: Irwin Law Inc., 2003) at 12.

- the necessity for scrupulous recording;
- the necessity for objective measurement of objectifiable qualities and quantities;
- the unreliability of verbal reports;
- the powerful impact of suggestibility on human beings, including experimenter bias and demand characteristics;
- the rules of logic and their application to conclusion-drawing;
- the omnipresence of chance as an explanation for any results;
- the meaning of base rates and why they are important;
- statistical phenomena such as regression to the mean (a form of chance phenomenon);
- the necessity of considering alternative explanations and hypotheses;
- the fundamental recognition that knowledge requires comparison: studying a target group gives you only suggestions; knowledge comes from studying a comparison group that differs from the target groups in the relevant aspects;
- correlation is not causation; and
- unfalsifiable claims are not science and their acceptance is a matter of taste, and not expertise.[21]

The mental health care expert should be cautious about providing opinions and testifying in areas where there is insufficient knowledge in the field to warrant an opinion offered with any measure of certainty. Such areas include dangerousness; propensity to commit an act; motivation; likelihood of recurrence; and the ability to detect lying and the credibility of witnesses. Above all, the expert should avoid incursion into the exclusive domain of the judge and jury, as would be the case if experts purported to offer opinions about the credibility of a witness or complainant.

1) Types of Experts and Their Credentials

An expert's curriculum vitae should be evaluated with respect to licensure/specialization, education, professional and academic affiliations, current and past professional positions, clinical and forensic experience, teaching and presentations, and especially publications.

---

21   Adapted from A.D. Gold, "Effective Expert Evidence" (Paper presented to "Where Law and Science Meet," the 46th Annual Conference of the Canadian Society of Forensic Science, Edmonton, AB, 18 November 1999) (unpublished). Reprinted with permission.

a) Psychiatrists

Psychiatrists are physicians who have completed a four-year residency training program in psychiatry and have completed written and oral examinations to entitle them to a fellowship (speciality designation) from the Royal College of Physicians and Surgeons of Canada. There are many areas of psychiatric subspecialization. Lawyers should select the area of subspecialty expertise most suitable to the subject matter:

- forensic psychiatrists (have particular expertise and a level of comfort appearing before most criminal and civil tribunals concerning a wide range of medico-legal issues);
- child and adolescent psychiatrists;
- geriatric psychiatrists;
- general hospital psychiatrists;
- psychotherapeutic/psychoanalytic therapists; and
- psychopharmacologists.

b) Psychologists and Neuropsychologists

These experts hold a Ph.D. (or equivalent degrees). Neuropsychologists are subspecialists who administer particular tests to determine which areas of the brain are responsible for a particular dysfunction. Psychological testing covers the following areas: personality, motivation, diagnosis, treatability, intelligence, specific brain function/dysfunction, psychological organization, and thought processes.

c) Social Workers

Usually experts in this group have a Bachelor's or Master's degree in social work. They assess individuals, couples, and families and they liaise between families and community and social service agencies. Generally, social workers are skilled in handling family dysfunction, child welfare issues, custody and access, and sexual abuse and incest.

d) Neurologists

Neurologists are experts who interpret the legal significance of conditions related to disorders of the brain and nervous systems such as epilepsy and congenital brain disorders.

e) Internists and Endocrinologists

Internists and endocrinologists have a specialty in internal medicine and a subspecialty in endocrinology, respectively. They are of particular use when a systemic illness and/or glandular disorder may have some significance to the matter giving rise to the legal proceeding; for example, the role hypoglycemia played in bringing about aggressive behaviour.

f) Sleep Experts

Sleep experts assess a patient's sleep cycle using polysomnography. These experts generally become involved when a case entails automatic behaviour that occurs during sleep; for example, violence associated with sleepwalking (somnabulism), or, a curious variant, sexomnia, which is sleep-related sexually assaultive behaviour.[22]

g) Toxicologists

Toxicologists offer opinions on blood levels of drugs and/or alcohol and the effects of these substances on the brain.

h) Pharmacologists

Pharmacologists are called upon in instances where the unique characteristics of a drug are thought to play a causative role in a criminal act, or where a drug is thought to have played a role in the client's ability to form specific intent.

2) Determining the Type of Expert Required

When deciding what kind of expert is needed it is important to consider a variety of factors, some of the more important being

- the nature of the case;
- whether more than one expert is required (that is, whether a multidisciplinary team is needed);
- whether a CT scan, MRI, EEG, and/or SPECT scan is required;
- whether hematologic, metabolic and endocrinologic laboratory evaluations are indicated;
- whether a sleep laboratory evaluation is required;
- whether there is a need for phallometric testing;
- whether the work-up should involve psychological or neuropsychological testing; and
- whether alcohol is implicated (that is, whether an alcohol tolerance test is required).

---

22   For a discussion of sexomnia, see C.M. Shapiro, N.N. Trajanovic, *et al.*, "Sexomnia—A New Parasomnia?" (2003) 48 Canadian Journal of Psychiatry 311.

I. THE IDEAL PSYCHIATRIC EVALUATION FOR COURT

1) General Concepts

Medico-legal evaluations are distinguishable from psychiatric evaluations that are carried out for general diagnostic and therapeutic purposes; for example, when a general medical practitioner refers a patient to a psychiatric colleague to assess the patient for depression, a psychotic disorder, or with respect to his candidacy for psychotherapy. A psychiatrist to whom a patient has been referred for diagnostic and/or therapeutic services has an inherently different relationship with the patient than is the case when an accused is sent to a psychiatrist for an assessment for court. The treating psychiatrist's allegiance is to the patient. It is both appropriate and expected that the psychiatrist advocate for the patient's interests. A treating clinician who has, for whatever reason, become involved in his patient's criminal prosecution (or civil action) should bring this consideration to the court's attention, either in the report or when asked to testify. The forensic psychiatric evaluator, on the other hand, should maintain a high index of suspicion about the quality and veracity of the information she receives from the subject of the assessment, knowing full well that the latter has not consulted the evaluator for diagnostic purposes and therapeutic relief. The premise of the consultation is some sort of financial gain, exemption from responsibility, or a mitigated disposition by the justice system.

2) Ethical Considerations

In contrast to a more general psychiatric examination, a psycho-legal assessment may be associated with a number of pitfalls, and could, in the end, prove adverse to the subject and cause her considerable misfortune. It is therefore incumbent upon examiners to review a number of key preliminary matters with the subject of an assessment before getting into the substantive aspects of it. The list of issues that examiners should take up with subjects prior to getting into the assessment include:

- lack of confidentiality;
- whether the subject consents to undergo the assessment;
- the fact that the examiner may be obligated, in certain instances, to disclose information provided in confidence; for example, if the examiner learns about child abuse, if the examiner is concerned that the subject is likely to inflict serious imminent physical or psychological

harm on an identifiable victim, or if the examiner is concerned about the evaluee's capacity to drive a motor vehicle;

- the manner in which the examiner will carry out the assessment;
- the issue of bias; and
- the implications for dishonesty, particularly if the court determines that what the expert has been told is significantly at odds with what the court has accepted as the facts in the case.

3) Clarity About the Retainer Question

Experts should be impeccably clear about their mandate before embarking on a potentially injurious fishing expedition.

4) Collateral Information

Experts should satisfy themselves that they have all of the relevant documentation in the case. If they do not, they should request it of the party retaining them or secure the subject's permission to pursue that information. In a similar vein, experts may, and often do, need to go beyond the subject of the assessment and interview collateral information sources; for example, spouses, family members, teachers, employers, probation officers, and former intimate partners.

5) Clinical Assessment

The clinical evaluation (that is, time spent with the subject in interview either by the psychiatrist and/or any other member of the team) must result in a thorough longitudinal history and cross-sectional evaluation of the subject's current functioning and mental status. There will obviously need to be special emphasis placed on obtaining the subject's account of the events giving rise to his charges. In the context of this discussion, the subject may need to be confronted with information that it is at odds with a version of the events that he presents. Experts should draw on any other available resources that are reasonable in the circumstances; for example, consultation with medical or psychiatric colleagues, laboratory investigations, neuroimaging, or psychological assessment and testing.

6) Diagnostic Formulation

At the end of the exercise, the clinician should provide a diagnostic formulation consistent with the method espoused by the DSM IV-TR. Experts get into difficulty when they use antiquated, eccentric, or imprecise diagnostic terms. Diagnostic formulation should include, wherever indicated, an appraisal of the accused's risk and a pronouncement as to her prognosis and motivation for treatment. It should go on to make meaningful recommendations as to what interventions would be of value in reducing the court's concerns about the offender.

7) The Ideal Psychiatric Report

Psychiatric reports are the essential vehicle for conveying an expert's psychiatric findings following an assessment of an accused. Psychiatric reports are the most basic product of a psychiatric evaluation. Although expert psychiatrists go to court in only a relatively small number of cases, they invariably prepare reports. If well written and thorough, a report may obviate the need for a court appearance. A report is often the only work product of an assessment that is formally introduced into a criminal proceeding. Needless to say, reports that are well-reasoned, balanced, and thorough; that synthesize all of the relevant information in the case; and that form a foundation for the opinions expressed in conclusion, will almost invariably be well-received by the parties. It is worthwhile for the forensic psychiatric evaluator to approach report writing with a fair measure of humility, understanding full well that every word contained in a report could expose him to rigorous cross-examination.

a) Guideline for Preparing Expert Psychiatric Reports

The following is a guideline for the preparation of an expert psychiatric report:

1. The beginning of the report should provide basic identifying and demographic information and deal with the expert's qualifications.
2. The report should make clear the specific psycho-legal issue the expert has been directed to address — for example, fitness to stand trial, criminal responsibility, or sentencing considerations — and should not address issues outside the scope of the referral.
3. Reports should be user friendly. Information should be compartmentalized so as to allow readers to navigate their way through the complexities of a report with comfort and ease.
4. Language should be intelligible to a wide cross-section of what is principally a lay readership. Technical terms should be explained, and, for the most part, jargon avoided. Where necessary, technical terms can be explained either in the body of the report, or in a glossary appended to it.

5. A report should contain a section which serves to demonstrate that the expert has attended to all ethical considerations and preliminary matters prior to getting into the substantive aspects of the assessment; for example, clarifying the relationship, ensuring that consent has been obtained, addressing confidentiality and legal obligations, reviewing the process of the assessment, and addressing the issue of bias.

6. Experts should include a section listing information relied upon in the formation of their opinions.

7. Reports should be well-balanced. Experts should be cognisant, on a moment-to-moment basis, of the need to be objective. In this regard, experts should demonstrate in their reports that they have entertained all hypotheses and the steps that they have taken to dismiss alternate hypotheses.

8. Psycho-legal reports must contain sufficient data to support the report's conclusions.

9. Reports should distinguish between what the subject of the assessment told the expert and what information has been gleaned from alternate sources.

10. Contradictions and inconsistencies in the data must be dealt with in the report.

11. Conclusions must be meaningful, and, in the end, rest on a solid factual foundation and database.

12. In the interest of objectivity, experts should feel free to declare their misgivings about the quality of the information and the accused's credibility (from a psychiatric perspective). Experts should also feel free to say so if they are uncertain about their conclusions, or lack confidence in one or more of the opinions they have expressed.

13. Experts must invariably deal with the issue of malingering. It must be posited as a hypothesis in any medico-legal matter and disposed of in a clear and well-reasoned manner.

J.   A CROSS-EXAMINER'S GUIDE TO THE CRITICAL APPRAISAL OF A PSYCHIATRIC EXPERT

1)   Introduction

It goes without saying that experts who fail to complete thorough evaluations, who rely on defective information, who approach evaluees in an unprofessional and unethical manner, who exhibit bias, and who write poor reports are highly vulnerable to being exposed as professionally incompetent, and, at times, even buffoons.

2) How Psychiatric Experts Flub Fitness Assessments

The following is a non-exhaustive list of errors that experts might make in carrying out a fitness assessment:

- assuming that the presence of a mental disorder is synonymous with being unfit to stand trial;
- failing to take the time to impart relevant information about the court process (information that the accused may never have had to begin with) before concluding that the accused lacks the requisite ability;
- failing to apply the appropriate test for unfitness (section 2 of the *Criminal Code*,[23] and the judicial interpretation of that test set out in *R. v. Taylor*[24]);
- confusing ignorance with inability;
- considering amnesia to be synonymous with unfitness; and
- failing to bear in mind that fitness is defined by the accused's overriding need to be able to conduct a defence, rather than by the boilerplate criteria such as knowing the job of the prosecutor.

3) How Psychiatric Experts Flub Bailworthiness Assessments

The errors experts might make in evaluating an accused's candidacy for judicial interim release, at least from a psychiatric perspective, include the following:

- failing to understand the criteria for bail;
- neglecting to clarify with counsel whether the expert is permitted to review the alleged offence with the accused, and otherwise, to address the implications of not being able to review that issue, if that is the case;
- failing to consider and describe the necessary detailed psychiatric management and supervision plan the court will require to be confident that the accused will be appropriately contained and treated while on bail;
- failing to address the issue of whether the accused has the wherewithal to attend court;
- failing to consider the accused's risk for harm to the public;
- failing to communicate with the accused's primary treating clinician(s), if there is one, and any other relevant collateral information sources so as to appraise realistic supervision in the community;
- failing to address treatment compliance; and

---

23   *Criminal Code*, R.S.C. 1985, c. C-46.
24   *R. v. Taylor* (1992), 11 O.R. (3d) 323 (C.A.).

- failing to address substance abuse issues.

4) How Psychiatric Experts Flub NCR Assessments

See Chapter 5, Section C.8(a).

5) How Psychiatric Experts Flub Dangerousness Assessments/Risk Assessments

A non-exhaustive list of some of the typical errors experts make in carrying out risk assessments and presenting them to the court includes the following:

- failing to understand the legal standard to be applied (that is, for the designation dangerous offender or long-term offender);
- failing to critically appraise the quality and veracity of information provided by the subject;
- failing to pursue a detailed description of all instances in the past when the accused has been aggressive/sexually inappropriate;
- over-reliance on actuarial risk appraisal tools to the exclusion of relevant clinical data (for a detailed discussion of this issue see Chapter 9);
- failing to carry out a thorough assessment;
- failing to use actuarial and clinical risk-appraisal tools;
- failing to acknowledge limitations in the field of risk assessment;
- lacking specific expertise to carry out a risk assessment;
- identifying risk without making concomitant risk reduction recommendations; and
- applying actuarial data to populations (that is, accused) for whom the tool was not created (that is, there is no normative data).

K. CONCLUSION

Psychiatrists and other mental health professionals play an important role in helping courts make meaningful decisions about the complexities of human behaviour. The "privilege" of participating in the legal process requires that experts approach the task objectively and honesty, and that they readily concede their own and their discipline's limitations. Experts are but invitees in the legal arena in which they work. Thoroughly understanding the legal tests and standards to be applied will help to guide the inquiry and its conclusions and will allow the expert to present the most meaningful, probative, and unassailable evidence.

CHAPTER THREE

Fitness to Stand Trial

A. INTRODUCTION/BRIEF HISTORY OF THE FITNESS RULES

The requirement that an accused be "fit to stand trial" stems from the ancient notion that an accused must be present to respond to accusations of the state. That basic requirement developed into a more refined view that the accused must not only be physically present but mentally present as well. Accordingly, rules originally developed at common law were codified in 1992 and are contained in section 2 of the *Criminal Code:*[1]

> *"unfit to stand trial"*
> "unfit to stand trial" means unable on account of mental disorder to conduct a defence at any stage of the proceedings before a verdict is rendered or to instruct counsel to do so, and, in particular, unable on account of mental disorder to
> (a) understand the nature or object of the proceedings,
> (b) understand the possible consequences of the proceedings, or
> (c) communicate with counsel;

The procedures for dealing with the issue of unfitness to stand trial, and mental disorder in general, are set out in Part XX.1 of the *Criminal Code.*

1) Current State of Affairs

Recently we have seen an unprecedented increase in the number of mentally disordered accused entering the criminal justice system in respect of whom the issue of "fitness" arises. Statistics show that over the last decade the num-

---

1   R.S.C. 1985, c. C-46.

ber of mentally disordered accused entering the criminal justice system has been escalating at a minimum of 10 percent annually while overall arrest and prosecution rates have been declining.[2]

There have been a number of hypotheses offered to explain this growth some of which include: 1) cutbacks in mental health care (civil) spending; 2) a perception that the new Part XX.1 of the *Criminal Code* is less harsh and is therefore inviting the issue; 3) inadequate civil legislation; and 4) a climate of "zero tolerance" regarding criminal activity, whether or not it is the product of mental disorder. These explanations are speculative and, if valid, may be complementary and overlapping. What is very clear is that the criminal justice system is having to deal with mentally disordered accused in volumes that are difficult to accommodate.

B. WHEN MAY THE ISSUE ARISE?

The issue of fitness may arise at any point in the proceedings. Most often, the issue arises at first appearance and is resolved prior to arraignment; however, the issue may arise during the course of a trial or preliminary hearing and may arise on multiple occasions (subsection 672.23(1)):

> *Court may direct issue to be tried*
>
> 672.23 (1) Where the court has reasonable grounds, at any stage of the proceedings before a verdict is rendered, to believe that the accused is unfit to stand trial, the court may direct, of its own motion or on application of the accused or the prosecutor, that the issue of fitness of the accused be tried.

As is apparent from the definition of "unfit to stand trial," now contained in section 2 of the *Criminal Code*, as set out above, the statutory provisions only relate to "unfitness" *prior to a verdict*. Where the issue arises after a verdict is pronounced and prior to sentencing or during the course of sentencing, the statutory provisions do not apply. It may be that, from a common law or *Charter of Rights* perspective, the prosecution may not be able to proceed. This issue, and the problem created by the definition in section 2, is currently being considered by Parliament and may result in an amendment which would resolve this rare but difficult situation.

---

2   See R.D. Schneider, *Statistical Survey of Provincial and Territorial Review Boards* (Ottawa: Department of Justice, 2000); Canadian Centre for Justice Statistics, *Canadian Crime Statistics* (Ottawa: Canadian Centre for Justice Statistics, 2002).

1) Unfitness Post-Verdict?

The relevant sections indicate that the statutory provisions dealing with unfitness to stand trial only pertain up to the point of a verdict. Therefore, if the accused becomes "unfit" after a verdict and prior to sentencing, Part XX.1 of the *Criminal Code* is not available.[3] Although not frequently encountered—because most accused are sentenced immediately upon their conviction—this problem does arise from time to time. The Standing Committee on Justice has recommended section 2 of the *Criminal Code* be amended so as to include the sentencing phase of the prosecution. As it stands now, the provisions have been modified (at least for Ontario) with Justice McWatt's recent decision in *R. v. G.B.*[4] Justice McWatt "read-in" the words "at any stage of the proceedings before a verdict is rendered or sentence imposed."[5]

2) "Reasonable Grounds" for a Judge to Order a Fitness Assessment

What amounts to "reasonable grounds" for a judge to order a fitness assessment (subsection 672.11(a)) and then direct a trial of that issue (672.23(1)1)? While there is no specific formula to answer that question, we invite the reader to consider that only those aspects of the accused's behaviour, words, or appearance that may bear on the issue of his fitness be considered. It must be reasonably inferred from how the accused has been acting since arrest, or how he is behaving in the courtroom, that his capacity to understand the constituent elements of the process is compromised. Psychotic symptoms or behaviour invariably qualify, although, to press the point, even a psychotic accused may be fit, provided the subject matter of the delusions or hallucinations neither impinges on his understanding of his legal predicament and the process, nor interferes with his participation in the process. The table below provides some guidelines of "appropriate" and "inappropriate" reasons. Fairness—the value upon which the process rests—dictates that any uncertainty enure to the accused's benefit.[6]

---

3   For a more thorough discussion of this problem, consult R.D. Schneider, "Fitness to be Sentenced" (1998) 41 Crim L.Q. 261.

4   *R. v. G.B.*, [2003] O.J. No. 784 (S.C.J.).

5   *Ibid.* at para. 48.

6   Note that the following represent guidelines. Evidence of a number of items listed under the "Inappropriate Reasons" column, taken together, may reasonably raise a question.

Reasons for a Judge to Order a Fitness Assessment	
Appropriate Reasons	*Inappropriate Reasons*
• Specific information seen or heard that accused does not understand and/or cannot participate in court process • Evidence of hallucinations and delusions affecting the accused's comprehension of the proceedings and/or ability to participate in it • Evidence of significant disordered thought—confusion • Evidence of difficulty processing information • Inability to concentrate • Apathy/Withdrawal • Muteness • Marked disruptive behaviour together with evidence of abnormal affect/perception/thought processes/delusions • Information or evidence of marked impairment of mood (significant depression or elation) • Patient is suicidal	• Accused has a psychiatric history (with no clear evidence of active mental illness) • Accused or counsel asks that the accused go to hospital • Accused is homeless • To understand how and why the accused became a habitual criminal • To provide treatment for an otherwise non-compliant accused under the guise of a need to assess him • Accused is angry and loud (with no evidence/history of mental disorder) • Accused's family conveys that the accused should be in hospital and not jail • Accused is unkempt, disheveled, or malodorous • Allegations are bizarre, or disclose that the accused's behaviour at the relevant time was bizarre (absent other information bearing on the issue of the accused's fitness) • Accused interrupts the proceedings (with no evidence/history of mental disorder) • Accused is seen muttering to himself.

C. WHO MAY RAISE THE ISSUE?

As indicated in subsection 672.23(1), set out above, the court may direct the trial of the issue upon its own motion or on application by the accused or the prosecutor.

D. COUNSEL

Where the court has reasonable grounds to believe that an accused may be unfit to stand trial and the accused is not represented by counsel, the court shall order that the accused be represented by counsel (subsection 672.24(1)). Therefore, counsel should be appointed prior to the making of an assessment order.

Counsel

> 672.24 (1) Where the court has reasonable grounds to believe that an accused is unfit to stand trial and the accused is not represented by counsel, the court shall order that the accused be represented by counsel.

1) Difficulties for Counsel

Where counsel is "retained" by someone other than the accused, usually a concerned family member, it must be remembered that the accused is nevertheless the client. Counsel will often encounter situations where the family members are offering advice and "instructions" that may sound more rational than those obtained from the accused. Counsel will nevertheless be required to take instructions from their client so long as they are not unethical or illegal, or would mislead the court in any way.

Family members may welcome, or even encourage, the laying of a criminal charge so that a process may unfold which will access assessment and treatment opportunities which had been difficult to obtain in the civil mental health care system. While this may objectively enure to the accused's clinical well-being, these opportunities may be resisted by the accused; counsel will nevertheless be bound to follow their client's instructions.

E. ASSESSMENTS

1) Jurisdiction to Order an Assessment

The court must have reasonable grounds to believe that medical evidence is necessary to determine the issue of fitness (section 672.11(a)), or, the court or review board may want to know whether the accused is permanently unfit and, if so, whether the accused constitutes a significant threat to the safety of the public (section 672.11(e)).

> *Assessment order*
>
> 672.11 A court having jurisdiction over an accused in respect of an offence may order an assessment of the mental condition of the accused, if it has reasonable grounds to believe that such evidence is necessary to determine
>
> (a) whether the accused is unfit to stand trial;
> (b) whether the accused was, at the time of the commission of the alleged offence, suffering from a mental disorder so as to be exempt from criminal responsibility by virtue of subsection 16(1);

(c) whether the balance of the mind of the accused was disturbed at the time of commission of the alleged offence, where the accused is a female person charged with an offence arising out of the death of her newly-born child;

(d) the appropriate disposition to be made, where a verdict of not criminally responsible on account of mental disorder or unfit to stand trial has been rendered in respect of the accused; or

(e) whether an order should be made under section 672.851 for a stay of proceedings, where a verdict of unfit to stand trial has been rendered against the accused.

An assessment order may be on a Form 48 (see Appendix A). "Assessment" means an assessment by a medical practitioner (section 672.1).

"assessment"

"assessment" means an assessment by a medical practitioner or any other person who has been designated by the Attorney General as being qualified to conduct an assessment of the mental condition of the accused under an assessment order made under section 672.11 or 672.121, and any incidental observation or examination of the accused;

In Part XX.1 of the *Criminal Code*, the court is not entitled to order that the accused be assessed at any hospital. It is limited to those hospitals that have been "designated" by the provincial/territorial Minister of Health.

"hospital"

"hospital" means a place in a province that is designated by the Minister of Health for the province for the custody, treatment or assessment of an accused in respect of whom an assessment order, a disposition or a placement decision is made;

While the above provisions pertain to the making of a court-ordered assessment, any witness who is able to give relevant information may be called at the actual trial of the issue. Mental health practitioners, such as psychologists, may be particularly appropriate.

2) Who May Request that an Assessment be Ordered?

For summary matters, where the prosecutor is seeking an assessment order, the court may only make the order where the accused raises the issue of fitness, or the prosecutor satisfies the court that there are reasonable grounds to doubt the accused's fitness (subsection 672.12(2).

Limitation on prosecutor's application for assessment of fitness

(2) Where the prosecutor applies for an assessment in order to determine whether the accused is unfit to stand trial for an offence that is prosecuted by way of summary conviction, the court may only order the assessment if

(a) the accused raised the issue of fitness; or

(b) the prosecutor satisfies the court that there are reasonable grounds to doubt that the accused is fit to stand trial.

As well, pursuant to the provisions of section 672.851(5), the court or review board (sections 672.11(e) and 6721.121) may order an assessment in order to determine whether a stay of proceedings should be made pursuant to the provisions of section 672.851. For a complete discussion of the "permanently unfit accused," see Chapter 3, Section N, below.

3) Custody

It is presumed that all assessments will take place out of custody, with certain exceptions imported from subsubsection 515(10) (section 672.16).

Presumption against custody

672.16 (1) Subject to subsection (3), an accused shall not be detained in custody under an assessment order of a court unless

(a) the court is satisfied that on the evidence custody is necessary to assess the accused, or that on the evidence of a medical practitioner custody is desirable to assess the accused and the accused consents to custody;

(b) custody of the accused is required in respect of any other matter or by virtue of any other provision of this Act; or

(c) the prosecutor, having been given a reasonable opportunity to do so, shows that detention of the accused in custody is justified on either of the grounds set out in subsection 515(10).

Note that while the presumption is that all assessments will take place on an "out-of-custody" basis, in practice, given the accused's clinical condition which has spawned the concern, most fitness assessments will take place on an in-custody basis. The accused may be floridly psychotic and not in a position to comply with any terms of release that might otherwise be imposed. Nevertheless, where appropriate supervision and arrangements can be made, the presumption should apply.

4) Duration of the Assessment

An assessment order to determine fitness shall be in force for no more than five days, excluding holidays and travel time. Where the accused and the prosecutor agree, this may be extended to thirty days or, in compelling circumstances, sixty days (sections 672.14 and 672.15).

General rule for period

672.14 (1) An assessment order shall not be in force for more than thirty days.

Exception in fitness cases

(2) No assessment order to determine whether the accused is unfit to stand trial shall be in force for more than five days, excluding holidays and the time required for the accused to travel to and from the place where the assessment is to be made, unless the accused and the prosecutor agree to a longer period not exceeding thirty days.

Exception for compelling circumstances

(3) Despite subsections (1) and (2), a court or Review Board may make an assessment order that remains in force for sixty days if the court or Review Board is satisfied that compelling circumstances exist that warrant it.

Extension

672.15 (1) Subject to subsection (2), a court or Review Board may extend an assessment order, of its own motion or on the application of the accused or the prosecutor made during or at the end of the period during which the order is in force, for any further period that is required, in its opinion, to complete the assessment of the accused.

Maximum duration of extensions

(2) No extension of an assessment order shall exceed thirty days, and the period of the initial order together with all extensions shall not exceed sixty days.

5) Variation of Assessment Orders

These may be granted upon application (section 672.18).

Application to vary assessment order

672.18 Where at any time while an assessment order made by a court is in force the prosecutor or an accused shows cause, the court may vary the terms of the order respecting the interim release or detention of the accused in such manner as it considers appropriate in the circumstances.

6) Treatment of an Accused During an Assessment

An assessment order shall not direct an accused to receive or submit to treatment (section 672.19).

> *No treatment order on assessment*
>
> 672.19 No assessment order may direct that psychiatric or any other treatment of the accused be carried out, or direct the accused to submit to such treatment.

7) Bail Hearings

No order for the release or detention of an accused shall be made while an assessment order is in force (section 672.17).

> *Assessment order takes precedence over bail hearing*
>
> 672.17 During the period that an assessment order made by a court in respect of an accused charged with an offence is in force, no order for the interim release or detention of the accused may be made by virtue of Part XVI or section 679 in respect of that offence or an included offence.

F. REPORTS

An assessment order may direct the assessor to submit an assessment report (subsection 672.2(1)).

> *Assessment report*
>
> 672.2 (1) An assessment order may require the person who makes the assessment to submit in writing an assessment report on the mental condition of the accused.

Where a report is ordered it shall be filed with the court as directed (subsection 672.2(2)).

> *Assessment report to be filed*
>
> (2) An assessment report shall be filed with the court or Review Board that ordered it, within the period fixed by the court or Review Board, as the case may be.

Copies shall be provided to the prosecutor, the accused, and counsel for the accused (subsection 672.2(4)).

Copies of reports to accused and prosecutor

(4) Subject to subsection 672.51(3), copies of any report filed with a court or Review Board under subsection (2) shall be provided without delay to the prosecutor, the accused and any counsel representing the accused.

1) Model Report Content

While we routinely see very complete and comprehensive reports tendered as exhibits, especially where they are produced by a "designated facility," a completely satisfactory report may be produced in a much more compressed manner. The issue of fitness to stand trial is typically an important but relatively straightforward matter which does not require an extensive report. If the immediate psycho-legal question is properly addressed, a complete report may be only a page or two in length. Often, the "extra" material provided is not relevant to the issue.

MODEL FORMAT FOR FITNESS TO STAND TRIAL REPORT:
- identifying data:
  - name
  - date of birth
  - charges
  - date(s) of interview
- referral source and reason for referral
- qualifications of examiner
- preliminary cautions reviewed with accused (for example, as to limits in confidentiality)
- concerns about accused's credibility (from a psychiatric perspective; that is, confused, contradictory, vague, guarded, or evasive)
- information reviewed:
  - police documents and witness statements
  - jail notes
  - medical and psychiatric records
- personal and family histories (briefly)
- medical and psychiatric histories
- substance abuse history
- legal/criminal history
- current mental status examination
- focused review of fitness evaluation:
  - understanding of charges and consequences of conviction
  - knowledge of role of courtroom personnel
  - knowledge of trial procedure, pleas and purpose of oath

- ▷ ability to communicate with and respond to counsel
- ▷ ability to challenge witness
- ▷ ability to testify
- ◆ opinions and conclusions:
  - ▷ diagnosis
  - ▷ malingering
  - ▷ concerns about safety (suicidal or violent)
  - ▷ fitness to stand trial
  - ▷ treatment—restoration of fitness to stand trial
- ◆ availability for court

G. TRIAL OF THE ISSUE OF FITNESS

1) Jurisdiction to Try Issue

As set out in subsection 672.23(1), above, reasonable grounds are required to believe that the accused is unfit to stand trial. Such grounds are often supported by medical evidence, although this is not strictly necessary.

2) Who Tries the Issue?

This responsibility falls to the trier of fact: either a judge, when sitting alone, or a jury (section 672.26).

> *Trial of issue by judge and jury*
>
> 672.26 Where an accused is tried or is to be tried before a court composed of a judge and jury,
>
> (a) if the judge directs that the issue of fitness of the accused be tried before the accused is given in charge to a jury for trial on the indictment, a jury composed of the number of jurors required in respect of the indictment in the province where the trial is to be held shall be sworn to try that issue and, with the consent of the accused, the issues to be tried on the indictment; and
>
> (b) if the judge directs that the issue of fitness of the accused be tried after the accused has been given in charge to a jury for trial on the indictment, the jury shall be sworn to try that issue in addition to the issues in respect of which it is already sworn.

3) When to Try the Issue?

The issue may not be tried until the prosecutor has made their election (if applicable) as to mode of trial (subsection 672.25(1)).

Postponing trial of issue

672.25 (1) The court shall postpone directing the trial of the issue of fitness of an accused in proceedings for an offence for which the accused may be prosecuted by indictment or that is punishable on summary conviction, until the prosecutor has elected to proceed by way of indictment or summary conviction.

The trial of the issue may be postponed, where it arises at a preliminary inquiry before the close of the prosecution's case, until a time that is not later than the time the accused is called upon to answer the charge (subsection 672.25(2)(a)); or, at a trial, to a time not later than the opening of the case for the defence; or, upon application of the accused, until any later time directed by the court (section 672.25(2)(b)).

Idem

(2) The court may postpone directing the trial of the issue of fitness of an accused

(a) where the issue arises before the close of the case for the prosecution at a preliminary inquiry, until a time that is not later than the time the accused is called on to answer to the charge; or

(b) where the issue arises before the close of the case for the prosecution at trial, until a time not later than the opening of the case for the defence or, on motion of the accused, any later time that the court may direct.

Where the trial of the issue is postponed and the accused is either discharged or acquitted prior to the trial of the issue of fitness, that issue shall not be tried (section 672.3).

Acquittal

672.3 Where the court has postponed directing the trial of the issue of fitness of an accused pursuant to subsection 672.25(2) and the accused is discharged or acquitted before the issue is tried, it shall not be tried.

H. UNFIT TO STAND TRIAL: THE TEST

1) Section 2

"Unfit to stand trial" is defined as unable on account of mental disorder to conduct a defence at any stage of the proceedings before a verdict is rendered, or to instruct counsel to do so, and, in particular, unable on account of mental disorder to: a) understand the nature and object of the proceedings,

b) understand the possible consequences of the proceedings, or c) communicate with counsel.

The test is not whether the accused *knows* his legal situation, etc., but whether he is *able* to understand the concepts and communicate with counsel. The accused's capacity is the central concern. Simple ignorance does not render an accused unfit.

"Mental disorder" is defined as "disease of the mind." Disease of the mind "embraces any illness, disorder or abnormal condition which impairs the human mind and its functioning"[7] The definition from the perspective of criminal law is broad and includes, for example, mental retardation.[8]

a) Psychopathology Associated with Fitness Problems

Clinical practice has made clear that psychosis, usually on the basis of schizophrenia, is the most frequently found condition leading to a finding of unfitness to stand trial. An American study found a strong correlation between psychosis and mental retardation, and unfitness to stand trial in patients with those conditions.[9] Other conditions well-represented in populations of unfit accused include organic mental disorders, particularly dementia, mania, and psychotic depression. Some form of psychotic disorder, particularly schizophrenia, will be the most common mental disorder or condition underpinning a concern and subsequently a finding that the accused is unfit to stand trial.[10]

According to Ogloff and Whittemore,[11] individuals referred for fitness evaluations are most often single, unemployed men living alone, the majority of whom have a previous psychiatric history. Observations on psychiatric wards and forensic units of individuals considered to be unfit indicate that they are more preoccupied, verbally abusive, hostile, assaultive, restless, so-

---

7   *R. v. Cooper*, [1980] 1 S.C.R. 1149.

8   For example, *R. v. Rouse*, [1996] O.J. No.4688 (Gen. Div.).

9   M.S. Heller, W.H. Taylor, S.M. Ehrlich *et al.* "Intelligence, Psychosis and Competency to Stand Trial" (1981) 9 Bulletin of the American Academy of Psychiatry and the Law 267.

10   A.E. Daniel, N.C. Beck, A. Herath, M. Schmidt, & K. Menning, "Factors Correlated with Psychiatric Recommendations of Incompetency and Insanity" (1984) 12 Journal of Psychiatry and Law 527. R. Roesch, D. Eaves, R. Sollner, M. Normandin, & W. Glackman, "Evaluating Fitness to Stand Trial: A Comparative Analysis of Fit and Unfit Defendants" (1981) 4 International Journal of Law and Psychiatry 145.

11   J.R.P. Ogloff & K.E. Whittemore, "Fitness to Stand Trial and Criminal Responsibility in Canada" in R.A. Schuller & J.R.P. Ogloff, eds., *Introduction to Psychology and Law: Canadian Perspectives* (Toronto: University of Toronto Press, 2001) 283.

cially isolated, thought disordered, and bizarre in their affect and behaviour than individuals considered fit.[12]

The following chart provides a crude overview of the relationship between specific symptoms a mentally disordered individual might experience and the potential impact of the symptom(s) on an area relevant to the individual's fitness to stand trial. Note that any one symptom, if experienced intensely, can impinge upon a number of areas of fitness. The chart's purpose is to suggest the more common relationship between a symptom/limitation and area of deficit with respect to fitness.

Area of Fitness	Conditions/Symptom Complex							
Potentially Compromised	Hallucinations	Delusions	Thought Disorder	Confusion	Depression & Self-Defeating Motivation	Mental Retardation (Mild)	Mental Retardation (Moderate)	Front Lobe Syndrome
Understand Charges	+/-	+/-	++	++	+/-	+/-	++	+/-
Understand Object Proceeding	+/-	+/-	++/-	++	+/-	+/-	++	++/-
Understand Consequences of Conviction	+/-	+/-	++/-	++	+/-	+/-	++	++/-
Understand Roles of Court Offices	+/-	+/-	++/-	++	+/-	+/-	++	++/-
Understand Pleas	+/-	+/-	++	++	+/-	+/-	++	++/-
Understand Strategies	+/-	+/-	++	++	++/-	+/-	++	++/-
Trust Counsel	+/-	+/- *	+/-	+/-	+/-	+/-	+/-	+/-
Relate to Counsel	+/-	+/-	++	++	++/-	++/-	++	++/-
Receive Guidance	+/-	+/-	++	++	+/-	+/-	++/-	++/-
Appraise Evidence	+/-	+/-	++/-	++	+/-	+/-	++/-	++/-
Testify	++/-	++/-	++	++	++/-	+/-	++	++
Act in Self-Preservational Manner	+/-	+/-	+/-	++	++	+/-	++	++
Self-Control	+/-	+/-	+/-	++/-	+/-	+/-	+/-	++/-

*   Likely not if the delusions are of a paranoid or grandiose nature.

---

12   R. Roesch *et al.*, above note 10.

Hallucinations and delusions do not render someone unfit, *per se,* unless the hallucinations and the delusions are implicated and impinge on one or more of the abilities referred to in section 2. Marked lack of insight, that is, a failure to see oneself as suffering from a condition others have diagnosed the individual with, is arguably also a factor to be taken into consideration when determining whether a person is fit or unfit to stand trial. An individual may appear to meet the barebones test for fitness to stand trial, and yet have a significant limitation in insight that prevents the individual from recognizing the disease process that may allow for exoneration through an NCR defence.

Amnesia for the events does not of itself render an accused unfit to stand trial. Memory impairment for the critical events is a common finding in violent crime. When it does not represent willful suppression, apparent memory difficulties are often attributable to substance consumption prior to the act, the inability to register memory because of the marked affective disruption the accused experienced at the time of the act, or both.

In *R. v. Morrissey,*[13] at the conclusion of the evidence at trial, the defence argued that the accused's inability to recall the events prior to and at the time he allegedly shot and killed his estranged girlfriend, due to an organic amnestic disorder/frontal lobe syndrome, made him unfit to stand trial. The principal concern here was that the accused's memory loss for the critical events and proneness to confabulation would prevent him from testifying relevantly in his defence. Counsel for the accused argued that his ability to testify in the circumstances, as a result of his brain condition, would result in a breach of his rights to life, liberty, and security of the person, and right to a fair trial, pursuant to sections 7 and 11(d), respectively, of the *Charter of Rights and Freedoms.*[14]

The trial judge essentially concluded that the accused's potential inability to testify as a result of a self-inflicted act, when it was unclear in any event whether he would have either been able to or chosen to testify for his own benefit, did not violate the *Charter of Rights and Freedoms.* The accused's limitations, for whatever reason, represented a sound tactical reason to keep him from testifying, but did not render his trial unfair. The case also touched on the policy concern that exempting individuals from prosecution on the basis

---

13   *R. v. Morrissey,* [2003] O.J. No. 5960 (S.C.J.).

14   *Canadian Charter of Rights and Freedoms,* Part I of the *Constitution Act, 1982,* being Schedule B to the *Canada Act 1982* (U.K.), 1982, c. 11.

of amnesia, which occurs commonly in violent crime (30 to 50 percent of cases), would lead to an untenable result.

To "conduct a defence" suggests that any dysfunction caused by a mental disorder that would render the accused unable to conduct his defence (or instruct counsel to do so), in addition to the examples contained in section 2, would make an accused unfit. The operative consideration is the accused's ability "to conduct a defence." The three particulars listed in subsections (a), (b), and (c) are seemingly examples of the most common domains of inquiry in the accused's ability to conduct a defence. In addition, given that a "defence" may require competence over a considerable period of time, depending on the nature of the litigation, fitness arguably requires a prospective component to the test.

"Before a verdict is rendered": the statutory provisions dealing with unfitness to stand trial only pertain to the point of a verdict. For a fuller discussion of this problem see Chapter 3, Sections B and B.1.

Traditionally, the criteria set out in section 2 have been explored through a set of questions such as the following:

- What are the roles of the various people in the courtroom?;
- What are the charges the accused is facing?;
- What are the available pleas?;
- What are the consequences of a conviction?;
- What is the meaning of an oath?; and
- What is perjury?

b) Fitness Interview Test[15]

The Fitness Interview Test (FIT) is a semistructured interview that takes thirty minutes to administer. All areas relevant to an accused's capacity to conduct his defence are inquired into and scored on a 3-point scale (2=impaired, 1=mildly impaired, and 0=not impaired.). The items of the FIT are outlined below.

- Section I: Understand the Nature or Object of Proceedings:
  - ▷ Item 1: Understanding of arrest process
  - ▷ Item 2: Understanding of current charges
  - ▷ Item 3: Understanding of the role of key participants
  - ▷ Item 4: Understanding of the legal process

---

15   R. Roesch, P.A. Zapf, D. Eaves, & C.D.Webster, *The Fitness Interview Test*, revised ed. (Burnaby, BC: Mental Health, Law, and Policy Institute, 1998) [FIT].

▷ Item 5: Understanding of pleas
▷ Item 6: Understanding of the court procedure
• Section II: Understand the Possible Consequences:
▷ Item 7: Appreciation of the possible penalties
▷ Item 8: Appraisal of available legal defences
▷ Item 9: Appraisal of likely outcome
• Section III: Communicate with Counsel:
▷ Item 10: Capacity to communicate facts
▷ Item 11: Capacity to relate to lawyer
▷ Item 12: Capacity to plan legal strategy
▷ Item 13: Capacity to engage in defence
▷ Item 14: capacity to challenge witnesses
▷ Item 15: Capacity to testify relevantly
▷ Item 16: Capacity to manage courtroom behaviour

2) Limited Cognitive Capacity Test

R. v. Taylor[16] sets the test for fitness to stand trial as the "limited cognitive capacity test." This test requires that the accused have only a rudimentary factual understanding of his legal predicament. A "rational" understanding is not required, nor is it necessary that the accused be able to act in her own best interests.[17]

a) Cases Missed by the *Taylor* Rules

The *Taylor* decision reflects the difficulty courts have in understanding the depth and scope of mental illness and its infiltrative quality, and the extent to which it can interfere with a person's capacity to enlist *normal* self-preservational functions; these functions do not just depend on cognitive abilities, but on other areas of intrapsychic functioning, such as motivation, insight, affect and volition. Cases where accused are unfit due to a reason other than cognitive impairment and overt psychosis are often more subtle. Both counsel and the forensic psychiatric examiner should maintain a high index of suspicion when certain information suggests the possibility or likelihood of a deficit. The test consequently fails to filter out a number of different types of accused who are probably not fit, and, having regard to the purpose and

16   *R. v. Taylor* (1992), 11 O.R. (3d) 323 (C.A.) [*Taylor*].
17   For a critique of the *Taylor* decision, see R.D. Schneider & H. Bloom, "*R. v. Taylor*: A Decision Not in the Best Interests of Some Mentally Ill Accused" (1995) 38 Crim. L.Q. 183.

intent of the fitness rules to begin with, should probably not be proceeding to trial.

THE DEPRESSED PATIENT

A seriously (psychotically) depressed patient's self-castigating mental state may produce a self-destructive posture inconsistent with being able to fend for his or her best legal interests. For example, a fifty-five-year-old psychotically depressed professional male kills a family member, believing that in so doing he is sparing that loved one the worse fate of life in a cruel and oppressive world. His understanding of trial process is intact, but he is guilt-ridden and punishment-seeking, and *indifferent* to his outcome. His willingness to engage in meaningful communication and strategizing that will result in the best disposition of his case is markedly impaired. He *understands* the nature, object, and possible outcome of the proceedings, and can confer with his lawyer in a relatively superficial way, but cannot, due to *impairment*, initiate or respond favourably to any action that might serve to exonerate, mitigate, etc.

THE MASOCHISTIC ACCUSED

Masochistic personality structure (not masochism in the sexual preference sense), by definition, predisposes the individual to engaging in self-sabotaging behaviour. A masochist's need to atone for actual and perceived misdeeds (often of a minor nature) may result in failure to enlist the necessary motivation to counter charges or mitigate a sentence.[18] Be suspicious when the accused fails to disclose potentially exonerative/mitigating information. The masochistic and depressed patient may overlap.

THE INTELLECTUALLY LIMITED AND SUGGESTIBLE ACCUSED

Intellectually limited persons often try to conceal their deficits. They are known to be much more vulnerable to suggestion.[19] An accused who, for whatever reason, has come to *falsely* believe that he or she is culpable for an act is more than likely incapable of appreciating the legal predicament itself. The issue here is not choice but capacity.[20]

---

18   K.L. Appelbaum, "Criminal Defendants Who Desire Punishment" (1990) 18 Bulletin of the American Academy of Psychiatry and the Law 385.

19   B. Tully & D.Cahill, *Police Interviewing of the Mentally Handicapped: An Experimental Study* (London: The Police Foundation, 1984).

20   I.C.H. Clare & G.H. Gudjonsson, "Interrogative Suggestibility, Confabulation, and Acquiescence in People With Mild Learning Disabilities (Mental Handicap): Implications for Reliability During Police Interrogations" (1993) 32 British Journal of Clinical Psychology 295.

THE PARANOID ACCUSED

The paranoid accused is likely to view the criminal prosecution as an extension of a conspiracy against him, and as such, as a perversion of justice. Paranoid delusions are not synonymous with mental illness. Paranoid accused often have well-preserved cognitive abilities. Their perspective on the world, however, is unique and skewed. Pervasive paranoia detracts from the "implicit assumption (that the accused's) primary goal is to be acquitted."[21]

For example, an intelligent middle-aged woman charged with mischief and harassment understood "the mechanical elements of court process," the (conjured up) charges against her, and the supposed benefit of having a lawyer. Believing that her lawyer was not to be trusted, she chose to forfeit representation, much the way Taylor did. She was found unfit to stand trial. Her rejection of the benefit of legal representation was the decision of a person suffering from active mental illness that was impinging on her *ability* to decide. The paranoia was so pervasive that she was "unable ... to conduct (her) defence."

THE MANIC ACCUSED

Grandiosity is often a central finding in mania. The grandiose patient may have preserved cognitive functioning so that he would easily be able to recite the basics of trial process. The accused may, however, have a distorted view of the trial process and his role in it. The accused may believe he is above the trial process; may see it as little more than a contrived source of amusement; or he may wish to use the trial as a vehicle for disseminating his delusional views.

For example, a forty-year-old manic man demonstrated a good understanding of trial process. He believed, however, that he was a powerful god-like being, and he therefore could not be tried by an ordinary person(s). Criteria (a) and (b) of the *Criminal Code* required that he only *understand* the trial process and the possible consequences of a conviction, as opposed to *appreciating* them, and he was able to meet that threshold. He could certainly communicate with counsel (criterion (c)), if he chose to, but his mental illness *prevented* him from taking advantage of legal representation.

---

21   R.D. Miller & E.J. Germain, "Evaluation of Competency to Stand Trial in Defendants Who Do Not Want To Be Defended Against the Crime Charged" (1987) 15 Bulletin of the American Academy of Psychiatry and the Law 371.

3) Time of Unfitness

While the assessment pertains to the accused's present abilities rather than his mental state at the time of the alleged offence, as mentioned above, the *conduct of a defence* may require assurance that, notwithstanding present competence, the accused will remain fit through to a specific point in the future. This *prospective* element is generally not recognized but, it is submitted, an individual whose condition is known to fluctuate in and out of "fitness" may be deemed unfit if his particular matter will require sustained attention and "fitness" over an expanse of time.

a) Fluctuating Fitness

The mental state of a mentally ill person, particularly a psychotic individual, is often not static and may fluctuate on an hour-to-hour (if not minute-to-minute) basis. What can then be said of an individual whose mental state has been fluctuating relative to his/her fitness to stand trial?

Courts are ever-mindful of the presumption of fitness in section 672.22:

> *Presumption of fitness*
> 672.22 An accused is presumed fit to stand trial unless the court is satisfied on the balance of probabilities that the accused is unfit to stand trial.

Courts may invite an expert to seize the moment, as it were, and provide an opinion that the accused is fit to stand trial, if that is what the clinical evaluation revealed moments earlier. It may be, however, that the accused was not fit to stand trial a short while before the assessment, nor will she predictably be fit to stand trial a short while thereafter.

The definition of "unfit to stand trial" in section 2 of the *Criminal Code*, however, requires that the accused be capable of "conduct(ing) a defence." To that end, it is reasonable to interpret that fitness to stand trial has a future connotation or element of prospectivity. This is a necessary interpretation in that, typically, the actual trial will be occurring days or weeks in the future. If it cannot be predicted that the accused will maintain fitness to stand trial for the foreseeable future, and endure and participate in a trial of some complexity, then he cannot be said to be fit to stand trial, even if the examiner catches him during a "fit interval."

Of course, an accused who intends to plead guilty and who will be sentenced in short order probably requires a narrower window of predictable fitness to stand trial. As well, it may be that this accused need not have the same "level" of fitness as the accused who is going to engage in a complex case of considerable duration.

4) Burden of Proof

Burden of proof must be met by the party asserting the accused's unfitness (subsection 672.23(2)).

> *Burden of proof*
> (2) An accused or a prosecutor who makes an application under subsection (1) has the burden of proof that the accused is unfit to stand trial.

Similarly, where a party subsequently asserts that the accused has become fit to stand trial, that party has the burden of proof (subsection 672.32(2)).

> *Burden of proof*
> (2) The burden of proof that the accused has subsequently become fit to stand trial is on the party who asserts it, and is discharged by proof on the balance of probabilities.

5) Presumption of Fitness

As is the case with criminal responsibility, an accused is presumed to be fit to stand trial unless the court is satisfied on the balance of probabilities that the accused is unfit to stand trial (see section 672.22, reproduced above).

I. IF THE ACCUSED IS FIT

If, upon a trial of the issue, the accused is found to be fit, the accused resumes his position in the process as if the issue had never arisen (section 672.28).

> *Proceeding continues where accused is fit*
> 672.28 Where the verdict on trial of the issue is that an accused is fit to stand trial, the arraignment, preliminary inquiry, trial or other stage of the proceeding shall continue as if the issue of fitness of the accused had never arisen.

If the accused is found fit to stand trial and has been detained in custody, the court may order the accused to remain in hospital until the completion of the trial if there are reasonable grounds to believe the accused would otherwise become unfit (section 672.29).

> *Where continued detention in custody*
> 672.29 Where an accused is detained in custody on delivery of a verdict that the accused is fit to stand trial, the court may order the accused to be detained in

a hospital until the completion of the trial, if the court has reasonable grounds to believe that the accused would become unfit to stand trial if released.

Parliament did not include a form for the making of such an order; however, one has been created (see Appendix D).

J. IF THE ACCUSED IS UNFIT

Where the issue is tried and the accused is found to be unfit, any plea that has been made shall be set aside and any jury shall be discharged (section 672.31).

Verdict of unfit to stand trial

672.31 Where the verdict on trial of the issue is that an accused is unfit to stand trial, any plea that has been made shall be set aside and any jury shall be discharged.

K. TREATMENT ORDERS

There is one narrow window of opportunity to order that an accused be treated without consent, and that is, upon a verdict of unfit to stand trial and prior to the making of any disposition under section 672.54 or section 672.58 which are reproduced below.

Dispositions that may be made

672.54 Where a court or Review Board makes a disposition under subsection 672.45(2) or section 672.47 or 672.83, it shall, taking into consideration the need to protect the public from dangerous persons, the mental condition of the accused, the reintegration of the accused into society and the other needs of the accused, make one of the following dispositions that is the least onerous and least restrictive to the accused:

(a) where a verdict of not criminally responsible on account of mental disorder has been rendered in respect of the accused and, in the opinion of the court or Review Board, the accused is not a significant threat to the safety of the public, by order, direct that the accused be discharged absolutely;

(b) by order, direct that the accused be discharged subject to such conditions as the court or Review Board considers appropriate; or

(c) by order, direct that the accused be detained in custody in a hospital, subject to such conditions as the court or Review Board considers appropriate.

The application for treatment, which may only be brought by the prosecutor, cannot exceed sixty days (section 672.58).

> *Treatment disposition*
>
> 672.58 Where a verdict of unfit to stand trial is rendered and the court has not made a disposition under section 672.54 in respect of an accused, the court may, on application by the prosecutor, by order, direct that treatment of the accused be carried out for a specified period not exceeding sixty days, subject to such conditions as the court considers appropriate and, where the accused is not detained in custody, direct that the accused submit to that treatment by the person or at the hospital specified.

Note that it has not been formally decided when the "clock starts ticking," although most would agree that the sixty-day window of time starts at the moment the order is made rather than the time the accused eventually arrives at the hospital. Treatment may be ordered in or out of custody and subject to any other terms the court considers appropriate.

1) Criteria: Section 672.59

Section 672.59 sets out the criteria a court must be satisfied exists, on the basis of expert testimony, before a treatment can be administered in order to make the accused fit to stand trial. The criteria set out below must be satisfied by the testimony of a medical practitioner.

1) The accused must have a verdict of "unfit to stand trial."
2) The proposed treatment will likely render the accused fit within sixty days.
3) Without treatment the accused will likely remain unfit.
4) Risk of harm is not disproportionate to anticipated benefits.
5) The treatment proposed is the least-restrictive and least-intrusive treatment option.
6) The proposed treatment facility or practitioner has consented to receive the accused (section 672.62).

In the interest of procedural fairness, the *Criminal Code* provides the accused with the right to be notified and respond accordingly (section 672.6).

> *Notice required*
>
> 672.6 (1) The court shall not make a disposition under section 672.58 unless the prosecutor notifies the accused, in writing and as soon as practicable, of the application.

Challenge by accused

(2) On receiving the notice referred to in subsection (1), the accused may challenge the application and adduce evidence for that purpose.

Consent of hospital required for treatment

672.62 (1) No court shall make a disposition under section 672.58 without the consent of

(a) the person in charge of the hospital where the accused is to be treated; or

(b) the person to whom responsibility for the treatment of the accused is assigned by the court.

Note that even where the statutory criteria have been met, there remains discretion with the judge as to whether the order is made.

2) Certain Treatments Excluded

Even where the criteria in section 672.59 are met and the court has prepared a treatment order for the circumscribed purpose of rendering the accused fit to stand trial, certain invasive interventions/treatments are excluded from consideration (section 672.61).

Exception

672.61 (1) The court shall not direct, and no disposition made under section 672.58 shall include, the performance of psychosurgery or electro-convulsive therapy or any other prohibited treatment that is prescribed.

Definitions

(2) In this section,

"electro-convulsive therapy"

"electro-convulsive therapy" means a procedure for the treatment of certain mental disorders that induces, by electrical stimulation of the brain, a series of generalized convulsions;

"psychosurgery"

"psychosurgery" means any procedure that by direct or indirect access to the brain removes, destroys or interrupts the continuity of histologically normal brain tissue, or inserts indwelling electrodes for pulsed electrical stimulation for the purpose of altering behaviour or treating psychiatric illness, but does not include neurological procedures used to diagnose or treat intractable physical pain, organic brain conditions, or epilepsy, where any of those conditions is clearly demonstrable.

3) Hearing the Application for a Treatment Order

1) The accused must have counsel.
2) The accused must have received written notice as soon as practicable.

Note that where a treatment order is made, the matter is returnable to court. The review board is not notified. At the conclusion of the treatment order the matter is retried—or, if no party is asserting the accused's fitness, the provisions of section 672.45 and following pertain.

L. DISPOSITION HEARING

Upon a verdict of unfit to stand trial, the court may, on its own motion, and shall, upon the application of the accused or the prosecution, hold a disposition hearing (subsection 672.45(1)).

> *Hearing to be held by a court*
> 672.45 (1) Where a verdict of not criminally responsible on account of mental disorder or unfit to stand trial is rendered in respect of an accused, the court may of its own motion, and shall on application by the accused or the prosecutor, hold a disposition hearing.

At the conclusion of a disposition hearing, the court shall make a disposition only if it is satisfied that it can do so readily and that a disposition should be made without delay (subsection 672.45(2).

> *Disposition to be made*
> (2) At a disposition hearing, the court shall make a disposition in respect of the accused, if it is satisfied that it can readily do so and that a disposition should be made without delay.

Disposition hearings are held in an informal manner adhering to procedures set out in section 672.5(2).

> *Hearing to be informal*
> (2) The hearing may be conducted in as informal a manner as is appropriate in the circumstances.

It is mandatory that the accused have counsel (subsection 672.5(8)).

> *Assigning counsel*
> (8) If an accused is not represented by counsel, the court or Review Board shall, either before or at the time of the hearing, assign counsel to act for any accused

At a disposition hearing the court may consider any "disposition information," which includes all or part of an assessment report and any other relevant written information (section 672.51(1)).

Definition of "disposition information"

> 672.51 (1) In this section, "disposition information" means all or part of an assessment report submitted to the court or Review Board and any other written information before the court or Review Board about the accused that is relevant to making a disposition.

Where the court makes a disposition it shall state its reasons on the record and shall provide all parties with a copy of the disposition and its reasons (subsection 672.52(3)).

Reasons for disposition and copies to be provided

> (3) The court or Review Board shall state its reasons for making a disposition in the record of the proceedings, and shall provide every party with a copy of the disposition and those reasons.

Where the court makes a disposition it shall send a transcript of the hearing, as well as all disposition information, and other exhibits to the review board (subsection 672.52(2)).

Transmittal of transcript to Review Board

> (2) If a court holds a disposition hearing under subsection 672.45(1), whether or not it makes a disposition, it shall send without delay to the Review Board that has jurisdiction in respect of the matter, in original or copied form, a transcript of the hearing, any other document or information related to the hearing, and all exhibits filed with it, if the transcript, document, information or exhibits are in its possession.

Note that where a disposition is not made by the court, the review board shall hold a hearing and make a disposition within forty-five days, or up to ninety days in exceptional circumstances (subsections 672.47(1) and (2)).

Review Board to make disposition where court does not

> 672.47 (1) Where a verdict of not criminally responsible on account of mental disorder or unfit to stand trial is rendered and the court makes no disposition in respect of an accused, the Review Board shall, as soon as is practicable but not later than forty-five days after the verdict was rendered, hold a hearing and make a disposition.

Extension of time for hearing

(2) Where the court is satisfied that there are exceptional circumstances that warrant it, the court may extend the time for holding a hearing under subsection (1) to a maximum of ninety days after the verdict was rendered.

Where a disposition is made by the court, that disposition will be reviewed by the review board within ninety days (subsection 672.45(3)).

Disposition made by court

(3) Where a court makes a disposition under section 672.54 other than an absolute discharge in respect of an accused, the Review Board shall, not later than ninety days after the disposition was made, hold a hearing and make a disposition in respect of the accused.

1) Custody of the Accused: *Status Quo* Presumed

Subject to the court's order, any order for the release or detention of the accused shall remain operative until a disposition is made. However, the court may, upon application, order that the accused be remanded to hospital pending a disposition hearing by the review board (subsections 672.46(1) and (2)).

Status quo pending Review Board hearing

672.46 (1) Where the court does not make a disposition in respect of the accused at a disposition hearing, any order for the interim release or detention of the accused or any appearance notice, promise to appear, summons, undertaking or recognizance in respect of the accused that is in force at the time the verdict of not criminally responsible on account of mental disorder or unfit to stand trial is rendered continues in force, subject to its terms, until the Review Board makes a disposition.

Variation of order

(2) Notwithstanding subsection (1), a court may, on cause being shown, vacate any order, appearance notice, promise to appear, summons, undertaking or recognizance referred to in that subsection and make any other order for the interim release or detention of the accused that the court considers to be appropriate in the circumstances, including an order directing that the accused be detained in custody in a hospital pending a disposition by the Review Board in respect of the accused.

Parliament did not include a form for an order of this sort; however, one has been created (see Appendix E).

2) Assessment Orders to Assist with Disposition

Where the court is considering a disposition hearing it may order an assessment to assist in the making of an appropriate disposition where it has reasonable grounds to believe that such evidence is necessary (section 672.11(d)).

> 672.11 A court having jurisdiction over an accused in respect of an offence may order an assessment of the mental condition of the accused, if it has reasonable grounds to believe that such evidence is necessary to determine ...
>
> (d) the appropriate disposition to be made, where a verdict of not criminally responsible on account of mental disorder or unfit to stand trial has been rendered in respect of the accused ...

3) Terms of the Disposition

Where a court makes a disposition it shall take into consideration:

1) the need to protect the public from dangerous persons,
2) the mental condition of the accused,
3) the reintegration of the accused into society, and
4) the other needs of the accused,

and shall impose the least onerous and least restrictive disposition.

The options for the unfit accused are:

1) discharge subject to appropriate conditions (while an "absolute discharge" is not available under section 672.54, a "stay" may be entered in certain circumstances set out below) [Observers note that it may be difficult to assume that the terms of a disposition will be understood or that the accused will have the wherewithal to comply with the terms of a disposition while "unfit"], or
2) detention in the custody of a hospital subject to appropriate conditions.

Where a disposition is made pursuant to subsection 672.54(c), the court shall issue a warrant of committal which may be in Form 49 (section 672.57).

> *Warrant of committal*
>
> 672.57 Where the court or Review Board makes a disposition under paragraph 672.54(c), it shall issue a warrant of committal of the accused, which may be in Form 49.

Note that a "discharge" under Part XX.1 should not be confused with the same terminology in the sentencing provisions of the *Crimimal Code*. Accordingly, probation is *never* part of such an order. "Treatment" shall not be a part of any disposition under section 672.54 unless the accused consents, and the court considers such a condition to be reasonable and necessary in the interests of the accused (subsection 672.55(1)).

M. *PRIMA FACIE* CASE

Within two years of a verdict of unfit to stand trial, or upon application at any other time, the court shall hold an inquiry to determine whether the prosecution is able to show a *prima facie* case (section 672.33).

Prima facie case to be made every two years

672.33 (1) The court that has jurisdiction in respect of the offence charged against an accused who is found unfit to stand trial shall hold an inquiry, not later than two years after the verdict is rendered and every two years thereafter until the accused is acquitted pursuant to subsection (6) or tried, to decide whether sufficient evidence can be adduced at that time to put the accused on trial.

Extension of time for holding inquiry

(1.1) Despite subsection (1), the court may extend the period for holding an inquiry where it is satisfied on the basis of an application by the prosecutor or the accused that the extension is necessary for the proper administration of justice.

Court may order inquiry to be held

(2) On application of the accused, the court may order an inquiry under this section to be held at any time if it is satisfied, on the basis of the application and any written material submitted by the accused, that there is reason to doubt that there is a *prima facie* case against the accused.

Burden of proof

(3) At an inquiry under this section, the burden of proof that sufficient evidence can be adduced to put the accused on trial is on the prosecutor.

Admissible evidence at an inquiry

(4) In an inquiry under this section, the court shall admit as evidence

(a) any affidavit containing evidence that would be admissible if given by the person making the affidavit as a witness in court; or

(b) any certified copy of the oral testimony given at a previous inquiry or hearing held before a court in respect of the offence with which the accused is charged.

Conduct of inquiry

(5) The court may determine the manner in which an inquiry under this section is conducted and may follow the practices and procedures in respect of a preliminary inquiry under Part XVIII where it concludes that the interests of justice so require.

Where prima facie case not made

(6) Where, on the completion of an inquiry under this section, the court is satisfied that sufficient evidence cannot be adduced to put the accused on trial, the court shall acquit the accused.

Where sufficient evidence cannot be adduced the accused shall be acquitted (subsection 672.33(6).

N. IF THE ACCUSED IS PERMANENTLY UNFIT

With the proclamation of Bill C-10 on 19 May 2005, a number of changes were made to Part XX.1 of the *Criminal Code* (and other legislation). The most significant aspect of the Bill pertains to the court's new ability to stay proceedings in respect of a permanently unfit accused. This and related provisions came into effect on 30 June 2005, whereas other changes came into force on 6 January 2006. The court is now permitted to hold an inquiry and order a judicial stay of proceedings for an accused found to be unfit to stand trial if the accused is not likely to ever become fit to stand trial, does not constitute a significant threat to the safety of the public, and a stay is in the interests of the proper administration of justice.

1) Background

Prior to the proclamation of Bill C-10, an unfit accused would remain subject to the jurisdiction of the review board indefinitely, so long as she remained unfit to stand trial (unless the Crown failed to show a *prima facie* case within every two years post-verdict (section 672.33)). Jurisdiction over the accused was not dangerousness-based (as is the case for accused found to be not criminally responsible (NCR)). Where the "mental disorder" mediating the unfitness was intellectual disability, brain injury, or some other intractable condition, the accused could remain subject to the jurisdiction of the review board forever. This situation was frustrating both for the accused and the review board who had no ability to discharge the accused as they might were the accused NCR. Stays, where entered, were the result of the Crown exercising its discretion on an *ad hoc* basis.

2) Specific Changes to the *Criminal Code*

a) Assessment Orders

The first significant change permits the court to order an assessment of the unfit accused to determine whether a stay should be entered (section 672.11(e)).

> 672.11 A court having jurisdiction over an accused in respect of an offence may order an assessment of the mental condition of the accused, if it has reasonable grounds to believe that such evidence is necessary to determine ...
>
> (e) whether an order should be made under section 672.851 for a stay of proceedings, where a verdict of unfit to stand trial has been rendered against the accused.

The review board may also order an assessment for this purpose (that is, making a recommendation for a stay to the court) (section 672.121(a)).

> *Review Board may order assessment*
>
> 672.121 The Review Board that has jurisdiction over an accused found not criminally responsible on account of mental disorder or unfit to stand trial may order an assessment of the mental condition of the accused of its own motion or on application of the prosecutor or the accused, if it has reasonable grounds to believe that such evidence is necessary to ...
>
> (a) make a recommendation to the court under subsection 672.851(1).

A new Form 48.1 (Appendix B) has been created for the review board, whereas the old Form 48 has been amended for the courts.

b) Stays

The key provisions are contained in the new section 672.851. Referrals back to the court for a hearing may be initiated by the review board if, after conducting a hearing of its own, it is of the view that the accused 1) remains unfit; 2) is not likely to ever become fit; and 3) does not pose a significant threat to the safety of the public.

Upon receiving such a recommendation from the review board, or upon its own motion, the court *may* hold an inquiry to determine whether a stay of proceedings should be ordered. If the court decides to hold an inquiry it *shall* order an assessment of the accused. At the conclusion of an inquiry the court may order a stay of proceedings if it is satisfied, on the basis of *clear information*, that the accused 1) remains unfit; 2) is not likely to ever become fit; 3) does not pose a significant threat to the safety of the public; and 4) that a stay is in the interests of the proper administration of justice.

Factors to be considered in deciding whether a stay of proceedings is in the interests of the proper administration of justice include:

1) the nature and seriousness of the alleged offence;
2) the salutary and deleterious effects of the order for a stay of proceedings, including any effect on public confidence in the administration of justice;
3) the time elapsed since the commission of the alleged offence;
4) whether a *prima facie* case has been proven under section 672.33; and
5) any other relevant factors.

3) Evidentiary Burden

At the time of writing there appears to be only one case on point: *R. v. Kearly*.[22] Here, the court decided that an inquiry pursuant to the provisions of section 672.851 would, as much as possible, be carried out in the same manner as a hearing pursuant to the provisions of section 672.54 and that to a large extent the Supreme Court of Canada's rulings in *Winko v. British Columbia (Forensic Psychiatric Institute)*[23] were applicable. Those key provisions are as follows (from *Kearly*):[24]

1) there is to be no presumption that the mentally disordered accused poses a significant threat to the safety of the public,
2) the accused is never in a position of having to disprove dangerousness—the accused is therefore relieved of any legal or evidentiary burden—the accused need do nothing (unless, of course, dangerousness is otherwise established),
3) this tactical incentive to adduce evidence is not properly described as a shifting of the legal or evidentiary burden to the accused,

---

22 *R. v. Kearly*, [2005] O.J. No. 5394 (Ct. J.) [*Kearly*].
23 *Winko v. British Columbia (Forensic Psychiatric Institute)*, [1999] 2 S.C.R. 625 [*Winko*].
24 *Kearly*, above note 22 at para. 13

4) if the court or Review Board is unable to conclude that the accused constitutes a significant threat to the safety of the public, he or she must be
absolutely discharged,

5) jurisdiction over the accused cannot be maintained where there is doubt
regarding dangerousness, continued jurisdiction requires an affirmative
finding of significant threat,

6) the threat posed must be more than speculative in nature; it must be supported by the evidence,

7) the threat must also be "significant," both in the sense that there must
be a real risk of physical or psychological harm occurring to individuals
in the community and in the sense that this potential harm be serious.
A miniscule risk of a grave harm will not suffice. Similarly, a high risk of
trivial harm will not meet the threshold,

8) the conduct or activity creating the harm must be criminal in nature,.

9) finally, it is up to the court or Review Board to ensure that it has sufficient
information in order to make the determination.

A reading of the Supreme Court's decision in *R. v. Demers*[25] makes it
quite clear that, to the extent possible, a permanently unfit accused who does
not constitute a significant threat to the safety of the public should be treated
the same as the NCR accused who does not pose a significant threat to the
safety of the public. Of course, the NCR accused has obtained a final verdict
on the merits after a trial whereas the permanently unfit accused has not
been tried. The permanently unfit accused is still presumed to be innocent
whereas there has been a finding of guilt in respect of the NCR accused.

The new statutory provisions are reproduced below.

Recommendation by Review Board
672.851 (1) The Review Board may, of its own motion, make a recommendation to the court that has jurisdiction in respect of the offence charged
against an accused found unfit to stand trial to hold an inquiry to determine
whether a stay of proceedings should be ordered if

(a) the Review Board has held a hearing under section 672.81 or 672.82 in
respect of the accused and

(b) on the basis of any relevant information, including disposition information within the meaning of subsection 672.51(1) and an assessment report made under an assessment ordered under paragraph 672.121(a), the
Review Board is of the opinion that

---

25   *R. v. Demers* (2004), 185 C.C.C. (3d) 257 (S.C.C.).

(i)   the accused remains unfit to stand trial and is not likely to ever become fit to stand trial, and

(ii) the accused does not pose a significant threat to the safety of the public.

Notice

(2) If the Review Board makes a recommendation to the court to hold an
inquiry, the Review Board shall provide notice to the accused, the prosecutor and any party who, in the opinion of the Review Board, has a substantial
interest in protecting the interests of the accused.

Inquiry

(3) As soon as practicable after receiving the recommendation referred to
in subsection (1), the court may hold an inquiry to determine whether a stay
of proceedings should be ordered.

Court may act on own motion

(4) A court may, of its own motion, conduct an inquiry to determine
whether a stay of proceedings should be ordered if the court is of the opinion,
on the basis of any relevant information, that

(a) the accused remains unfit to stand trial and is not likely to ever become
fit to stand trial; and

(b) the accused does not pose a significant threat to the safety of the public.

Assessment order

(5) If the court holds an inquiry under subsection (3) or (4), it shall order
an assessment of the accused.

Application

(6) Section 672.51 applies to an inquiry of the court under this section.

Stay

(7) The court may, on completion of an inquiry under this section, order
a stay of proceedings if it is satisfied

(a) on the basis of clear information, that the accused remains unfit to stand
trial and is not likely to ever become fit to stand trial;

(b) that the accused does not pose a significant threat to the safety of the
public; and

(c) that a stay is in the interests of the proper administration of justice.

Proper administration of justice

(8) In order to determine whether a stay of proceedings is in the interests
of the proper administration of justice, the court shall consider any submis-

sions of the prosecutor, the accused and all other parties and the following factors:

(a) the nature and seriousness of the alleged offence;

(b) the salutary and deleterious effects of the order for a stay of proceedings, including any effect on public confidence in the administration of justice;

(c) the time that has elapsed since the commission of the alleged offence and whether an inquiry has been held under section 672.33 to decide whether sufficient evidence can be adduced to put the accused on trial; and

(d) any other factor that the court considers relevant.

Effect of stay

(9) If a stay of proceedings is ordered by the court, any disposition made in respect of the accused ceases to have effect. If a stay of proceedings is not ordered, the finding of unfit to stand trial and any disposition made in respect of the accused remain in force, until the Review Board holds a disposition hearing and makes a disposition in respect of the accused under section 672.83.

The new legislation includes at least one serious inconsistency. Subsection 672.851(5) clearly contains a mandatory requirement that the court holding an inquiry order an "assessment" of the accused. Subsection 672.11(e), on the other hand, is clear that such an assessment may only be ordered where the court has "reasonable grounds to believe that such evidence is necessary." Where the court receives a recommendation from the review board it will inevitably have the benefit of its record which will typically include an assessment report focused upon the same issue. It may be that the court is left without "reasonable grounds," notwithstanding subsection 672.851(5), to order yet another assessment. In any event, the court need not order an assessment "report." It may be that the process can be greatly abbreviated with an "oral report" or confirmation of a previously performed assessment.

The court's holding of an inquiry in response to the review board's "recommendation" would appear to be, with the use of the word "may," discretionary. It is not at all clear why the court would decline to hold such an inquiry where a recommendation was made or, after it had initiated the process, on its own motion.

4) Clinical Considerations

From a practical perspective, the issue of permanent unfitness in accused who are otherwise not a significant threat to the safety of the public is likely to arise infrequently. Only a small percentage of chronically unfit accused fall into this category. Most unfit accused who come under the review board's jurisdiction are rendered fit through treatment and returned to court. The lapse of time is one key factor in establishing the permanent nature of an accused's unfitness, even apart from the condition causing him or her to be unfit. It is, in fact, reasonable to suggest that the preponderance of accused who may be eligible for a recommendation pursuant to section 672.851 who are "on the books" of their respective provincial or territorial review board as chronically unfit and not a significant threat will have this issue addressed within the next one to two years as existing cases are looked at more closely by hospitals, clinicians, counsel, and by review boards at annual hearings.

Although this represents an oversimplification, permanently unfit accused are more likely to suffer from intractable or deteriorating congenital or acquired conditions associated with intellectual limitations that have either prevented them from acquiring the information relevant to fitness in the first instance, learning it through deliberate efforts to educate them, or retaining information relevant to this capacity as a result of marked memory deficits. A review of conditions more likely to be associated with permanent unfitness is provided below.

- *Congenital Conditions*
  - ▷ mental retardation (especially moderate to severe)
  - ▷ severe fetal alcohol effect
  - ▷ congenital metabolic disorders associated with significant intellectual limitations

- *Acquired Conditions*
  - ▷ pervasive developmental disorder
  - ▷ brain injury
  - ▷ cerebrovascular disease
  - ▷ dementia (for example, Alzheimer's disease)
  - ▷ Huntington's disease
  - ▷ alcohol-related dementive conditions

- *Functional Mental Disorders*
  - ▷ severe chronic schizophrenia

The figure below provides a crude schematic representation of the types of timelines associated with either promoting or restoring fitness based on the nature and degree of the mental disorder in question.

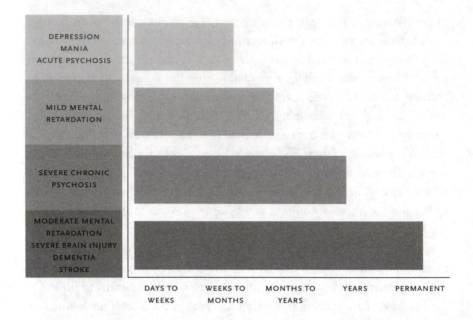

| | DAYS TO WEEKS | WEEKS TO MONTHS | MONTHS TO YEARS | YEARS | PERMANENT |

Clinicians and hospitals who address routine fitness considerations at initial (sections 672.47(1) and 672.48(1)) or annual (sections 672.81(1) and 672.48(1)) hearings of unfit accused ordinarily provide opinions based on "here and now" assessments of the accused's fitness, both presently and for the foreseeable future, as well as the dispositional considerations listed in section 672.54 (that is, least onerous and lease restrictive disposition) and expanded upon recently by the Supreme Court of Canada in *Penetanguishene Mental Health Centre v. Ontario (Attorney General)*[26] (least onerous and least restrictive conditions).

Clinicians who assess an accused with respect to his eligibility for a recommendation pursuant to section 672.851 will need to go beyond providing an opinion concerning the accused's present fitness to stand trial and forecast whether the accused is ever likely to become fit to stand trial, and then, if it is the clinician's opinion that the accused is in fact permanently unfit, go on to address whether he represents a significant threat to the safety of the public. The assessment of whether an individual represents a significant threat to the safety of the public—the statutory test for the discharge or retention of an NCR accused (section 672.54)—is beyond the scope of this

---

26   *Penetanguishene Mental Health Centre v. Ontario (Attorney General)* (2003), [2004] 1 S.C.R. 498.

chapter. The reader is referred to the key case in this area, *Winko*,[27] and to Chapter 8 for a general review of clinical factors experts consider in assessing an individual's risk for future violence.

From a practical perspective, many unfit accused suffer from deteriorating conditions that progressively limit their physical and cognitive abilities to engage the public (they are both physically and psychologically institutionalized) and act out violently. With respect to whether an accused is permanently unfit, the court and review board having jurisdiction over the accused will want the expert to address the following issues:

- Is the accused's diagnosis consistent with a condition frequently associated with permanent unfitness?
- How long has it been since the accused was found unfit to stand trial in the first instance?
- What has the accused's course in hospital been?
- What clinical parameters have or have not improved?
- How often has the treatment team attempted to address the accused's fitness to stand trial, and what is the most recent assessment of this kind?
- What efforts have been made to educate the accused with respect to the charges and other areas inherent in being fit to stand trial?
- What specific deficits are responsible for the permanent unfitness, that is, inability to acquire new information, extreme apathy, confusion, memory problems, etc.?
- Are there any therapies or interventions on the horizon likely to positively impact on the accused's fitness to stand trial; and
- Has the possibility of malingering of unfitness been addressed? (It would be certainly be in an accused's interest to be declared permanently unfit in order to avoid prosecution for a serious charge.)

---

27   Above note 23.

CHAPTER FOUR

Pre-Trial Issues

It should be noted that while the formal psycho-legal issues of fitness to stand trial and criminal responsibility are certainly the most common situations for psychiatric evidence to be sought or adduced, there are other junctures at which it can be most important. Psychiatric consultation and evidence may be of use in a wide variety of scenarios. The need for psychiatric expertise can arise in any instance where a mental health, psychological, or behavioural issue becomes a focus of concern or interest in a proceeding before a criminal court. There is a great deal of room for the creative use of psychiatry, provided it meets the threshold test of relevance and reliability.[1]

A. JUDICIAL INTERIM RELEASE OR "BAIL"

1) Psychiatric Aspects of Bailworthiness

Mentally disordered offenders may experience difficulty obtaining judicial interim release because their mental condition may have implications for both the primary and secondary grounds. The bailworthiness of a mentally disordered accused may depend on whether he has sufficient psychiatric supervision in place. Psychiatric evaluations with respect to judicial interim release can raise some strategic concerns for defence counsel. The clinician will often find it necessary to review the current allegations against the accused as they may well have implications for his suitability for release; however, that information may turn out to be inculpatory or otherwise prejudicial.

---

1   *R. v. Mohan*, [1994] 2 S.C.R. 9; *R. v. Olscamp*, [1994] O.J. No. 2926 (Gen. Div.).

2) Primary Ground

Psychiatric evidence may be called by the defence to address the concern that because of the accused's mental disorder she may not attend court when required if released. Alternatively, the Crown may call psychiatric evidence to show that because of the accused's mental condition she would not be inclined to attend court. Aside from the general probability of attendance or non-attendance, psychiatric evidence may suggest terms to be included in an order for judicial interim release which would reduce those concerns.

The accused's eligibility on the primary ground (subsection 515 (10)(a))

> *Justification for detention in custody*
>
> (10) For the purposes of this section, the detention of an accused in custody is justified only on one or more of the following grounds:
>
> (a) where the detention is necessary to ensure his or her attendance in court in order to be dealt with according to law;
>
> (b) where the detention is necessary for the protection or safety of the public, including any victim of or witness to the offence, having regard to all the circumstances including any substantial likelihood that the accused will, if released from custody, commit a criminal offence or interfere with the administration of justice ...

may depend on his understanding of the charge and need to appear in court (fitness may be an issue here); on whether any cognitive limitation would affect his ability to attend court; on whether he has support; and on his risk for substance abuse or medication non-compliance due to the mental disorder. Some mentally disordered accused are so ill (psychotic) that they cannot process information meaningfully, or so paranoid that they would do anything to avoid the clutches of the criminal justice system.

3) Secondary Ground

The concern on the secondary ground is whether detention is necessary for the protection of the public, having regard to all the circumstances including any substantial likelihood that the accused will, if released from custody, commit a criminal offence or interfere with the administration of justice. It is in respect of these concerns that psychiatric evidence is more typically adduced. The accused's current mental disorder and its implications for dangerous behaviour in the community are the key considerations with respect to the secondary ground (see subsection 515(10)(b), above). In this regard, the court should be satisfied that a proper risk assessment has been carried out (see Chapter 8).

B. CALLING OF PSYCHIATRIC EVIDENCE

While it is now accepted that mental disorder should not be equated with dangerousness, there are features of some mental disorders which may render an accused a risk if released. Psychiatric evidence may be called by either party in order to address these issues and the extent to which they should concern the court or could be alleviated with appropriate terms of release.

C. PSYCHIATRIC ASSESSMENTS

Curiously, section 672.11, which sets out the general provisions with respect to psychiatric assessments in Part XX.1 of the *Criminal Code*, does not provide for psychiatric assessments for the purposes of either judicial interim release or sentencing (as mentioned in Chapter 9).

> *Assessment order*
>
> 672.11 A court having jurisdiction over an accused in respect of an offence may order an assessment of the mental condition of the accused, if it has reasonable grounds to believe that such evidence is necessary to determine
>
> (a) whether the accused is unfit to stand trial;
>
> (b) whether the accused was, at the time of the commission of the alleged offence, suffering from a mental disorder so as to be exempt from criminal responsibility by virtue of subsection 16(1);
>
> (c) whether the balance of the mind of the accused was disturbed at the time of commission of the alleged offence, where the accused is a female person charged with offence arising out of the death of her newly-born child;
>
> (d) the appropriate disposition to be made, where a verdict of not criminally responsible on account of mental disorder or unfit to stand trial has been rendered in respect of the accused; or
>
> (e) whether an order should be made under section 672.851 for a stay of proceedings, where a verdict of unfit to stand trial has been rendered against the accused.

1) *Mental Health Act* (MHA)

Sections 21 and 22 (for out-of-custody and in-custody, respectively) of the *Mental Health Act*,[2] however, may be used for the purposes of obtaining a psychi-

---

2   R.S.O. 1990, c. M.7 [MHA].

atric assessment in Ontario.[3] In other provinces the civil legislation may be relied upon to fill the gap in section 672.11 where the provisions permit.

Judge's order for examination

21(1) Where a judge has reason to believe that a person who appears before him or her charged with or convicted of an offence suffers from mental disorder, the judge may order the person to attend a psychiatric facility for examination.

Senior physician's report

(2) Where an examination is made under this section, the senior physician shall report in writing to the judge as to the mental condition of the person.

Judge's order for admission

22(1) Where a judge has reason to believe that a person in custody who appears before him or her charged with an offence suffers from mental disorder, the judge may, by order, remand that person for admission as a patient to a psychiatric facility for a period of not more than two months.

Senior physician's report

(2) Before the expiration of the time mentioned in such order, the senior physician shall report in writing to the judge as to the mental condition of the person.

Note that where legislation outside of the *Criminal Code* is relied upon to obtain psychiatric assessments, the array of protective provisions attached to section 672.11 do not apply. It is recommended that the court attach similar conditions as part of any order made outside of the *Criminal Code*.

D. BAIL AND FITNESS TO STAND TRIAL

As discussed in Chapter 3, the accused is presumed to be fit to stand trial (section 672.22) and may be released on bail prior to the issue being tried. Even where there are reasonable grounds to believe medical evidence is necessary to determine the issue (subsection 672.11(a)) a subsequent order for assessment is presumed to take place on an out-of-custody basis (section 672.16). As well, there is no necessary requirement that an accused be fit in order to be granted judicial interim release. While, for the most part, an ac-

---

3   *R. v. Lenart* (1998), 123 C.C.C. (3d) 353 (Ont. C.A.).

cused who is so compromised as to put fitness in issue may not be amenable to terms of release, where an adequate "plan" can be put in place, judicial interim release is appropriate.

As set out in section 672.16, the provisions from section 515, dealing with judicial interim release generally, have been imported into Part XX.1:

> *Presumption against custody*
>
> 672.16 (1) Subject to subsection (3), an accused shall not be detained in custody under an assessment order of a court unless
>
> (a) the court is satisfied that on the evidence custody is necessary to assess the accused, or that on the evidence of a medical practitioner custody is desirable to assess the accused and the accused consents to custody;
>
> (b) custody of the accused is required in respect of any other matter or by virtue of any other provision of this Act; or
>
> (c) the prosecutor, having been given a reasonable opportunity to do so, shows that detention of the accused in custody is justified on either of the grounds set out in subsection 515(10).

E. DIVERSION

The availability of formal "diversion" programs for mentally disordered accused will vary from province to province. In Ontario, as of 1994, there has been a formal diversion program for mentally disordered accused contained in the *Crown Policy Manual*.[4] While of great interest to the judiciary, the discretion to "divert" is entirely that of the prosecution. It is widely recognized that for most of the mentally disordered accused who come through the courthouse doors, the most efficacious and appropriate course is to divert accused back into the civil mental health system from which they have somehow become disconnected or insufficiently well-connected. In Ontario, if an accused is charged with a divertible (generally non-violent) offence and agrees to participate in a rehabilitative program, the Crown will stay or withdraw the charge. No admission of guilt is required. It is not necessary that the accused be "fit to stand trial."

The Ministry of the Attorney General has issued a *Crown Policy Manual* entitled "Diversion of Mentally Disordered Accused" that provides a protocol for routing patients from court to either hospital or community care. Diver-

---

4   Ontario Ministry of the Attorney General, "Diversion of Mentally Disordered Accused," *Crown Policy Manual*, looseleaf (Toronto: Ministry of the Attorney General, 1993).

sion is defined as a pre-trial procedure where Crown counsel uses her discretion on a case-by-case basis to not prosecute a mentally disordered accused and, instead, route him to psychiatric intervention. For an accused to be eligible for diversion, a number of criteria and conditions need to be met. First, there has to be a reasonable prospect of conviction. It would be inequitable to divert an accused when the Crown would never have been in a position to convict him. Second, public safety is the paramount consideration. There is no diversion in instances where public safety would be compromised. Third, an individual's past criminal history, or even past history of diversion, does not preclude him from pursuing diversion this time, but it is a factor that can be considered. The obvious is stated by the fourth criterion: a mental disorder has to be presumed as the basis for the criminal conduct in question. Not every offence is divertible, for obvious reasons. Divertible offences will generally be of a minor nature; for example, involving property, fraud, or trespass. These are called Class I offences. Any Crown attorney can proceed to divert these offenders. An outline of diversion programs and their criteria is provided below.

CRITERIA FOR DIVERSION PROGRAMS:
1. Reasonable prospect of conviction.
2. Public safety is not compromised.
3. Previous diversion or criminal record are considered; they do not automatically preclude diversion.
4. A mental disorder is presumed to underlie the criminal conduct.
5. The class of offence is appropriate/proportionate to severity:
   - Class 1: property and minor (Okay),
   - Class 2: break and enter, simple assault, utter threats, assault of police officer (Consent of local Crown attorney needed), and
   - Class 3: Serious offence (No).
6. Accused must be advised of right to trial, counsel, etc.; choice for diversion is volutary.
7. Accused need not admit responsibility for the act.
8. Candidate likely to respond to treatment (*Quaere* section, 22 MHA assessment) (Ontario Ministry of Health criteria).
9. A suitable candidate appears to be suffering from discernible psychiatric symptoms (delusions, hallucinations) (Ontario Ministry of Health criteria).
10. The contemplated facility must accept patient (Ontario Ministry of Health criteria).
11. Charge is stayed.

The consent of the local senior Crown attorney is needed when some measure of violence, albeit a fairly limited one, is involved. Class III offences involving serious violence, use of weapons, sexual offences, or arson, are not divertible. The accused must make a decision about diversion in an informed manner. It must be her choice, and she must know in the alternative that she has available a right to counsel and a right to proceed to trial. Since a divertible accused may have had the benefit of an NCR, she need not admit responsibility for the act.

There are several Ministry of Health criteria. Candidates for diversion must have a reasonably good prognosis—they would not be good candidates for diversion if they were not amenable to treatment. They must at least appear, even before being formally diagnosed, to be suffering from discernible psychiatric symptoms such as hallucinations or delusions. Finally, a patient cannot be diverted until the receiving facility or agency accepts her.

1) Where There is No Diversion Program

"Diversions" were taking place on an informal *ad hoc* basis long before the implementation of formal programs. Generally, this had been accomplished on a cooperative basis with the Crown attorney's office. Counsel would approach the Crown and indicate—with some support—that the alleged offence was really more reflective of a mental health problem than "criminality."

Where there is no diversion program, the case may be adjourned while counsel documents that position with an expert opinion and, having put a plan in place, the Crown may elect to withdraw the charge. In more serious cases, the Crown may elect to wait until a report is available indicating that the accused had actually been successfully treated before exercising its discretion. Again, this procedure is not one that involves any judicial discretion.

2) Police Diversion

Police have always been first-line intervenors when it comes to the mentally disordered persons they frequently encounter on a day-to-day basis, particularly on the streets of large urban centres. Except in more serious cases, police have a substantial amount of discretion to make a decision against charging a person with a minor criminal offence—for example, mischief or minor theft—and can instead deliver the person to some form of intervention.

Police discretion is derived from two concepts: the first is the police officer's primary function of protecting members of the public; the second derives from the police officer's *parens patrie* or paternalistic role in safeguarding disabled individuals. One fairly recent paper referred to police in their role of dealing with mentally disordered accused as "frontline mental health workers" and another called them "street corner psychiatrists."[5] In this role, however, many police officers are not functioning in a criminal justice capacity; that is, catching felons and putting them in jail. Instead, they are dealing with situational problems, and for the most part, controlling a nuisance.

Whether the police happen upon an individual engaged in bizarre and unlawful behaviour or are brought in through a 911 call, they have the authority pursuant to section 17 of the *Mental Health Act* (Ontario) to apprehend individuals who are acting in a dangerous and disorderly manner. Police unaware of their section 17 authority may wind up charging the individual with a criminal offence—usually for offences such as common assault, mischief, or threatening.

Action by police officer

17. Where a police officer has reasonable and probable grounds to believe that a person is acting or has acted in a disorderly manner and has reasonable cause to believe that the person,

(a) has threatened or attempted or is threatening or attempting to cause bodily harm to himself or herself;

(b) has behaved or is behaving violently towards another person or has caused or is causing another person to fear bodily harm from him or her; or

(c) has shown or is showing a lack of competence to care for himself or herself,

and in addition the police officer is of the opinion that the person is apparently suffering from mental disorder of a nature or quality that likely will result in,

(d) Serious bodily harm to the person;

(e) Serious bodily harm to another person; or

(f) Serious physical impairment of the person,

and that it would be dangerous to proceed under section 16, the police officer may take the person in custody to an appropriate place for examination by a physician.

---

5   T.M. Green, "Police as Frontline Mental Health Workers: The Decision to Arrest or Refer to Mental Health Agencies" (1997) 20 International Journal of Law and Psychiatry 469; L.A. Teplin & N.S. Pruett, "Police as Street Corner Psychiatrists: Managing the Mentally Ill" (1992) 15 International Journal of Law and Psychiatry 139.

Some studies have shown that police prefer to bypass either option, and will instead use whatever discretion and "street sense" they have to bring about a more informal solution—a temporary patch or band-aid, as it were—that involves persuading the patient to attend hospital, see his doctor, or abide by the will of concerned family members. The reason for this strategy has to do with the frustration and demoralization many police officers who have dealt with the mentally ill and with the mental health system experience in these encounters. An officer's altruistic wish to get a patient treated, may, in many instances, make him feel that the effort has been in vain when hospitals release the patient back to the street within hours because she does not meet the criteria for involuntary detention. The hospital may have justifiably decided that the patient cannot be held involuntarily as she may have become outwardly placid since the officer first encountered her, and, besides, bed space has been at a premium for years. In addition, experienced police officers will often get bogged down with the need to remain with patients waiting to be assessed by doctors or residents (a safeguard in hospitals with limited security resources), as well as with the need to complete the paperwork involved in this process.

Many officers come to understand that the *Criminal Code* is the *Mental Health Act* of last resort, but unlike the *Mental Health Act*, it has enough teeth to hold onto the patient for long enough to offer the prospect of some meaningful intervention. They consequently charge the patient in the hope that he will get trapped in the filter of the criminal justice system. Clinicians see many police synopses of arrests of likely mentally disordered accused conclude with words to the effect "this accused should be held for a psychiatric evaluation."

F. PRE-TRIAL ISSUES

1) Mental Illness, Confessions, Voluntariness and Inculpatory Statements

The threshold for voluntariness is higher in instances where mental debility is a factor.[6]

a) The "Operating Mind" Test

The essential test to be met in determining the voluntariness of an accused's statement is the "operating mind" test. A psychiatric expert may be of assis-

---

6   *R. v. Evans*, (1991), 4 C.R. (4th) 144 (S.C.C.).

tance here in helping the court determine whether the accused had an "operating mind" at the time she made a statement; that is, that she understood what was being said; that she understood what was occurring and the consequences of her behaviour; or that the she was not so psychotically disturbed that her utterances could be said not to reflect her mind.

From a psychiatric perspective, an accused may not have an operating mind in instances where she:

- is impaired by an intoxicant;
- suffers from an organic brain syndrome, such as Alzheimer's disease;
- is suffering from the effects of a recent head injury;
- has experienced an emotional shock prior to giving the statement;
- is intellectually limited;
- is psychotic; and
- is apathetic (due to depression) and consequently does not care about what she says.

2) False Confessions

A psychiatric expert may provide assistance in identifying whether an accused's psychological make up, intellectual limitations, need to please, suggestibility, or any other factor might make him susceptible to a false confession. A psychiatric evaluation of an accused asserting that a confession was involuntary or induced involves:

- a detailed review of the accused's past criminal, medical, and psychiatric records; school records, etc.; and as much information as is available about the circumstances in which the statement or confession was made;
- a clinical evaluation; and
- psychological testing, which should include tests to evaluate intellectual abilities, reading skills, personality make up, and suggestibility.

3) Testimonial Capacity

Assessments of this kind are carried out rather infrequently, but essentially involve an evaluation of an accused to determine whether she understands the nature and purpose of an oath; has the ability to distinguish fact from fiction; and can not only recollect the salient information about which she will testify, but also has an ability to communicate that information. Experts cannot provide opinions concerning a witness's credibility, but can be called to assist the court in understanding whether a mental disorder impacts upon a witness's ability to testify reliably.[7]

---

7   *R. v. Osolin* (1991), 10 C.R. (4th) 159 (B.C.C.A.).

CHAPTER FIVE

Criminal Responsibility: Part I

A. NOT CRIMINALLY RESPONSIBLE: INTRODUCTION

In 1992, Parliament replaced the "insanity defence" with the defence of "not criminally responsible on account of mental disorder" (NCR). The statutory changes consist largely of a modernization of the language employed. Section 16 of the *Criminal Code* of Canada[1] articulates the principle that no person who committed an offence while suffering from a mental disorder may be convicted. The test to be met is given consideration below. It should be emphasized at the outset that the test is strictly legal, not medical.

Defence of mental disorder

16. (1) No person is criminally responsible for an act committed or an omission made while suffering from a mental disorder that rendered the person incapable of appreciating the nature and quality of the act or omission or of knowing that it was wrong.

Presumption

(2) Every person is presumed not to suffer from a mental disorder so as to be exempt from criminal responsibility by virtue of subsection (1), until the contrary is proved on the balance of probabilities.

Burden of proof

(3) The burden of proof that an accused was suffering from a mental disorder so as to be exempt from criminal responsibility is on the party that raises the issue.

---

1   R.S.C. 1985, c. C-46.

B. WHEN MAY THE ISSUE ARISE?

As with any defence, the accused may assert this defence at the outset of
the trial or may raise it at the conclusion of the Crown's case if, and only if,
there is a case to meet calling for a defence. This may be done as late as upon
a finding of guilt, but prior to conviction. As a result of the Supreme Court
of Canada decision in *R. v. Swain*,[2] a new common law rule established that
the Crown may also raise the "defence" over the accused's objection at one
of two junctures.

1) When the Crown May Raise the Issue

The Crown may raise the issue where 1) during the accused's own defence,
the accused puts his or her mental capacity for intent in issue; or 2) after the
trier of fact has concluded that the accused is otherwise guilty.

   This common law rule provides procedurally for a "bifurcated trial." If
the issue is not raised by the accused at the outset of the trial, the issue may
be raised by either party—but only after the accused is proven otherwise
guilty. The accused may call evidence at the first phase of the bifurcated trial
and may raise other issues or defences such as "identification," or alibi, etc.,
while reserving the right to respond with the defence of NCR only if the trier
of fact finds him guilty.[3]

2) Should the Court Raise the Defence on its Own Motion?

Comments made in *obiter* in *Swain* have caused some jurists to believe they
have an obligation to raise the defence of NCR even in situations where neither the defence nor the Crown are seeking such a verdict. In *Swain*, Lamer
C.J.C. said the following:

> An accused person has control over the decision of whether to have counsel,
> whether to testify on his or her own behalf, and what witnesses to call. This is
> a reflection of our society's traditional respect for individual autonomy within
> an adversarial system. In *R. v. Chaulk, supra*, I indicated that the insanity
> defence is best characterized as an exemption to criminal liability which is
> based on an incapacity for criminal intent.[4]

---

2   [1991] 1 S.C.R. 933 [*Swain*].

3   *Ibid.*

4   *Ibid.* at 972.

Parenthetically, it is *not* the law that the NCR defence principally operates to negative the requisite *mens rea*. If *mens rea* is not proved there is no need for any defence. The NCR defence, as set out in section 16, is a supervening defence which assumes that *mens rea* has been proved but which, in some cases, may operate collaterally to disprove the otherwise proven *mens rea*. The classic example is the accused who plans and deliberates and specifically intends to kill his neighbour, but believes the neighbour to be Satan about to eliminate the entire human population. All elements of the offence are proved.

> In my view, the decision whether or not to raise this exemption as a means of negating criminal culpability is part and parcel of the conduct of an accused's overall defence. ...[5]
>
> Thus, although it is a principle of fundamental justice that an accused has the right to control his or her own defence, this is not an "absolute" right. If an accused chooses to conduct his or her defence in such a way that that accused's mental capacity for criminal intent is somehow put into question, then the Crown will be entitled to "complete the picture" by raising its own evidence of insanity and the trial judge will be entitled to charge the jury on s. 16 ...
>
> The Crown has indicated, however, that the Crown's ability to raise independently evidence of insanity conforms with a second principle of fundamental justice; namely, that a person who was insane at the time of the offence (and was therefore incapable of having criminal intent) ought not to be convicted under the criminal law. In other words, it is argued that the Crown must have the ability to raise evidence of insanity when the accused chooses not to do so, because it would violate the principles of fundamental justice for the accused to be convicted of a criminal offence when there is a real question about the accused's criminal culpability (and, therefore, about the accused's guilt) ...
>
> *I agree that it is a principle of fundamental justice that the criminal justice system not convict a person who was insane at the time of the offence* [Emphasis added].[6]

It is this passage that has caused courts to believe they have a "supervisory" obligation to raise the defence on their own motion. However, as Madam Justice Wilson observed in *Swain*,

---

5   *Ibid.*
6   *Ibid.* at 976.

Also of interest in these two articles is the examination of the American case law on the subject. Both writers identify two lines of American authority. The first is found in *Whalem v. United States*, 346 F.2d 812 (D.C. Cir. 1965), where the court held that since society only has an interest in punishing those who are morally culpable, trial judges have a discretion to raise the defence over the objections of the defendant. On the other hand in *Frendak v. United States*, 408 A.2d 364 (D.C. Ct. App. 1979), the court held that the trial judge must defer to the wishes of an accused if the defence is waived "intelligently and voluntarily." *If an accused freely and with full knowledge of the alternatives and consequences waives the insanity defence, then the court cannot independently impose the defence.* Other courts' responses to these two conflicting authorities have been mixed. Some jurisdictions follow *Whalem* and others *Frendak* [Emphasis added].[7]

In *R. v. Piette*,[8] the court on its own motion sent the accused off for an assessment pursuant to the provisions of section 672.12 to determine his criminal responsibility in the face of argument against such an order by the accused and the Crown. The trial judge then, after obtaining an assessment which suggested that the accused was significantly impaired, including with respect to his ability to "appreciate," proceeded to find that the accused's condition brought him within the ambit of section 16 without first finding the requisite mental element. The Crown and the defence were content that the accused's mental disorder simply negatived the requisite *mens rea*.

At appeal, the court observed that the new provisions contained in Part XX.1 of the *Criminal Code* no longer result in an "acquittal" upon a finding of NCR, but rather a hybrid verdict which is neither an acquittal nor a conviction. It is arguably right to say that Lamer, C.J.C.'s admonition in *Swain* has been rendered difficult, if not impossible, to interpret in the context of the new statutory regime. We are no longer speaking of "acquittals." The hybrid verdict may, on a case-by-case basis, prove to be more onerous than a conviction would have been. The appeal court found that the raising of the issue of criminal responsibility was something to be done by either the accused or the Crown, at the appropriate juncture. And further, for the court to pursue the defence on its own motion deprived the accused of his constitutional right to control the conduct of his defence at trial.

---

7   *Ibid.* at 1030.
8   2005 BCSC 1724.

C. ASSESSMENTS

1) Jurisdiction to Order an Assessment

The court must have reasonable grounds to believe that medical evidence is necessary to determine the issue of criminal responsibility (section 672.11(b)).

> *Assessment order*
>
> 672.11 A court having jurisdiction over an accused in respect of an offence may order an assessment of the mental condition of the accused, if it has reasonable grounds to believe that such evidence is necessary to determine (b) whether the accused was, at the time of the commission of the alleged offence, suffering from a mental disorder so as to be exempt from criminal responsibility by virtue of subsection 16(1);

"Assessment" will most often mean an assessment by a medical practitioner (section 672.1).

> *"Assessment"*
>
> "Assessment" means an assessment by a medical practitioner or any other person who has been designated by the Attorney General as being qualified to conduct an assessment of the mental condition of the accused under an assessment order made under section 672.11 or 672.121, and any incidental observation or examination of the accused;

"Form 48" may be used in the making of the order (see Appendix A).

While the above provisions pertain to the making of a court ordered assessment, any witness who is able to give relevant information may be called at the actual trial of the issue. Mental health practitioners such as psychologists may be particularly appropriate.

2) Who May Request that an Assessment be Ordered?

The accused may request that an order for assessment be made at any time. Where the prosecutor applies for an assessment order to determine criminal responsibility, the court may only order the assessment if (a) the accused puts his or her mental capacity to form criminal intent into issue; or (b) the prosecutor satisfies the court that there are reasonable grounds to doubt the accused is criminally responsible (section 672.12(3)).

3) Custody

It is presumed that all assessments will take place out of custody, with certain exceptions imported from section 515(10) (section 672.16). (See Chapter 3, Section E.3.) Notwithstanding this presumption, it should be noted that some designated "hospitals" (section 672.1) may require that assessments of criminal responsibility be conducted on an in-patient basis given the complexity and logistics of the assessment.

"Hospital"

"Hospital" means a place in a province that is designated by the Minister of Health for the province for the custody, treatment or assessment of an accused in respect of whom an assessment order, a disposition or a placement decision is made.

4) Duration of the Assessment

An assessment order to determine criminal responsibility shall be in force for more than thirty days (subsection 672.12(1)). Notwithstanding subsection 672.14(1), a court may make an order that remains in force for up to sixty days where there are compelling circumstances (subsection 672.14(3)).

General rule for period

672.14 (1) An assessment order shall not be in force for more than thirty days.

Exception in fitness cases

(2) No assessment order to determine whether the accused is unfit to stand trial shall be in force for more than five days, excluding holidays and the time required for the accused to travel to and from the place where the assessment is to be made, unless the accused and the prosecutor agree to a longer period not exceeding thirty days.

Exception for compelling circumstances

(3) Despite subsections (1) and (2), a court or Review Board may make an assessment order that remains in force for sixty days if the court or Review Board is satisfied that compelling circumstances exist that warrant it.

5) Variation of Assessment Orders

Variation may be made upon application (section 672.18).

6) Treatment of an Accused During an Assessment

Involuntary treatment of an accused during an assessment is not permissible.

No treatment order on assessment

672.19 No assessment order may direct that psychiatric or any other treatment of the accused be carried out, or direct the accused to submit to such treatment.

7) Bail Hearings

No order for the release or detention of an accused shall be made while an assessment order is in force (section 672.17).

8) Reports

An assessment order may direct the assessor to submit an assessment report (section 672.2(1). Where a report is ordered it shall be filed with the court as directed (section 672.2(2). It shall be provided to the prosecutor, the accused, and counsel for the accused (section 672.2(4).

Assessment report

672.2 (1) An assessment order may require the person who makes the assessment to submit in writing an assessment report on the mental condition of the accused.

Assessment report to be filed

(2) An assessment report shall be filed with the court or Review Board that ordered it, within the period fixed by the court or Review Board, as the case may be.

Court to send assessment report to Review Board

(3) The court shall send to the Review Board without delay a copy of any report filed with it pursuant to subsection (2), to assist in determining the appropriate disposition to be made in respect of the accused.

Copies of reports to accused and prosecutor

(4) Subject to subsection 672.51(3), copies of any report filed with a court or Review Board under subsection (2) shall be provided without delay to the prosecutor, the accused and any counsel representing the accused.

a) Critical Appraisal of an Expert's Criminal Responsibility Report

A non-exhaustive list of the errors experts make in evaluating accused with respect to the accused's criminal responsibility includes:

- failure to understand the legal standard for absent criminal responsibility;
- assuming that mental disorder is synonymous with lack of criminal responsibility;
- failing to hypothesize and deal with the prospect the accused is malingering;
- relying on inadequate information; and
- failing to address the accused's mental state with respect to each and every offence with which she is charged. (The error here is assuming that the same mental state was operative so as to exempt the accused from responsibility with respect to each and every charge.)

D. TRIAL OF THE ISSUE OF CRIMINAL RESPONSIBILITY

1) Jurisdiction to Try Issue

The trier of fact may try the issue (see Chapter 5, Section C.1) where 1) the accused raises the issue; 2) the Crown raises the issue after, in the opinion of the trial judge, the accused has put his mental capacity for criminal responsibility in issue; or 3) the Crown raises the issue upon a finding of guilt and prior to conviction.

2) Who Tries the Issue?

The trier of fact tries the issue—either a judge, when sitting alone, or a jury (section 672.34).

> *Verdict of not criminally responsible on account of mental disorder*
>
> 672.34 Where the jury, or the judge or provincial court judge where there is no jury, finds that an accused committed the act or made the omission that formed the basis of the offence charged, but was at the time suffering from mental disorder so as to be exempt from criminal responsibility by virtue of subsection 16(1), the jury or the judge shall render a verdict that the accused committed the act or made the omission but is not criminally responsible on account of mental disorder.

3) The Verdict

Where the trier of fact finds that an accused committed the act or made the omission that formed the basis of the offence, but was at the time suffering from mental disorder so as to be exempt from criminal responsibility by virtue of subsection 16(1), a verdict that the accused committed the act or made the omission but is not criminally responsible on account of mental disorder shall be rendered and may be used for limited purposes in the future (section 672.35).

> *Effect of verdict of not criminally responsible on account of mental disorder*
>
> 672.35 Where a verdict of not criminally responsible on account of mental disorder is rendered, the accused shall not be found guilty or convicted of the offence, but
>
> (a) the accused may plead autrefois acquit in respect of any subsequent charge relating to that offence;
>
> (b) any court may take the verdict into account in considering an application for judicial interim release or in considering what dispositions to make or sentence to impose for any other offence; and
>
> (c) the National Parole Board or any provincial parole board may take the verdict into account in considering an application by the accused for parole or pardon in respect of any other offence.

A verdict of NCR does not constitute a previous conviction for the purposes of any offence under any Act of Parliament for which a greater punishment is provided by reason of previous conviction (section 672.36).

> *Verdict not a previous conviction*
>
> 672.36 A verdict of not criminally responsible on account of mental disorder is not a previous conviction for the purposes of any offence under any Act of Parliament for which a greater punishment is provided by reason of previous convictions.

a) The Psychiatric Assessment

The psychiatric assessment of an accused's eligibility for an NCR defence must begin with the premise of an objective stance, a high index of suspicion about the potential for malingering, and respect for the notion that no person's mental state, let alone a person's mental state some time ago (at the time of the index offence) can be precisely known. Mental state is invariably surmised. As such, a clinician needs to be exceedingly thorough, pay scrupulous attention to detail, and be investigative and reconstructive in his or her orientation. In this regard, clinicians should consider the following:

- the context of the offence and potential motives;
- pre-existing animus;
- "similar fact" behaviours or episodes of deranged mental functioning in the past;
- the accused's affective state at the time (was the accused simply in a rage?); and
- the precise role of the mental disorder in bringing about the behaviour in question.

Serious mental disorder or psychosis is not synonymous with absent criminal responsibility. A background mental disorder, as defined in section 2 (see Chapter 3, Section H.1), is a necessary criterion for a successful defence under section 16, but it is only one of several. From a psychiatric perspective, the symptoms of the mental disorder need to have expressed themselves robustly enough at the critical time before a clinician can reasonably say that the symptoms of the mental disorder were instrumental in bringing about the behaviour under consideration.

i)   The Information to be Relied upon

The investigative approach requires a detailed database as well as the best information available concerning the accused's state of mind at the time. A non-exhaustive list of data (subject to admissibility) required includes:

- the Crown brief, including witness statements, officer's notes, relevant videos and audios, crime scene video, forensic reports, etc.;
- any statement given by the accused;
- the accused's criminal record;
- the accused's probation and previous supervision records;
- medical and psychiatric records;
- a detailed clinical assessment of the accused;
- information gathered from collateral informants; and
- psychological testing.

The psychiatric interview generally proceeds along the lines of the standard medical/psychiatric model of assessment, but special emphasis is placed on eliciting information with respect to the accused's state of mind at the critical time. The components of a psychiatric assessment for a possible NCR defence include the following:

THE BASIC HISTORY

- a history of the current psychiatric illness;
- past medical and mental health care histories;
- substance use history;
- legal history;
- personal history with emphasis on violence;
- family history; and
- a detailed current mental state examination.

THE CRIMINAL RESPONSIBILITY ISSUE

- This begins with an account of the patient's mental state leading up to the critical event, going back months, weeks, days, and especially the twenty-four hours immediately preceding the event.
- Use of prescribed drugs, street drugs, alcohol proximal to the event and whether they played a primary role (that is, drug-induced psychosis or confusional state) or secondary role of exacerbating the underlying mental disorder.
- Meaning of the behaviour to the accused (that is, potential psychotic motive).
- Detailed description of the accused's relationship with the victim, and feelings about him, recent changes in that relationship, misperceptions by the accused of the victim's behaviour or demeanour.
- Environmental factors (that is, was the act committed in circumstances that demonstrate an ability to take steps to avoid detection).
- Situational factors—persons in the environment or situational variables that might have played an instigating or provocative role.
- Presence or absence of delusions related to the event.
- Presence of auditory hallucinations, whether they were command in nature, the extent to which the accused was experiencing them that day (as opposed to any other time) and their impact on the accused that day. If the accused resisted the hallucinations in the past, why act on them that day?
- How precise or vague were the delusions? If, for example, an accused said that he believed killing the victim was "God's will," it still needs to be asked how the accused came to interpret that relatively vague direction as an instruction to cause harm to the victim.
- To what extent can a non-psychotic motive be teased out of the otherwise psychotic appearing picture, and what degree of role did it play?
- Could the accused "appreciate" the nature and quality of the act? In the case of a homicide, the clinician might ask these questions:

▷ What happened?

▷ What were you thinking?

▷ What were you feeling?

▷ What was to be gained (by doing whatever the accused did)?

▷ What did you want to happen?

▷ What was the result?

▷ How was the victim reacting to all of this: was he afraid, did he seem to be in pain, did you notice blood?

▷ What did you think was happening to him?

- Note that the wrongfulness prong of the test in section 16, particularly lack of knowledge (or inability to apply knowledge) of the moral wrongfulness of the behaviour, is the one most frequently relied upon to justify an NCR defence. Paranoid or grandiose accused often operate on the belief that the behaviour resulting in the charge(s) was necessary for self-preservation, or to achieve a higher purpose, respectively.

- The clinician must determine whether the accused made any attempts to arrest what she was doing. This inquiry is relevant to the accused's knowledge of the wrongfulness of her actions. Immediate and unquestioning obedience to the command of voices is strong evidence that the accused's capacity to reason and refrain from certain actions became overpowered.

- What did the accused understand of the legal and moral wrongfulness of her actions at the time? This information can sometimes be obtained by asking the accused to imagine that the examiner was present at the time and asking questions about the accused's mental state, and about her understanding of the wrongfulness of the behaviour. In this regard, the examiner might ask any one or more of the following questions:

▷ Why did you make that choice?

▷ What might have happened if you didn't?

▷ Where did your right to do that action come from?

▷ Are there laws that might have something to say about that kind of behaviour?

▷ Are there laws that you feel are more important that exempt you from the laws most people have to abide by?

▷ Were you concerned about getting caught, and what would have happened to you had you been caught?

▷ Do you think you would have done what you did if someone else had been there in the room (for example, a friend, a member of the clergy, a parent)?

Many accused are unable and/or unwilling to engage in a dialogue (of the kind envisioned above) that would allow an examiner to better understand the accused's mental state at the critical time. Many accused claim amnesia for the event(s) giving rise to their charge(s). *Apropos* the earlier discussion concerning the relevance of amnesia in a fitness to stand trial issue (see Chapter 3, Section H.1(a), amnesia (including partial amnesia and fragmented recollection) is a common finding in violent crime, particularly when alcohol and drugs are implicated.

Factors contributing to the potential for amnesia/fragmented memory include, apart from the ingestion of substances, the emotional state the accused was in prior to, during, and after the critical event(s); his preparedness to be forthcoming; and the potential impact of psychotic symptoms. Significant psychosis at the time of the event may have played an interfering role in recording the event(s), perhaps because of the distracting effect of internal stimuli (for example, auditory hallucinations), or because of an element of confusion. A psychotic process at the time of the assessment can, apart from limiting an accused's cooperation, interfere with his ability to retrieve memory of the event(s) that might otherwise be accessible but for the accused's mental state at the time of the assessment.

From a psychiatric perspective, amnesia is, in and of itself, little or no evidence in support of an NCR defence. It should do no more than raise a number of hypotheses that run the gamut between genuine amnesia (or fragmented recollection) caused by any one or number of the factors touched on above, to outright malingering.

ii) Conditions Justifying the NCR Defence

The condition that qualifies the accused for an NCR defence must be a recognized condition, and for the most part, one that is capable of compromising the accused's appreciation of the nature and quality of her acts or knowing their wrongfulness. Again, it is not so much the diagnosis that is important, but the condition's effect on the brain functions that mediate the various capacities touched on in section 16.

1. Common conditions that are often found in the background to an NCR defence
a) *Schizophrenia* (see Chapter 1, Section C). Brief overview of schizophrenia:
   * delusions
   * hallucinations

- disordered thought
- inappropriate affect
- deteriorated social, educational, vocational functioning
- biological basis
- onset: male—late teens to early twenties; female—early to mid-twenties;
- poor insight common
- medication compliance problems common

b) *Delusional Disorder* (see Chapter 1, Section C). Brief overview of delusional disorder:
- characterized by one or more delusions (hallucinations and other psychotic phenomena either not present or not prominent)
- types:
  ▷ somatic type
  ▷ persecutory type
  ▷ grandiose type
  ▷ erotomanic type
  ▷ jealous type

c) *Major Depressive Episode—with Psychotic Features* (see Chapter 1, Section C). Brief overview of major depressive episode:
- pervasively depressed mood +/- loss of interest in usually sustaining activities
- + neurovegetative signs and symptoms:
  ▷ loss or increased appetite
  ▷ loss or gain weight
  ▷ decrease or increase of sleep
  ▷ fatigue, lethargy, low energy
  ▷ poor concentration
  ▷ bleak future outlook
  ▷ poor self-esteem
  ▷ suicidal ideation
  ▷ deteriorated self-care
- +/- psychotic component:
  ▷ delusions and hallucinations, often with self-deprecating, guilt-laden, and nihilistic themes

d) *Mania — Bopolar Disorder* (see Chapter 1, Section C). Brief overview of mania—bipolar disorder:

- elevated, expansive, and/or irritable mood
- increased activity
- accelerated and disjunctive thought and speech
- grandiosity
- decreased need for sleep
- foolish, high risk, and poor judgment behaviour:
  - ▷ spending sprees
  - ▷ promiscuity
  - ▷ substance abuse

e) *Organic Mental Disorders* (see Chapter 1, Section C). Brief overview of organic mental disorders:
- delirium:
  - ▷ clouded consciousness, confusion, disorientation, memory problems
  - ▷ disorganized thought
  - ▷ perceptual disturbance and delusions
  - ▷ inability to focus
  - ▷ agitation (for example, delirium tremens; (see Chapter 1, Section C)

2. Less common conditions that occasionally underpin an NCR defence
- Alcohol and drug withdrawal. For example, a forty-year-old male with a chronic severe alcohol dependency problem stopped drinking abruptly within twelve hours of taking a transcontinental flight. He developed the symptoms of delirium tremens (see definition for delirium tremens in Chapter 1). In his deluded and confused state he thought the pilot was going to crash the plane. His behaviour and violent conduct towards others (who were trying to settle him) led to a series of charges.
- Dissociative disorders (see Chapter 1, Section C).
- Cerebral trauma
- Dementia

3. Uncommon conditions that rarely justify a finding of NCR
- post-traumatic stress disorder
- paraphilias
- personality disorders and psychopathy. Prior to the decision in *R. v. Chaulk*,[9] the prong of the test in section 16 that exempted an individ-

---

9   [1990] 3 S.C.R. 1303.

ual from criminal responsibility if the individual could not, on account of mental disorder, know that the act was wrong, was limited to an inability to know the legal wrongfulness of the action. *Chaulk* expanded that branch of the wrongfulness component to include an inability to know the moral wrongfulness of the behaviour. There was understandable concern thereafter that antisocial personality disordered individuals/psychopaths would consequently be eligible for exemption from criminal responsibility because of the inherent moral defect in their conditions. (Their condition—antisocial personality disorder/psychopath—qualifies as a disease of the mind). The distinction, and an important one at that, however, is that antisocial personality disordered or psychopathic accused most often do not lack an ability to understand the moral wrongfulness of their actions. They engage in the behaviours that lead to their criminal charges because of their preference for their own moral code over that of society's.[10]

iii) Psychopathology Frequently Found to Justify an NCR Finding

The following three symptoms are frequently relied upon to justify the degree of impairment envisioned by section 16 of the *Criminal Code*:

1.   Delusions (see Chapter 1, Section C.2)

Delusions can impinge upon an accused's appreciation of the nature and quality of his act, or more commonly, his ability to know that an act was legally or morally wrong. Delusions may create moral justifications for the behaviour in some of the following ways:

- The act was a preemptive strike against an (imagined) danger.
- The behaviour was used to fend off an alien or evil force.
- The delusion dictated the need to act in order to bring about a new order.
- An attack on a victim may be motivated by the delusional belief that she is an imposter.
- Psychotically depressed individuals sometimes kill because of some delusional notion about the health of the victim or to end the victim's suffering on earth and bring about a better life in heaven.

---

10   See *R. v. Simpson* (1977), 77 D.L.R. (3d) 507 (Ont. C.A.).

2. Hallucinations (see Chapter 1, Section C.2)

Hallucinations frequently justify an NCR finding when the hallucination involves a voice commanding the action, particularly one that the accused can not resist and feels compelled to abide by. Hallucinations may at times be so pervasive and disturbing, and create so much background noise, confusion and disorganization, that they cause the accused to behave in an unpredictable and angry fashion.

3. Confusion

A number of serious psychiatric conditions (psychotic depression, post-traumatic stress disorder, psychosis, mania, and organic brain syndromes) are associated with some measure of disorientation or confusion, and some conditions (delirium) are specifically defined by that symptom. Confusion can have implications for either branch of the tests in section 16 (appreciation of the nature and quality of the act or knowing its wrongfulness). Confusion could cause the accused to misapprehend the nature of her physical actions towards the victim and may have implications for her ability to understand the impact of the behaviour and the vulnerability of the victim. Confusion could also have the effect of making information about the legal and moral wrongfulness of the behaviour otherwise known to the accused inaccessible to her in that instant.

In the end, a successful NCR defence is more likely to be made out when the stars align, that is, there is a condition in the background, causing significant symptoms that have a specific effect, which has implications for the capacities described in section 16. Some examples of the way in which the various conditions that are most often implicated in an NCR defence and their symptoms may correlate to a particular defect in the capacities described in section 16 of the *Criminal Code* are provided in Figures 5-1 to 5-6 below.

Figure 5-1, below, illustrates the case of an individual suffering from a diagnosis of schizophrenia whose hallucinations and delusions cause him to feel concerned about his safety and an imminent attack. His preemptive strike against the victim (*qua* suspected foe) results in a subsequent NCR defence based on him being incapable of knowing the moral wrongfulness of his act, in that he felt morally justified in taking the self-protective steps that resulted in the charge.

Figure 5-1: Potential NCR Configuration in a Schizophrenic Accused

Constructing an NCR Defence			
Condition	Symptom	Effect	Section 16 Branch
Schizophrenia	Hallucinations	Irresistible command to commit act	Incapable of appreciating nature and quality of act or omission
Delusional disorder	Delusions • Persecutory • Grandiose • Nihilistic	Distorted reality that supplants existing reality • People are conspiring • People are evil • People are aliens • People are imposters • People are controlling	
Psychotic depression	Confusion		
Mania	Affective dysregulation • Elation • Depression • Irritability • Anger	Disorganization • Information inaccessible	Incapable of knowing act is legally wrong
Organic brain syndrome • Delirium • Dementia	Cognitive limitations/ distortion	• Information jumbled	Incapable of knowing act is morally wrong
	Thought disorder	Impaired judgment	
Mental retardation	Psychomotor agitation/ retardation	Lack of understanding	Feels morally justified

Figure 5-2: Potential NCR Configuration in an Accused with Delusional Disorder

Constructing an NCR Defence			
Condition	Symptom	Effect	Section 16 Branch
Schizophrenia	Hallucinations	Irresistible command to commit act	Incapable of appreciating nature and quality of act or omission
Delusional disorder	Delusions • Persecutory • Grandiose • Nihilistic	Distorted reality that supplants existing reality • People are conspiring • People are evil • People are aliens • People are imposters • People are controlling	
Psychotic depression	Confusion		
Mania	Affective dysregulation • Elation • Depression • Irritability • Anger	Disorganization • Information inaccessible	Incapable of knowing act is legally wrong
Organic brain syndrome • Delirium • Dementia	Cognitive limitations/ distortion	• Information jumbled	Incapable of knowing act is morally wrong
	Thought disorder	Impaired judgment	
Mental retardation	Psychomotor agitation/ retardation	Lack of understanding	Feels morally justified

The pattern in a patient suffering from a delusional disorder could well resemble the illustrative pattern picked up on by Figure 5-2, above.

A psychotically depressed accused, for example, may have experienced delusions with nihilistic and guilty themes, such that she believed a family member would inevitably suffer a horrible demise as a result of an illness he truly did not have. As a result, she devises a murder-suicide scenario to send them both to heaven and spare them both from the horrible outcome she felt was in store for them. This accused believed her actions were morally justified. The configuration that perhaps best describes the pathway to an NCR defence for her is covered in Figure 5-3, below.

Figure 5-3: Potential NCR Configuration in a Psychotically Depressed Accused

Constructing an NCR Defence			
Condition	*Symptom*	*Effect*	*Section 16 Branch*
Schizophrenia	Hallucinations	Irresistible command to commit act	Incapable of appreciating nature and quality of act c omission
Delusional disorder	Delusions • Persecutory • Grandiose • Nihilistic	Distorted reality that supplants existing reality • People are conspiring • People are evil • People are aliens	
Psychotic depression	Confusion	• People are imposters	
Mania	Affective dysregulation • Elation • Depression • Irritability • Anger	• People are controlling Disorganization • Information inaccessible	Incapable of knowing act is legally wrong
Organic brain syndrome • Delirium • Dementia	Cognitive limitations/ distortion Thought disorder	• Information jumbled Impaired judgment	Incapable of knowing act is morally wrong
Mental retardation	Psychomotor agitation/ retardation	Lack of understanding	Feels morally justified

Figure 5-4 demonstrates the potential flow from condition to exonerative branch(es) of section 16 in the case of a manic accused.

The example illustrated below, in Figure 5-5, is of a delirious accused (that is, organic brain syndrome) whose acute state has caused a plethora of disturbances. Not only is he confused, disorganized in thought, and highly agitated, but he is suspicious and experiencing visual hallucinations. The symptom profile has caused him to lash out and seriously injure a staff member in the chronic care facility in which he resides. His various impairments

Figure 5-4: Potential NCR Configuration in a Manic Accused

Constructing an NCR Defence			
Condition	Symptom	Effect	Section 16 Branch
Schizophrenia	Hallucinations	Irresistible command to commit act	Incapable of appreciating nature and quality of act or omission
Delusional disorder	Delusions • Persecutory • Grandiose • Nihilistic	Distorted reality that supplants existing reality • People are conspiring • People are evil • People are aliens • People are imposters	
Psychotic depression	Confusion		
Mania	Affective dysregulation • Elation • Depression • Irritability • Anger	• People are controlling Disorganization • Information inaccessible • Information jumbled	Incapable of knowing act is legally wrong
Organic brain syndrome • Delirium • Dementia	Cognitive limitations/ distortion Thought disorder	Impaired judgment	Incapable of knowing act is morally wrong
Mental retardation	Psychomotor agitation/ retardation	Lack of understanding	Feels morally justified

Figure 5-5: Potential NCR Configuration in an Accused with Delirium

Constructing an NCR Defence			
Condition	Symptom	Effect	Section 16 Branch
Schizophrenia	Hallucinations	Irresistible command to commit act	Incapable of appreciating nature and quality of act or omission
Delusional disorder	Delusions • Persecutory • Grandiose • Nihilistic	Distorted reality that supplants existing reality • People are conspiring • People are evil • People are aliens • People are imposters	
Psychotic depression	Confusion		
Mania	Affective dysregulation • Elation • Depression • Irritability • Anger	• People are controlling Disorganization • Information inaccessible • Information jumbled	Incapable of knowing act is legally wrong
Organic brain syndrome • Delirium • Dementia	Cognitive limitations/ distortion Thought disorder	Impaired judgment	Incapable of knowing act is morally wrong
Mental retardation	Psychomotor agitation/ retardation	Lack of understanding	Feels morally justified

have resulted in an inability to appreciate either the nature or quality of his act. As well, any information concerning its legality or morality is inaccessible to him, in light of his highly disorganized mental state.

The potential configuration in the case of a mentally retarded accused demonstrates (see Figure 5-6 below) that the primary pathway to an NCR defence is based principally on limited appreciation of the impact (that is, the quality) of the act and limited understanding of its legal and/or moral wrongfulness. Note that from a practical perspective, significantly cognitively limited accused are frequently found unfit to stand trial and frequently remain so permanently, and thus they do not get to the NCR stage at trial.

Figure 5-6: Potential NCR Configuration in a Mentally Retarded Accused

Constructing an NCR Defence			
Condition	*Symptom*	*Effect*	*Section 16 Branch*
Schizophrenia	Hallucinations	Irresistible command to commit act	Incapable of appreciating nature and quality of act or omission
Delusional disorder	Delusions • Persecutory • Grandiose • Nihilistic	Distorted reality that supplants existing reality • People are conspiring • People are evil • People are aliens • People are imposters • People are controlling	
Psychotic depression	Confusion		
Mania	Affective dysregulation • Elation • Depression • Irritability • Anger	Disorganization • Information inaccessible • Information jumbled	Incapable of knowing act is legally wrong
Organic brain syndrome • Delirium • Dementia	Cognitive limitations/ distortion Thought disorder	Impaired judgment	Incapable of knowing act is morally wrong
Mental retardation	Psychomotor agitation/ retardation	Lack of understanding	Feels morally justified

E. NOT CRIMINALLY RESPONSIBLE ON ACCOUNT OF A MENTAL DISORDER: THE TEST

1) Section 16

(1) No person is criminally responsible for an act committed or an omission made while suffering from a mental disorder that rendered the person

incapable of appreciating the nature and quality of the act or omission or of knowing that it was wrong.

(2) Every person is presumed not to suffer from a mental disorder so as to be exempt from criminal responsibility by virtue of subsection (1), until the contrary is proved on the balance of probabilities.

(3) The burden of proof that an accused was suffering from a mental disorder so as to be exempt from criminal responsibility is on the party that raises the issue.

Mental disorder: "Mental disorder" (section 2, *Criminal Code*) means "disease of the mind." Disease of the mind embraces any illness, disorder or abnormal condition which impairs the human mind and its functioning.[11] Thus, personality disorders may constitute disease of the mind. The definition from the criminal law's perspective is broad and includes, for example, mental retardation[12] or delerium tremens.[13]

Appreciating and knowing: In using the two words "appreciating" and "knowing,'" Parliament clearly intended that different tests be used. The verb "know" has a positive connotation requiring a base awareness while "appreciate" involves a degree of analysis of knowledge or experience.[14]

Nature and quality: Appreciation of the "nature and quality" of the act refers to an incapacity by reason of disease of the mind to appreciate the physical consequences of the act.[15]

Wrong: Wrong means "morally wrong" and not simply "legally wrong."[16] Furthermore, the accused must have the ability to apply this knowledge at the time of the otherwise criminal act.[17] And, it is not necessary that, where an accused was delusional at the time of the act, the delusion, if true, would provide a defence.[18]

---

11   *R. v. Cooper*, [1980] 1 S.C.R. 1149.
12   See, for example, *R. v. Rouse*, [1996] O.J. No. 4688 (Gen. Div.).
13   See, for example, *R. v. Malcolm*, [1989] M.J. No. 375 (C.A.).
14   *R. v. Barnier*, [1980] 1 S.C.R. 1124.
15   *R. v. Landry*, [1991] 1 S.C.R. 99.
16   *R. v. Chaulk*, above note 9.
17   *R. v. Oommen*, [1994] 2 S.C.R. 507.
18   *Ibid.*

2) No Evidence of Insanity

Where, at the conclusion of trial, the trial judge is of the view that there is no evidence to support the defence of insanity, she should inform counsel prior to making their jury addresses.[19]

3) Adverse Inference

While an accused asserting a defence of NCR is not obligated to submit to an examination by a psychiatrist retained by the Crown, an adverse inference may be drawn from a failure to do so.[20]

F. WHERE NCR FOUND

Upon a verdict that the accused was NCR at the relevant time, the provisions of section 672.54 apply (section 672.54 is set out above in Chapter 3, Section K). The accused may be detained in hospital, discharged subject to conditions, or, if not a significant threat to the safety of the public, discharged absolutely.[21]

1) Does the Accused Want to Taise the "Defence"?

A very important question for counsel to ask their experts (especially when retained privately) is "do I want to raise the NCR defence?" The answer to this question will require very careful questioning of the expert and discussion with the client. Upon a verdict of NCR the accused will have a disposition hearing and a disposition will be rendered, either by the court at first instance, or later by the review board (see Chapter 9).

Given that the objective of most accused is the fastest path to liberty, the raising of an NCR defence may be counterproductive. Counsel must inquire of the expert — hopefully an expert in forensic psychiatry with intimate knowledge of the review board system — whether, upon a verdict of NCR, the accused is likely to be found a "significant threat to the safety of the public" and, if so, what likely is the "least onerous and least restrictive disposition"? If the opinion of the expert is that it cannot be shown that the accused is a

---

19   See *R. v. Charest* (1990), 57 C.C.C. (3d) 312 (Que. C.A.).

20   See *R. v. Sweeney (No. 2)* (1977), 16 O.R. (2d) 814 (C.A.); *R. v. Worth* (1995), 98 C.C.C. (3d) 133 (Ont. C.A.).

21   See Chapter 9, Section B for a complete discussion of the making of dispositions and the jurisdictional threshold.

significant threat to the safety of the public, the accused may look forward to an absolute discharge. His matter will then be terminated with no further obligation to the review board or the courts. If, on the other hand, the accused is likely going to be found a significant threat to the safety of the public there are a wide range of possible outcomes. These range from detention in a maximum secure hospital (which looks very much like a jail) to being discharged from hospital and living in the community with minor encumbrances upon the accused's liberty.

Knowing the likely post-NCR verdict outcome is critical information for counsel to impart to the accused prior to the receiving of instructions. While, of course, the expert cannot make guarantees, counsel will be able to determine with a high degree of certainty what the post-verdict outcome will be. There is no predictable correlation between the seriousness of the offence and the final disposition. And, this is logically appropriate. An accused charged with a very minor offence may, upon assessment, be viewed as a very dangerous person. On the other hand, an accused charged with a very serious offence may be viewed as not a significant threat. Significant weight is accorded to the accused's condition at the time of the assessment. The accused's mental state at the time of the offence becomes considerably less important.

So, the question to be asked of the expert is not so much whether the accused has a potential NCR defence, but rather, does he want one? In working through these questions it is imperative that a forensic expert be retained in order to provide the accused with the best information to base his instructions upon.

G. MENTAL DISORDER SHORT OF NCR

The *Criminal Code* does not recognize a defence of diminished responsibility.[22] Nevertheless, where the accused is charged with an offence requiring the proof of specific intent or planning and deliberation, the evidence of mental disorder, while falling short of NCR, must be considered and may negate the required mental element.[23]

---

22   See *R. v. Chartrand*, [1977] 1 S.C.R. 314.

23   See, for example, *R. v. Hilton*, [1977] O.J. No. 550 (C.A.); *R. v. Allard* (1990), 57 C.C.C. (3d) 397 (Que. C.A.).

H. AUTOMATISM

1) Legal Considerations

The defence of automatism is not included in the *Criminal Code* but, if found, is dealt with according to common law as an adjunct to the general provisions regarding criminal responsibility. Two sorts of automatism are recognized at common law: mental disorder and non-mental disorder automatism; differentiating between the two requires a two-step procedure.[24] First, the trial judge must decide whether the accused has satisfied the evidentiary burden for the defence of automatism and, if so, whether it is attributable to mental disorder.[25] As with NCR generally, the law presumes that the accused acted voluntarily and, therefore, the accused bears the burden of establishing on a balance of probabilities the he or she acted involuntarily by reason of automatism.[26] Typically, this burden will be established by calling expert evidence. Once automatism is established, the accused will once again bear the burden of proving that it was caused by a psychological blow. Typically, this will require evidence of a trigger equivalent to a "shock."[27]

R. v. Stone maps out very nicely the procedure to be followed and the tests to be met. It effectively replaces much of the previously decided case law. With the recent Supreme Court of Canada decision in *R. v. Fontaine*,[28] it is now clear that the trial judge is not responsible for appraising the likely success of an automatism defence and therefore required to engage in a weighing of evidence. An assertion of involuntariness, supported by the logically probative opinion of a qualified expert (supporting either mental disorder or non-mental disorder automatism) will generally provide a sufficient evidentiary foundation for putting the defence to the trier of fact. *Stone* must be read in light of *R. v. Cinous*.[29] What needs to be established is an "air of reality." Where the automatism is produced by a mental disorder, the accused is treated as if she were found NCR and the provisions of Part XX.1 apply. Where the automatism is not produced by a mental disorder the accused is acquitted.

---

24 See *R. v. Stone*, [1999] 2 S.C.R. 290.
25 *Ibid.*
26 *Ibid.*
27 *Ibid.*
28 (2004), 183 C.C.C. (3d) 1 (S.C.C.).
29 (2002), 162 C.C.C. (3d) 129 (S.C.C.).

In deciding whether the automatism was caused by mental disorder, the judge should consider a number of factors, including 1) was the automatism caused by internal or external factors? and 2) does the accused constitute a recurring danger? It should be noted that these were the same tests applied prior to *Stone* in differentiating between "insane" and "non-insane" automatism. Both "tests" have their origins in pre-*Stone* decisions. The rather obvious objective in both is to contain potentially dangerous accused and avoid their outright acquittal. That is, automatism caused by an "internal" condition was seen as reflective of a mental disorder naively thought to render the accused "dangerous," whereas automatism caused by an "external" force was, for some reason, seen as benign and not reflective of dangerousness (that is, the accused was a simple victim of circumstance). The same logic is applied with the "recurring danger" test. This logic contains an implicit presumption that mental illness is a sign of dangerousness. This, it should be noted, is out of keeping with all current scientific literature and inconsistent with the Supreme Court of Canada's own decision in *Winko*[30] where the court clearly states that there is to be no presumption that the mentally disordered accused poses a significant threat to the safety of the public. Furthermore, if the automatism defence were to be codified and formally incorporated into the provisions of section 16 there would be no need to search for artificial "dangerousness differentiators" as all accused would be subject to the provisions of section 672.54. Where the accused is not shown to be a significant threat to the safety of the public, he is discharged absolutely.

2) Psychiatric Considerations

Since *Stone,* the long-standing distinction between "insane" and "non-insane" automatism has really been "re-packaged" using different terminology. As before, the key distinction following *Stone* lies in determining whether the automatism is the result of a mental disorder (in which case the accused follows the NCR pathway) or is a non-mental disorder automatism (for example, a psychological blow or other condition that can lead to an acquittal).

The conditions that might underpin an automatism defence have remained more or less the same. Each has the potential, depending on a number of factors, to result in involuntary behaviour. From a psychiatric perspective, automatism denotes physical behaviour that occurs in the absence of conscious direction of that behaviour. Involuntary behaviour, a relatively

---

30   *Winko v. British Columbia (Forensic Psychiatric Institute)*, [1999] 2 S.C.R. 625.

rare phenomenon at that, ordinarily flows from some form of serious de-rangement of mental functioning, whether as a result of a biological (organ-ic) or psychological disturbance. In other instances, the accused may have been conscious and aware of his behaviour which was being performed "in-voluntarily." What follows is a list of a variety of conditions, some illustrated with examples, that can potentially cause involuntary behaviour.

a) Seizure Disorders—Epilepsy

Put simply, epilepsy is a disturbance of the brain's electrical activity. It can affect the brain in either a focal or diffuse manner and be associated with a wide array of clinical presentations that include a circumscribed emotional disturbance or outburst (that is, the seizure activity is limited to the part of the brain that regulates affect), or a grand mal seizure (falling to the ground, loss of consciousness, shaking, and loss of control of bodily functions).

Of the various seizure disorders or combinations thereof, complex partial seizures (previously more commonly referred to as temporal lobe epilepsy) are more likely to be associated with automatisms—stereotyped non-purposeful movements or behaviours—than any other type of seizure disorder. Patients experiencing a complex partial seizure often lose touch with their environment (experience depersonalization and/or derealization) as a prelude to demon-strating the characteristic automatic movements that may include lipsmack-ing, chewing, pacing, repetitive movements, or fumbling of the hands; for example, unbuttoning a garment. The automatisms described above that are characteristic of complex partial seizures are almost invariably limited in scope, and rarely lead to behaviours of the degree and complexity that might form the substance of a criminal charge. If aggression were to be associated with a complex partial seizure, then it would likely be a more amorphous kind of ag-gression, rather than aggressive behaviour that requires a number of steps and the degree of skill and agility seen in conscious functioning.

Grand mal seizures are rarely, if ever, associated with automatic behav-iours that may be implicated in criminal conduct. The degree of debility as-sociated with a grand mal seizure would generally not permit actions of this kind to occur. If grand mal seizures are the underlying condition, automa-tisms are more likely to occur in a post-seizure confusional state (that is, the "post-ictal" state). The following classic quote from Holmes describes this issue well:

> The automatic states and conditions of altered consciousness which occur
> after major or minor seizures ... are very important from the medico-legal

aspect, as in these states the patient is not consciously aware of what he does and is unable to distinguish between right and wrong, and as he preserves no memory of his actions on return to his normal level, he is unable to place them in a rational relationship to his ordinary life.[31]

For a discussion of how a seizure (induced by hypoglycemia) resulted in an automatism that exonerated the accused, see *R. v. Bohak*.[32]

b) Cerebral Tumor

An intra-cerebral growth or tumor would indeed be a rare cause of automatic behaviour. The fact is that any intra-cerebral pathology (that is, brain infarct, arteriosclerosis, abscess, or other type of infection) could, either through the seizure it induces or through compression and ensuing disruption of brain activity, lead to automatic behaviour.

c) Concussion

Formerly thought of as falling into the category of "non-insane automatism," a concussion (a violent shock or jarring of the brain often associated with loss of consciousness) may rarely be associated with automatic behaviour that results in a criminal charge. The mechanism or derangement can include a seizure-induced automatism secondary to the blow, or involuntary action that is a function of a post-concussion confusional state.

d) Drugs and Alcohol

From a legal perspective, the greater issue here is whether the ingested substances were consumed involuntarily or with no intent or wish to become intoxicated—as might occur when the accused is authentically naïve to the effects of the substance, misapprehended the nature of the substance, or has had a reaction to a voluntarily ingested substance that is idiosyncratic or out of keeping with the expected effect.

For example, a twenty-five-year-old soft-spoken, lawful, and gentle man with a chronic back problem was helping his aunt strip old carpets from the floor. After working fifteen hours without a break, he took one tablet of a narcotic analgesic and two barbiturates (tranquilizers), both of which he had used sparingly in the past for back pain and sleep respectively. The

---

31   G. Holmes, "The Mental Abnormalities Associated with Epilepsy," in The Lancet, quoted by Sir N.W. East, *An Introduction to Forensic Psychiatry in the Criminal Courts* (New York: William Wood & Company, 1927).

32   [2004] M.J. No. 172 (Prov. Ct.).

young man had little or no experience with either street drugs or prescribed drugs. He had no recollection of the events after ingesting these drugs. He had evidently been awakened early by a relative's telephone call, and asked to run an errand. He appeared "dazed (and) ill" to the person to whom he delivered the items. He could not recollect entering the store, stealing the items, striking security personnel, running down the street waving a hammer, or hiding in the back of a van until he was apprehended. A defence of non-insane automatism was accepted based on psychiatric evidence that the accused's behaviours were involuntary—carried out in the course of a drug-induced semi-somnambulistic state. The court was also invited to consider his overall vulnerability to that state as a result of his fatigue, pain, possible hypoglycemia (he had eaten little) and the potential effects of the toxins (carpet-glue fumes) to which he had been exposed.

e) Psychosis

As a general rule, individuals suffering from the effects of a psychotic disorder are not automatons. They have conscious control over their actions, but they may not understand the true nature of their behaviour, or have some difficulty stopping themselves from engaging in the act(s) in question. There are some instances, however, where a psychosis may be so intense as to cause a confusional state of a degree that has implications for the voluntariness of the action. In other words, the behaviour is arguably "unguided," as opposed to "misguided."

f) Somnambulism/Sleepwalking

Automatisms that occur in the context of sleepwalking are one of the best-known, most-frequently occurring, and often the most highly publicized forms of automatic behaviour. In *R. v. Parks*,[33] the accused was acquitted of the murder of his mother-in-law on the basis of sleepwalking. He evidently drove 23 kilometers to his in-laws' home, located a kitchen knife, then proceeded to kill his mother-in-law and severely injure his father-in-law. Parks reportedly got along well with his in-laws, and there was no evident underlying *animus*. Parks had no recollection of the events, purportedly because he was in a somnambulistic state; such was the uncontroverted evidence of experts who testified, and corroborated by sleep laboratory findings. A defence of non-insane automatism based on sleepwalking had never previously been the basis of any acquittal in Canada. (*Quaere*, had the experts been

---

33   (1992), 75 C.C.C. (3d) 287 (S.C.C.).

asked whether somnambulism was an abnormal condition which impairs the human mind and its functioning (that is, *Cooper*, at Chapter 5, Section E.1, above), would the same result have been obtained. The experts were asked whether somnambulism was a "mental disorder." It is likely that this was interpreted in a medical sense and the answer was, as a result, "no.")

g) Hypoglycemia

Although some individuals may experience spontaneous hypoglycemia (low blood sugar), hypoglycemia of such severity to result in a derangement of mental functioning is much more likely to occur in diabetics who have either delayed eating or eaten too little to counteract the effects of their diabetic medication, most often insulin. Physical symptoms of hypoglycemia include fatigue, tremulousness, sweating, blurred vision, or headaches, to name a few. Mental symptoms include anxiety, irritability, restlessness, cognitive impairment, and occasionally, disruption of conscious functioning and aggressivity. For an excellent example of the manner in which hypoglycemia can lead to the degree of brain dysfunction that could result in an automatism, see *R. v. Frost*.[34]

h) Dissociative States

A dissociative state (derangement of the integrated functions of consciousness), like somnambulism, was a notably characteristic example of what was previously referred to as a non-insane automatism. Having regard to *Stone*, dissociative state is likely to be seen as falling more into the category of "non-mental disorder automatism" (particularly if external factors are the cause of the episode and it does not constitute a recurring danger).

---

34   [2003] B.C.J. No. 2947 (S.C.).

CHAPTER SIX

Criminal Responsibility: Part II

A. INTRODUCTION

In Part I we considered mental disorder as a central or primary factor in an accused's criminal responsibility. In Part II we consider mental disorder as an ingredient in what would otherwise constitute a "free standing" defence. We are considering mental disorder—whether caused by external factors, internal factors, or the ingestion of drugs—where its effect may be to *reduce* rather than *eliminate* an accused's criminal responsibility.

B. INTOXICATION

1) Common Law

A drug may intoxicate an individual to an extent that the requisite intent is negatived. Where the offence is one which requires "specific intent," a drug may diminish an accused's capacity to form the required specific intent.[1]

2) Diminished Responsibility—Intoxication and Intent

Keiter has described the history of the intoxication defence in North America, tracing its origins in English law as far back as 1551, when the voluntary consumption of alcohol, even when it was associated with lack of understanding or memory of the act, did not lead to an acquittal on a murder charge.[2] More

---

1   *D.P.P. v. Beard*, [1920] A.C. 479 (H.L.) [*Beard*], as adopted by the Supreme Court of Canada in *R. v. Bernard* (1988), 67 C.R. (3d) 113 (S.C.C.).
2   M. Keiter, "Just Say No Excuse: The Rise and Fall of the Intoxication Defense" (1997) 87 Journal of Criminal Law and Criminology 482.

recently, courts have developed the notion of "specific intent" and "general intent" crimes to distinguish circumstances in which the intoxication defence might be permissible. A general intent crime requires only the intent to commit that act, whereas a specific intent crime goes beyond that, with an intent, for example, to strike a blow in order to kill a person. Specific intent crimes include murder, whereas common assault is a general or basic intent crime. The courts have carefully categorized crimes as general or specific intent crimes, although the basis for deciding whether they are one or the other has not always been clear. Impaired driving is a general intent crime.

a) The *Beard* Rules

Canadian law was influenced by *Beard*, an English case which was reaffirmed by the Canadian Supreme Court.[3] The implications of the *Beard* case in Canada are as follows. Intoxication is different from mental disorder. If, however, intoxication induces a mental disorder, and it meets the test in section 16 of the *Criminal Code*, then the verdict should be "not guilty by reason of insanity" (now NCR) and should lead to a custodial or community order or an absolute discharge, that is, a special verdict. An intoxication defence is only relevant to a crime of specific intent, and if successful, would lead to an absolute acquittal. Under the *Beard* rules, a level of intoxication falling short of preventing a person from having the capacity to form the intent necessary for committing a specific intent crime would be irrelevant.

b) The Expert's Role

Expert evidence may assist the court in determining whether a person had the capacity to form intent, not whether intent existed. It may also shed light on the extent to which the accused's actions were "voluntary." For example, a toxicologic expert can help establish the fact of intoxication and provide an opinion regarding the accused's blood alcohol level (BAL) at the time of the event (see Chapter 6, Section B.4(b), below). In particular, the expert evidence will be of assistance in determining whether the accused's deficits were the result of some abnormal condition, or whether he was simply intoxicated under normal circumstances. As with other defences where psychiatric evidence is adduced, the question for the expert is not whether a particular defence has been established. That is a function for the court. Policy concerns regarding self-induced intoxication will, again, be matters for the court to determine. The expert will give her best interpretation of the

---

3   Above note 1.

facts and offer the court the most parsimonious explanation for the behaviour of the accused.

3) Public Policy

While intoxication can negative the *mens rea* of specific intent offences, on public policy grounds and until the Supreme Court of Canada's decision in *R. v. Daviault*,[4] it could not negative the *mens rea* for general intent offences.[5]

a) The *Daviault* Case

The *Daviault* case changed the law on intoxication. In 1989, Henri Daviault was charged with sexual assault against an elderly, infirm woman. He was very intoxicated at the time, and had no recollection of the actual events. He was acquitted by the lower court judge on the grounds that there was a reasonable doubt that he had even the capacity to form the minimal intent to commit a general intent assault. The decision was overturned by the Quebec Court of Appeal. Intoxication was historically, and on policy grounds, not a defence to a general intent crime such as sexual assault. In 1994, however, the Supreme Court ruled that preventing Daviault from asserting compromised mental functioning to an extent where he could not form the general intent for a sexual assault amounted to a violation of Daviault's rights under the *Charter of Rights and Freedoms*, and it ordered a new trial. *Daviault* was never, in fact, re-tried as the complainant died from unrelated causes before a new trial could take place.

There was an immediate public reaction to the ruling, even though the court indicated that it would only be in unique and rare circumstances that the defence might succeed. Nevertheless, the perception created was that any drunken person could argue an intoxication defence for criminal charges that had previously been exempt from that fact. It had been calculated by an expert witness that Daviault had a blood alcohol level in excess of 400 mg percent, although he was a chronic alcoholic and therefore may have had some greater tolerance to very high levels of alcohol ingestion. To be successful, the *Daviault* defence requires that the person be rendered so insensible by intoxication that he is in a state akin to automatism. That state must be borne out, on the balance of probabilities.

---

4   (1994), 33 C.R. (4th) 165 (S.C.C.) [*Daviault*].
5   *R. v. Leary* (1977), [1978] 1 S.C.R. 29.

b) Factors Relevant to the Defence Not Succeeding

1) evidence of either a pre-intoxication wish or intention to commit the act, or, evidence of that intention during a lesser state of intoxication than the one purportedly giving rise to the defence;

2) evidence that the intoxication was to steel the accused's nerves;

3) evidence of purposeful and guided actions;

4) evidence of lucidity during supposed extreme intoxication;

5) insufficient or weak evidence of intoxication;

6) weak toxicologic and psychiatric expert evidence;

7) an accused who lacks credibility; and

8) a pattern of the same or similar behaviour while intoxicated.

c) Statutory Response to *Daviault*

The *Criminal Code*[6] has since been changed (section 33.1):

When defence not available

33.1 (1) It is not a defence to an offence referred to in subsection (3) that the accused, by reason of self-induced intoxication, lacked the general intent or the voluntariness required to commit the offence, where the accused departed markedly from the standard of care as described in subsection (2).

Criminal fault by reason of intoxication

(2) For the purposes of this section, a person departs markedly from the standard of reasonable care generally recognized in Canadian society and is thereby criminally at fault where the person, while in a state of self-induced intoxication that renders the person unaware of, or incapable of consciously controlling, their behaviour, voluntarily or involuntarily interferes or threatens to interfere with the bodily integrity of another person.

Application

(3) This section applies in respect of an offence under this Act or any other Act of Parliament that includes as an element an assault or any other interference or threat of interference by a person with the bodily integrity of another person.

Section 33.1 returns the law to the situation which existed prior to the *Daviault* case with regard to offences against the person. A person is criminally at fault if in a state of self-induced intoxication she becomes unaware of or incapable of consciously controlling her behaviour when interfering with or

---

6   R.S.C. 1985, c. C-46.

threatening to interfere with the bodily integrity of another person. Assault and sexual assault are therefore covered by this section. It remains to be seen whether this enactment will stand the test of further *Charter* challenges.

i)   Exception

If a state akin to automatism is induced by the involuntary consumption of drugs or alcohol, then the defence of automatism is available. This might occur if drugs were added to an alcoholic drink, or if a drink was laced with spirits unbeknownst to the consumer. There have been successful cases where prescribed drugs have been given without adequate explanation of the dangers, or where there have been interactions with other drugs, which resulted in charges of impaired driving. Psychiatric evidence would be relevant in such a case. Expert evidence would be called to determine whether a person's act was voluntary or whether the accused had the capacity to form intent.

4)   Role of Alcohol and Drugs in Crime

a)   Generally

A recent study carried out by the Canadian Centre for Substance Abuse[7] confirmed alcohol's pre-eminent role in violent crime. Key findings of the study include the following:

- alcohol-dependent federal inmates were much more likely to have committed a violent crime than drug-dependent inmates;
- drug-dependent inmates were more likely to have committed a gainful crime, such as theft;
- alcohol abuse was a key contributing factor in a third of homicides (30 percent of attempted murders and 39 percent of assaults); and
- the proportion of crimes committed by federal and provincial inmates attributed to the use of alcohol and/or illicit drugs in Canada is estimated to be between 40 and 50 percent.

b)   Alcohol Intoxication

Alcohol (and other substances) can play a number of roles in criminal proceedings. A clinician may be called upon to assess an accused and provide an opinion regarding alcohol intoxication—specifically, the effects of alcohol on an individual's behaviour and capacity to form the requisite intent for the of-

---

7   K. Pernanen, M. Cousineau, S. Brochu, & F. Sun, *Proportions of Crimes Associated with Alcohol and Other Drugs in Canada* (Ottawa: Canadian Centre on Substance Abuse, 2002).

fence charged. DSM IV-TR[8] describes the criteria for substance intoxication as the development of a reversible substance-specific syndrome due to recent ingestion of (or exposure to) a substance, and clinically significant maladaptive behavioural or psychological changes that are due to the effect of the substance on the central nervous system (for example, belligerence, mood lability, cognitive impairment, impaired judgment, and impaired social or occupational functioning) and develop during or shortly after use of the substance.

The clinical presentation of alcohol intoxication is well known. Listed below are the behavioural and psychological manifestations of alcohol consumption that generally correlate with measured blood alcohol levels (BAL).

- 30 mg percent: motor skills begin to be impaired
- 50 mg percent: lifting of inhibitions and reduction in anxiety
- 80 mg percent: legally impaired for the purpose of driving a motor vehicle
- 100 mg percent: disinhibited, altered speech pattern, motor impairment
- 200 mg percent: coordination problem, slowed reflexes, impaired judgment, slurred speech, rambling speech
- 300 mg percent: sedated, somnolent, confused, marked motor impairment, approaching coma
- 400 mg percent: severe coma and death

The effects of alcohol consumption on individuals in specific circumstances depend on a number of factors:

- the nature of the beverage, especially the concentration of alcohol;
- the rate of ingestion (BAL peaks a half an hour to three hours after rapid ingestion);
- the size of the person;
- the rate of absorption (food inhibits absorption);
- individual differences in metabolism; and
- a previous history of exposure to alcohol.

A blood level of 80 mg percent, the legal limit for driving in Canada, would be reached by an average-sized person consuming four beers in a one-hour period. Since an average-sized person metabolizes alcohol at a rate

---

8   American Psychiatric Association, *Diagnostic and Statistical Manual of Mental Disorders*, 4th ed., Text Revision (Arlington, VA: American Psychiatric Association, 2000) at 201 [DSM IV-TR]. Reprinted with permission of the American Psychiatric Association. © 2000.

of 15–20 mg percent (one beer, one glass of wine, or 1 oz. of liquor) per hour, breathalyzer or blood levels can help to pinpoint a person's likely blood level at a point in the near past. Such estimates are often critical in determining the impact of alcohol consumption, though laboratory evidence should always be supplemented by observation of witnesses, history and examination, and scrutiny of hospital records, if available, to determine a person's mental state at a particular point in time. Blood and urine tests can confirm the presence of other drugs that may be relevant.

c) Alcohol Withdrawal and Delirium Tremens

Criminal (usually aggressive) behaviour committed during a severe withdrawal state may lead to a successful NCR or automatism defence. For example, a forty-five-year-old chronic alcohol abuser had been consuming very high amounts of alcohol in the several weeks preceding the event. He resolved, however, to become abstinent and, consequently, reduced his consumption to what was for him a negligible amount over the day preceding a precipitous decision to fly across the country to visit family. Delirium tremens manifested with two hours of boarding the plane. In a confused and paranoid state, the accused twice charged the cockpit in the belief that the pilots were going to crash the plane; he subsequently assaulted a physician who tried to calm him. The accused was found NCR on the basis of delirium tremens.

d) Alcohol Induced Psychotic Disorder/Automatism

DSM IV-TR requires that the symptoms are not due to a general medical condition and are not better accounted for by another mental disorder. In actual practice, it is common to find that intoxication contributes to pre-existing psychopathology and thereby complicates a given clinical picture. Dual diagnosis — for example, schizophrenia and alcohol or drug abuse — is a common finding. Chronic amphetamine or other stimulant abuse can create a clinical syndrome similar to schizophrenia; the true picture emerges only when the drugs are discontinued after weeks or even months. Head injury is a frequent complication of alcohol abuse. For example, a forty-seven-year-old man smoked a joint of marijuana and drank several pints of beer over a three-hour period. He subsequently drove his car into a pole and was knocked unconscious. On recovery, he was confused and belligerent. He refused a breathalyzer request and was charged with refusal. The next day, he had no memory of the events surrounding his arrest. He successfully advanced an automatism defence.

e) Pathological Intoxication

This rare condition, if successfully argued in court, results in a complete acquittal. The lack of culpability flows from the notion that the accused never set out to become intoxicated and thereby create potential risk for others (and self) as a result of impaired judgment and disinhibition. The intoxication was unintended, idiosyncratic, or unexpected. Pathological intoxication has been described by Maletzky as "an extraordinary severe response to alcohol, especially to small amounts, marked by apparently senseless violent behaviour and usually followed by exhaustion, sleep, and amnesia for the episode."[9]

DSM III-R, the predecessor edition to DSM IV-TR, included pathological intoxication, but referred to it as alcohol idiosyncratic intoxication, which it defined by the following:[10]

- ◆ maladaptive behavioural changes, for example, aggressive or assaultive behaviour, occurring within minutes of ingesting an amount of alcohol insufficient to induce intoxication in most people;
- ◆ behaviour is atypical of the person when not drinking;
- ◆ biologic intolerance, perhaps a vulnerability of the limbic system has been postulated; and
- ◆ not due to any physical or other mental disorder.

Several researchers have administered alcohol, in a laboratory setting, to individuals thought to have this condition. The very few studies available on the subject have yielded conflicting results.[11] DSM IV-TR[12] consequently abandoned the diagnostic entity. Presentations previously thought to be pathological intoxication or alcohol idiosyncratic intoxication would now likely be diagnosed as simple alcohol intoxication, or as an alcohol-related disorder, not otherwise specified.

The controversy regarding "pathological intoxication" has been explored in some detail by Lawrence P. Tiffany and Mary Tiffany.[13] These authors

---

9   B.M. Maletzky, "The Diagnosis of Pathological Intoxication" (1976) 37 Journal of Studies on Alcohol 1215.

10   American Psychiatric Association, *Diagnostic and Statistical Manual of Mental Disorders*, 3d ed., revised (Washington, DC: American Psychiatric Association, 1987) [DSM III-R]. Reprinted with the permission of the American Psychiatric Association. © 1987.

11   See G. Bach-y-Rita, J.R. Lion, & F.R. Ervin, "Pathological Intoxication: Clinical and Electroencephalographic Studies" (1970) 127 American Journal of Psychiatry 698.

12   Above note 8.

13   L.P. Tiffany & M. Tiffany, "Nosologic Objections to the Criminal Defense of Pathological Intoxication: What do the Doubters Doubt?" (1990) 13 International Journal of Law and Psychiatry 49.

describe a syndrome associated with brain damage or disease in which a small amount of alcohol will trigger an outburst of rage or senseless violence of short duration, followed by sleep or amnesia. Whether such a condition merits an independent diagnosis or not remains unclear. A number of forensic clinicians have come across, albeit rarely, explosive conditions associated with (occasionally relatively low amounts of) alcohol consumption, but without the usual features of intoxication. The presence of an underlying neurological or metabolic condition —for example, epilepsy or hypoglycemia, respectively—should be ruled out and distinguished from intermittent explosive disorder. The diagnostic criteria for intermittent explosive disorder are described below:

- several discrete episodes of failure to resist aggressive impulses that result in serious assaultive acts or destruction of property;
- the degree of aggressiveness expressed during the episodes is grossly out of proportion to any precipitating psychosocial stressors; and
- the aggressive episodes are not better accounted for by another mental disorder (for example, antisocial personality disorder, borderline personality disorder, a psychotic disorder, a manic episode, conduct disorder, or attention-deficit/hyperactivity disorder) and are not due to the direct physiological effects of a substance (for example, a drug of abuse, a medication) or a general medical condition (for example, head trauma, Alzheimer's disease).[14]

Dr. Eric Fine considers the exclusion of alcohol idiosyncratic intoxication from DSM IV-TR to be imprudent. He cites the "small, but important number of individuals (who) do indeed become quickly and severely intoxicated with very small quantities of alcohol"[15]

5) Alcohol and Aggression

The causal relationship between alcohol and violent crime remains uncertain, although crime statistics, accident reports, and clinical wisdom and experience suggest there is a strong connection. The literature bears out that the relationship is complex and involves sociocultural, individual, and situational factors, in addition to alcohol's presumed aggression-promoting ac-

14   DSM IV-TR, above note 8 at 667. Reprinted with the permission of the American Psychiatric Association. © 2000.

15   E. Fine, *Alcohol Intoxication: Psychiatric, Psychological, Forensic Issues* (Balboa Island, CA: ACFP Press, 1996) at 36–37.

tion. Relatively recent research has shown a fairly clear association between low levels of the brain neurotransmitter serotonin (5-HIAA) and aggressive and suicidal behaviour. Relevant to this discussion, alcoholic patients have significantly lower levels of serotonin than control subjects matched for age and other variables. Further, according to Dr. Fine,[16] a significant number of alcoholic patients attempt and often succeed in committing suicide. Personality variables, particularly those brought into the foreground through the disinhibitory role of alcohol, are likely critically important. It appears that alcohol and drugs only modify the judgment and self-control of a predisposed individual who in a specific situation may become violent.[17] The association or causal attribution of violence and crime to alcohol can be explained by a number of theories.[18] It is likely, however, that the theories overlap considerably in many instances of alcohol-related aggression and crime.

6) Verdict

Where the intoxication defence is established for a specific intent offence, it results in either a conviction for the lesser included general intent offence (for example, murder to manslaughter) or an outright acquittal if there is no lesser included offence.[19] In Canada, "diminished responsibility" has never been formally recognized as a defence. Nevertheless, the effect is essentially the same. That is, where an accused's capacity to form the requisite *mens rea* is compromised, the accused's culpability may be attenuated.

7) Drugs

Virtually any drug, when taken in sufficient quantities, can have an intoxicating effect sufficient to produce diminished capacity to form criminal intent. Some of the more common drugs which come before the courts are amphetamines (colloquially known as "speed" or "bennies"); cannabis; cocaine; phencyclidine (known as "PCP," "angel dust," "crystal," "rocket fuel," "peace pill"); sedatives; hypnotics, or anxiolytics; hallucinogens (such as LSD); inhalants (such as glue, gasoline, paint, paint thinner, solvents); opiates (such as opium, morphine, heroin, codeine, methadone, demeral); and steroids.

---

16   *Ibid.*
17   H.P. Moss & R.E. Tarter, "Substance Abuse, Aggression, and Violence" (1993) 2 American Journal on Addictions 149.
18   K. Pernanen, M. Cousineau, S. Brochu, & F. Sun, *Proportions of Crimes Associated with Alcohol and Other Drugs in Canada*, above note 7.
19   *R. v. Quin* (1988), 67 C.R. (3d) 162 (S.C.C.).

The quantitative and qualitative effects of these various drugs upon an individual accused will typically be established with the assistance of expert testimony. Psychiatrists can testify as to the impact of a substance on an individual, but often need to collaborate with a toxicologist colleague, particularly when there are questions about the quantity ingested or its interaction with other prescribed and/or non-prescribed psychoactive substances etc.

8) Mistake of Fact

Mistake of fact caused by intoxication is not a defence to a general intent offence.[20]

C. IRRESISTIBLE IMPULSE

The so-called "irresistible impulse" defence is based upon mental disorder which renders the accused incapable of resisting the impulse to commit an act, even though the accused may be conscious and able to appreciate the nature and consequences of the act and know that it was "wrong." The defence undermines the requisite volitional element of the *actus reus* rather than operating upon the *mens rea*.

In Canada, this defence has yet to be formally recognized although defences "packaged" as intoxication often appear to be based upon essentially the same clinical phenomenon. The defence is recognized in some American jurisdictions where it is alternatively known as the "but-for-the-policeman-at-the-elbow" test. While Canadian courts have carefully avoided recognizing defences squarely framed as irresistible impulse, in reality, the defence may win or lose depending upon its "delivery." That is, while the evidence of mental disorder may not be accepted to found a formal defence of irresistible impulse, the same medical evidence of a psychiatric condition rendering the accused susceptible to an impulse disorder may found a defence of not criminally responsible on account of mental disorder. For example, in *R. v. Abbey*,[21] the Court cites *R. v. Borg*[22] with approval: "if there is medical evidence of disease of the mind as there was here and yet the only symptoms of that disease of the mind are irresistible impulses, the jury may conclude that the accused is insane." This is a curious statement. It should be noted that

---

20   *R. v. Moreau* (1986), 51 C.R. (3d) 209 (Ont. C.A.); *R. v. O'Grady*, [1987] 3 All E.R. 420 (C.A.).
21   [1982] 2 S.C.R. 24.
22   [1969] S.C.R. 551 at 570, Hall J.

were a defence of irresistible impulse driven by mental disorder to receive acceptance as a defence, it would be treated precisely the same was as a defence of automatism caused by mental disorder.

In *R. v. Courville*,[23] there is the suggestion that while irresistible impulse caused by self-induced intoxication is not a defence, irresistible impulse caused by other circumstances, such as mental disorder, may be a defence: "[t]he fact that the respondent's conduct was caused by a loss of control or an irresistible impulse which in turn was caused by delusions resulting from self-induced intoxication does not constitute a defence *in the circumstances* [emphasis added]."[24]

In an extreme case, it may be that the impulse to perform an act is so overwhelming that it completely overrides or obliterates conscious thought processes and, in this way, irresistible impulse would become subsumed as a traditional defence of NCR in that there would be no ability to appreciate the nature and consequences of the act.

D. PROVOCATION

Provocation includes provocation by blows, words, or gestures (*Criminal Code*, section 36).

> *Provocation*
> 36. Provocation includes, for the purposes of sections 34 and 35, provocation by blows, words or gestures.

1) The Role of the Psychiatric Expert

An expert may be of particular assistance with respect to the subjective component, and here, the expert may inform the court as follows:

- whether the accused was incapable of controlling his actions, such that he would be more susceptible to acting suddenly and in the heat of passion;[25]
- factors concerning the accused's background, temper, character, general mental condition, unique psychological vulnerabilities, and idiosyncrasies; and

---

23   *R. v. Courville* (1982), 2 C.C.C. (3d) 118 (Ont. C.A.).
24   *Ibid.* at 125.
25   See *R. v. Parnerkar* (1973), [1974] S.C.R. 449.

- the effects of intoxication on the accused's capacity for self-control.[26]

Under certain specified circumstances, the defences of self-defence, provocation, or duress may be raised by a person accused of a crime before a court of law. As the guilt of an accused must be proven beyond a reasonable doubt, it therefore follows that a defence of provocation need only be raised when the guilt of the accused has otherwise been proved beyond a reasonable doubt. For instance, a defence of provocation will only become an issue if the accused would otherwise be found guilty of murder.

As noted above, provocation includes, for the purposes of sections 34 and 35, provocation by blows, words, or gestures. Provocation may further be evoked to reduce a charge of murder to manslaughter when the crime is committed by a person in the "heat of passion" caused by sudden provocation. For the purposes of section 232 of the *Criminal Code*, provocation is defined by a wrongful act or insult of a sufficient nature to deprive an ordinary person of the power of self-control.

Murder reduced to manslaughter

232. (1) Culpable homicide that otherwise would be murder may be reduced to manslaughter if the person who committed it did so in the heat of passion caused by sudden provocation.

What is provocation

(2) A wrongful act or an insult that is of such a nature as to be sufficient to deprive an ordinary person of the power of self-control is provocation for the purposes of this section if the accused acted on it on the sudden and before there was time for his passion to cool.

Questions of fact

(3) For the purposes of this section, the questions

(a) whether a particular wrongful act or insult amounted to provocation, and

(b) whether the accused was deprived of the power of self-control by the provocation that he alleges he received, are questions of fact, but no one shall be deemed to have given provocation to another by doing anything that he had a legal right to do, or by doing anything that the accused incited him to do in order to provide the accused with an excuse for causing death or bodily harm to any human being.

---

26   See *R. v. Olbey*, [1980] 1 S.C.R. 1008.

Death during illegal arrest

(4) Culpable homicide that otherwise would be murder is not necessarily manslaughter by reason only that it was committed by a person who was being arrested illegally, but the fact that the illegality of the arrest was known to the accused may be evidence of provocation for the purpose of this section.

E. SELF-DEFENCE

1) Subjective and Objective Issues

Self-defence, like provocation, involves both an objective element (the reasonableness of the accused's perceptions) as well as consideration of the accused's subjective perceptions.

Self-defence against unprovoked assault

34. (1) Every one who is unlawfully assaulted without having provoked the assault is justified in repelling force by force if the force he uses is not intended to cause death or grievous bodily harm and is no more than is necessary to enable him to defend himself.

Extent of justification

(2) Every one who is unlawfully assaulted and who causes death or grievous bodily harm in repelling the assault is justified if

(a) he causes it under reasonable apprehension of death or grievous bodily harm from the violence with which the assault was originally made or with which the assailant pursues his purposes; and

(b) he believes, on reasonable grounds, that he cannot otherwise preserve himself from death or grievous bodily harm.

Self-defence in case of aggression

35. Every one who has without justification assaulted another but did not commence the assault with intent to cause death or grievous bodily harm, or has without justification provoked an assault on himself by another, may justify the use of force subsequent to the assault if

(a) he uses the force

    (i) under reasonable apprehension of death or grievous bodily harm from the violence of the person whom he has assaulted or provoked, and

    (ii) in the belief, on reasonable grounds, that it is necessary in order to preserve himself from death or grievous bodily harm;

(b) he did not, at any time before the necessity of preserving himself from death or grievous bodily harm arose, endeavour to cause death or grievous bodily harm; and

(c) he declined further conflict and quitted or retreated from it as far as it was feasible to do so before the necessity of preserving himself from death or grievous bodily harm arose.

As seen above, sections 34(1) and 34(2) are different inasmuch as the former deals with repelling an attack that was not initiated by the accused and involves using "no more (force) than is necessary to enable (the accused) to defend himself," in the case where he had not provoked the original assault upon him. Section 34(2), on the other hand, can apply in instances where the accused provoked the assault or was the initial aggressor. Unlike section 34(1), section 34(2) does not require the accused to use no more harm than is necessary in the circumstances, but rather, that he believe on reasonable grounds that he would be the victim of death or grievous bodily harm if he did not repel the assault.

Section 34(2) requires three elements for the defence of self-defence: 1) the existence of an unlawful assault; 2) a reasonable apprehension of a risk of death or grievous bodily harm; and 3) a reasonable belief that it is not possible to preserve oneself from that harm without harming the adversary. The criteria elaborated in section 34(1) are fairly objective. There is a limit on the amount of force the accused may apply to repel an assault. It is generally accepted that the force used must be proportionate to the force of the attacker and no more than is necessary for the purpose of defending oneself.

Sections 34(2) and 35 rely on a more subjective standard where the accused has caused death or grievous bodily harm in repelling the assault. An often quoted excerpt from *R. v. Reilly* describes the criteria for the requisite subjective belief and the accused's reasonable basis for those beliefs:

> Section 34(2) places in issue the accused's state of mind at the time he caused death. The subsection can only afford protection to the accused if he apprehended death or grievous bodily harm from the assault he was repelling and if he believed he could not preserve himself from death or grievous bodily harm otherwise than by the force he used. Nonetheless, his apprehension must be a reasonable one and his belief must be based upon reasonable and probable grounds.[27]

There are two aspects of self-defence pursuant to section 34(2). These two components blend subjective and objective elements, the latter being that

---

27　*R. v. Reilly* (1984), 15 C.C.C. (3d) 1 at 7 (S.C.C.), Ritchie J.

the accused's belief rests on a reasonable basis. Psychiatric assessment may be relevant to the subjective component with respect to both elements, as discussed below.

a) Reasonable Apprehension of Death or Grievous Bodily Harm

The accused's emotional experience—the subjective element—is a key component in understanding the manner in which the accused processed the degree of jeopardy he was in, what type of jeopardy, and the extent of the response. Cases involving battered woman syndrome (BWS) are particularly instructive with respect to the synergy between the subjective and objective elements contemplated by section 34(2). In *R. v. Lavalee*,[28] the Supreme Court held that the accused was not legally required to face an imminent act from the deceased until she acted. In that case, the accused had anticipatorily shot her abusive spouse in the back of the head after he threatened that he would harm her after guests had left their house. Psychiatric evidence demonstrated that the accused had reasonable grounds to believe that she was in immediate danger and that her circumstances were life-threatening. Madame Justice Wilson noted in *Lavalee* that it would be unreasonable for a woman to apprehend grievous bodily harm or death only when the physical assault was actually in progress, and she went on to say that expert evidence might disclose that "it may in fact be possible for a battered spouse to accurately predict the onset of violence before the first blow is struck, even if an outsider to the relationship cannot."[29] The expert evidence assists in explaining any heightened sensitivity the accused might have with respect to the batterer, and in essence, what appears to the world as a pre-emptive step, is a self-defensive one.

The reasonableness of the accused's actions in the above context—the imported objective element—was made apparent by elucidating the nature of abusive relationships and their impact on the victim of the battering. To assist the court in establishing battered woman syndrome and the subjective susceptibility, a psychiatric expert will likely canvass the following issues and make reference to them in either a report or *viva voce* evidence, or both:

- childhood abuse;
- a history of domestic violence or family violence in the victim's family of origin;
- having been victimized in a previous relationship;

---

28   *R. v. Lavalee* (1990), 55 C.C.C. (3d) 97 (S.C.C.).
29   *Ibid.* at 119.

- an expanded history of the current relationship, especially as regards repeated physical, emotional, and/or sexual victimization;
- medical records, especially with respect to attendance at hospital for injuries;
- physical examination;
- collateral information regarding abuse of the victim/accused;
- emphasis on the existence of post-traumatic symptoms;
- emphasis on the presence of current symptoms and findings consistent with having been victimized; and
- information with respect to any woman's shelter the victim may have attended.

Particular information with respect to BWS includes:

- a history of intensifying threats against the victim as background to her legitimate cause for fear;
- a history of increasing dependency; being cut-off from social connections and other supports; being progressively controlled, and rendered resourceless; and
- the absence of a previous history of violence, and the absence of a history of planning or premeditation.

b) Reasonable Belief in the Lack of Alternatives

Reflecting back on the *Lavallee* case, evidence concerning what occurs to women who are battered spouses explains why a woman would not have left an abusive relationship sooner. With respect to this criterion, the accused must be found to subjectively believe that the infliction of grievous bodily harm or death is the only way to protect herself. The objective component requires some measure of reasonableness and probable grounds for the accused's actions, modified by understanding of the accused's perceptions and judgments. *R. v. Pétel*[30] is illustrative of that point. In that case, the Supreme Court of Canada confirmed the importance of prior assaults suffered by the accused and her daughter in deciding the reasonableness of her belief that she could not escape grievous bodily harm or death if she did not kill the attacker.

A particular situation arises when excessive force is used in what otherwise constitutes a self-defence situation. This had led to the acceptance, by many Canadian courts, of a partial defence of excessive force within the following parameters:

---

30   (1994), 26 C.R. (4th) 145 (S.C.C.).

1. There must have been reasonable and probable grounds for the accused to apprehend serious danger to himself;
2. The accused must believe that he used a necessary degree of force to preserve himself; and
3. The force used was excessive in the sense that it was unreasonable in the given circumstances.

The result of the partial defence of excessive force in a charge of murder will not negative the intent but may excuse it partially, leading to a conviction on a lesser charge (for example, manslaughter).

Provocation is a factor to consider in sections 34 and 35 dealing with self-defence, or in a charge of murder where provocation, if proven, may reduce the accused's culpability resulting in a conviction for manslaughter (section 232.1).

CHAPTER SEVEN

Sex Offenders and the Paraphilias

A. INTRODUCTION TO THE PARAPHILIAS

It goes without saying, but it is nevertheless worth mentioning at the outset of this chapter, that even a treatise, let alone a chapter that focuses on the legal aspects of sexual behaviour in a primer of this kind, will not do justice to the complexities of human sexuality, the various normal and "abnormal" ways of expressing it, and the bountiful theories regarding the causes of sexual pathology. This chapter introduces the reader to the phenomenology of sexual offending and the psychopathological processes associated with sexual deviation (paraphilias). "Paraphilias" is the proper psychiatric terminology for the various kinds of sexually anomalous behaviours identified in the *Diagnostic and Statistical Manual* of the American Psychiatric Association (DSM IV-TR).[1] The prefix "para" denotes a deviation, and the suffix "philia" denotes that the deviation is in relation to sexual attraction.

The intensity of the drive to pursue sexual gratification, and the degree to which the individual's life may be taken up with that pursuit, is one of the more notable clinical features of paraphilic (and hypersexual, albeit to normal stimuli) patients. "Pathological sexuality," which in today's age can be more easily indulged (and arguably fostered), by internet access to pornography was described more than one hundred years ago by Krafft-Ebing:

> It permeates all his thoughts and feelings, allowing of no other aims in life, tumultuously, and in a rut-like fashion demanding gratification without granting the possibility of moral and righteous counter-presentations, and

---

1   American Psychiatric Association, *Diagnostic and Statistical Manual of Mental Disorders*, 4th ed., Text Revision (Washington, DC: American Psychiatric Association, 2000) [DSM IV-TR].

resolving itself into an impulsive, insatiable succession of sexual enjoyments ... This pathological sexuality is a dreadful scourge for its victim, for he is in constant danger of violating the laws of the state and of morality, of losing his honor, his freedom and even his life.[2]

Paraphilias are defined by either (or both) sexually anomalous fantasies and urges or deviant sexual behaviours. Fantasies, urges, and behaviours are paraphilic when their subject matter or object involves children, unconsenting partners, non-human subjects, or the infliction of pain and suffering on oneself or another. DSM IV-TR stipulates that a diagnosis can only be made if symptoms have been present for at least six consecutive months.

Paraphiliacs experience deviant fantasies, urges, and behaviours to varying degrees of exclusivity (over non-paraphilic interests) and levels of intensity. There are individuals for whom the paraphilic subject matter or object is obligatory, in that the behaviour or person of interest must invariably be included in sexual activity in order for the paraphiliac to become erotically aroused. There are other cases, however, where the problematic interests and preferences (for example, voyeurism, or exhibitionism) occur only episodically; these behaviours are commonly brought out by stress. Individuals in this category are generally able to function sexually without reliance on the paraphilic component. Pedophilia is another example. There are exclusive pedophiles, who cannot be aroused by anyone other than a prepubescent child, and non-exclusive pedophiles who may be equally or more attracted to age-appropriate partners. They may appear sexually "normal."

Predecessor editions of the *Diagnostic and Statistical Manual* (for example, DSM II[3]) considered homosexuality to be a disorder. Reflecting advancements in the understanding of human sexuality (and no doubt the times), a subsequent edition (DSM III-R[4]) de-listed homosexuality as a disorder, and instead included the diagnostic designation "ego dystonic homosexuality" as a psychopathological characterization of a condition that may result when an individual fails to accept his homosexual orientation. DSM IV-TR preserved the construct of ego-dystonic homosexuality under the rubric sexual

---

2   As quoted by D.J. Stein, D.W. Black, N.A. Shapira, & R.L. Spitzer, "Hypersexual Disorder and Preoccupation with Internet Pornography" (2001) 158 American Journal of Psychiatry 1590–94, online: ajp.psychiatryonline.org/cgi/content/full/158/10/1590.

3   American Psychiatric Association, *Diagnostic and Statistical Manual of Mental Disorders*, 2d ed. (Washington, DC: American Psychiatric Association, 1968) [DSM II].

4   American Psychiatric Association, *Diagnostic and Statistical Manual of Mental Disorders*, 3d ed., revised (Washington, DC: American Psychiatric Association, 1987) [DSM III-R].

disorders, and calls it "sexual disorder not otherwise specified" (NOS); it is characterized by "persistent and marked distress about sexual orientation." Note that cross-examiners, hoping to denigrate psychiatry's status as a medical science, have occasionally drawn on homosexuality's history in the DSM to highlight the arbitrariness of the inclusion or exclusion of diagnoses as a little more than a function of changing tides.

From a psychiatric and sexologic perspective, there is a grey-zone between sexual practices (however bizarre) engaged in by consenting adults in privacy, and true paraphilic sexual practices. Ostensibly deviant or counter-cultural sexual practices may be "normalized" provided no laws are broken and both (or all) participants consent (and are capable of consenting). Sadistic and masochistic activities — whether pain is inflicted or blood is drawn — are within the realm of acceptable behaviour, provided two capable adults have consented to the activity.

B. BASIC DEFINITIONS

Paraphilias: The essential feature of this group of psychosexual disorders is the necessity of unusual, deviant, or bizarre images, urges, or behaviours for sexual arousal. The arousing fantasies or activities involve either non-human objects, the use of children or adult non-consenting individuals, or causing one's partner (or oneself) to experience either suffering or humiliation. Paraphilia is a clinical descriptive term that subsumes various sub-types of erotic preferences, thoughts and behaviours. Having a paraphilia is not synonymous with being a sex offender. Although, in the case of certain paraphilias, there is a high co-occurrence rate between the clinical and legal designations. A list of some of the more common paraphilias follows below.

Ephebophilia: Sexual activities and/or fantasies in which post-pubertal but adolescent subjects are the preferred or exclusive method of attaining sexual arousal and gratification.

Exhibitionism: Exposure of the genitals to unsuspecting others as a (often the primary) vehicle for achieving sexual gratification.

Fetishism: The individual strongly prefers or requires the use of inanimate objects as a means of sexual arousal. Fetishes are rarely implicated in criminal proceedings, although they may be associated with other paraphilic inclinations that have brought the individual to the attention of the authorities.

Telephone Scatalogia: Obscene phone calls for the purpose of gratifying the caller's erotic interests.

Transvestic Fetishism: A paraphilia in which a heterosexual male either experiences intense sexually arousing fantasies or urges, or engages in behaviours that involve cross-dressing. This type of interest/preference, which, like fetishism, rarely involves criminal behaviour, can either occur in males who are comfortable in their gender role or identity, or persistently uncomfortable in that role/identity.

Frotteurism: The individual purposefully and repeatedly seeks sexual arousal by rubbing against (invariably) women, most often in crowded public environments, where detection is unlikely.

Hebephilia: Sexual activities with and/or fantasies of children in the peri-pubertal/pubertal age range.

Pedophilia: Sexual activities or fantasies involving pre-pubertal children are the preferred or exclusive method of achieving sexual arousal.

Sexual Sadism: Intense sexual urges, arousing fantasies, and/or activities where sexual gratification is obtained by inflicting pain or humiliation on a partner.

Toucheurism: The individual deliberately and regularly pursues sexual arousal by touching other people, usually surreptitiously, and in circumstances where his identity is unlikely to be disclosed.

Voyeurism: Often referred to as "peeping." In this paraphilic disturbance, the individual experiences sexual fantasies or urges, or engages in activities that involve observing unsuspecting individuals (almost always women) who are partially unclad, naked or engaged in some form of sexual activity.

Zoophilia: Sexual fantasies/activities involving animals.

C. CATEGORIES OF PARAPHILIAS

1) Pedophilia

Pedophilia was formally recognized as a specific sexual disorder as early as 1886:[5]

---

5   R.V. Krafft-Ebing, *Psychopathia Sexualis*, 12th ed., trans. by F.J. Rebman (New York: Rebman Company, 1912).

[I]n addition to the aforesaid categories of moral renegades, and those afflicted with psychico-moral weakness—be this congenital or superinduced
by cerebral disease or episodical mental aberration—there are cases in
which the sexually needy subject is drawn to children not as a consequence
of degenerated morality or psychical or physical impotence, but rather by a
morbid disposition, a *psychosexual perversion*, which may at present be named
paedophilia erotica.[6]

a) Distinction Between the Terms "Pedophile" and "Child Molester"

Although "pedophile" and "child molester" are often used interchangeably
by the lay public, these are clearly distinguishable entities. The former is a
diagnostic category reserved for individuals who experience intense sexually
arousing fantasies, behaviours or urges towards prepubescent children (generally age thirteen or younger) on a recurring basis. The "child molester"
designation contemplates men who have offended against (and have usually
been convicted for having sexual contact with) a person under the legal age
of consent (a male or female minor).

b) Diagnostic Criteria

An individual diagnosed with pedophilia must be at least sixteen years old,
and there must be at least a five-year age difference between the pedophile
and the child, except where the pedophile is a late adolescent. In that instance, clinical judgment is used rather than specifying a specific age difference. The diagnostic criteria for pedophilia are as follows:

A. Over a period of at least six months, recurrent, intense sexually arousing
   fantasies, sexual urges, or behaviors involving sexual activity with a pre-
   pubescent child or children (generally age thirteen years or younger).
B. The person has acted on these urges, or the sexual urges or fantasies
   cause marked distress or interpersonal difficulty.
C. The person is at least age sixteen years and at least five years older than
   the child or children in criterion A. *Note*: Do not include an individual
   in the late adolescence involved in an ongoing sexual relationship with a
   twelve- or thirteen-year-old. Specify if sexually attracted to males; sexually
   attracted to females; sexually attracted to both; limited to incest; exclusive
   type (attracted only to children); nonexclusive type.[7]

---

6   *Ibid.* at 555.
7   DSM IV-TR, above note 1 at 572. Reprinted with the permission of the American Psychi-
     atric Association. © 2000.

Pedophiles are divided into categories of individuals who prefer pre-pubescent females (usually between the ages of eight and ten), and those who prefer males (generally slightly older prepubescent boys). Pedophiles who offend against boys have been found to recidivate at a higher rate (estimated to be roughly twice as much as pedophiles who offend against pre-pubescent girls). Pedophiles are further grouped into an exclusive subtype (sexually attracted only to children), and a non-exclusive subtype (those who are sometimes attracted to adults).

The extent to which pedophilia occurs (incidence and prevalence) is unknown (as self-reports of pedophiles are notably unreliable). In light of what is known, however, about how extensively pedophiles use minimization and denial, it is estimated that the incidence of pedophilia is, in fact, considerably greater than has been apparent thus far.

c) Cognitive Distortions and Rationalizations of Pedophiles

Many sex offenders harbour and offer distorted views to explain their conduct towards the children against whom they have offended. They do so to minimize and rationalize their behaviour. The explanations are frequently genuinely believed by the offender; if accepted by others they may serve to minimize the heinous nature of the offender's behaviour, and mitigate his culpability. These anomalous views (which are not unique to pedophilia, and occur in many other paraphilias) are commonly referred to as "cognitive distortions." A number of better-known examples of cognitive distortions of pedophiles are provided below.

- The behaviour was an attempt to "educate" the child, purportedly to protect him from learning about sex in a more harmful way, that is, from peers on the street.
- The child derived sexual pleasure from the activity.
- The child was experienced in sexual activity and was willing or interested in participating.
- The precocious child actively collaborated in the exchange as he or she was much more aware of sexual behaviour than is normal for a child that age, or, being sexually provocative, instigated it.
- The child is unlikely to have been harmed by the behaviour.

d) Behaviours of Pedophiles

Pedophiles can engage their victims in a variety of sexual activities. Many limit their involvement to undressing the child, fondling the child, or masturbating in his or her presence, whereas a number of other pedophiles involve the child in more invasive activities. Physical force and gratuitous violence are uncommon. Instead, perpetrators go about accessing a child by "grooming" him or her in preparation for, and in anticipation of, the intended contact using varying degrees of persuasion, coercion or inducements. Grooming a child also involves getting the child to become more trusting of and reliant on the perpetrator.

Many pedophiles do not experience their pedophilic fantasies, urges, or behaviours as distressing (thoughts, fantasies and behaviours that do not pose a problem for the person's sense of self are referred to as ego-syntonic). The absence of distress does not preclude the diagnosis, in as much as the arousal pattern itself, as well as acting on the fantasies and urges with a child, is sufficient to qualify for the diagnosis.

Pedophiles are adept at gaining access to children. They may accomplish this goal by grooming the prospective victim's mother, by gaining the mother's trust, by marrying a woman with a child whom the pedophile sees as attractive, or by involving him or herself in a collaborative relationship with other pedophiles that allows for the exchange of children. In extreme examples, a pedophile might take in foster children or abduct children from strangers in order to access them sexually.

The explosion of internet child pornography (exchange of still pictures, video clips of children being sexually abused, and chat lines (which has led to a number of luring charges)) has been met by an understandably strong negative reaction by a number of concerned stakeholders, a strategic response by law enforcement, and both research and clinical interest by sexologists and behavioural scientists. Are men who access child pornography on the internet invariably pedophiles, or more likely to be pedophiles than not?

There is as yet no clear answer to this question as research in the area is currently underway. Early indicators suggest that pedophiles are overrepresented in a group of offenders convicted of child pornography, such that child pornography offending is a strong diagnostic indicator of pedophilia.[8] At the same time, however, accessing child pornography or being charged with child pornography should not be understood as synonymous with a diagnosis of pedophilia. No studies to date have identified any correlation between the quantity (percentage of pornographic images) and quality (nature

---

8   See M.C. Seto, J.M. Cantor, & R. Blanchard, "Child Pornographic Offenses are a Valid Diagnostic Indicator of Pedophilia" *Journal of Abnormal Psychology* (forthcoming).

and type) of images on an offender's internet browser or hard drive relative to other imagery that defines the likelihood of a diagnosis of pedophilia.

Any so inclined individual can access the widest conceivable variety of pornographic imagery on the internet. Many individuals with so-called internet pornography "addictions" (there is no such addiction in medicine) are hypersexual individuals with polymorphous interests for whom photos and videos of children is but one type of erotic imagery downloaded in the pursuit of increasingly arousing stimuli. Again, accessing any type of internet pornography—legal or illegal—is not synonymous with a paraphilic diagnosis.

From a psychiatric perspective, one key issue is whether the downloaded images or chat line discussions, however much they stand out as red flags, are indicative of a paraphilia, are symptomatic of another condition or diagnosis (for example, hypomania or substance abuse), or disclose hypersexual symptoms or disorder. Although this latter entity has been proposed for inclusion as a sexual disorder in a subsequent edition of DSM, hypersexual disorder, by definition, is characterized by normative (but excessive) arousal patterns.[9]

Equally unclear is the extent to which viewing child pornography is either associated with, or predictive of, a contact sexual offence with a child. A recent study by Seto and Eke[10] of 201 adult male child pornography offenders determined that 56 percent of the sample had a prior criminal record, 24 percent had prior contact sexual offences, and 15 percent had prior child pornography offences. Over a 2.5 year period of time, 17 percent of the group offended again in some way and 4 percent committed a new contact sexual offence over the (2.5 year period) at-risk follow-up period. Of significance, child pornography offenders with prior criminal records were much more likely to offend again in any way during the follow-up period. And of this group, child pornography offenders who had committed a prior or concurrent contact sexual offence were the most likely to offend again. Research that compares groups of men who view child pornography who are found to be pedophilic and who have never been charged or convicted, with pedophilic child pornography viewers convicted of a sexual offence, may shed some light on the factors that differentiate men with pedophilic interests they do not act upon from those who have acted out those same interests against child contacts.

---

9   See Stein *et al.*, "Hypersexual Disorder," above note 2.

10   M.C. Seto & A.W. Elke, "The Criminal Histories and Later Offending of Child Pornography Offenders" (2005) 17 Sexual Abuse: A Journal of Research and Treatment 201.

Pedophiles are also skilled at creating situations that facilitate their access to children; for example, coaching boys' or girls' athletic teams, teaching children, serving as Big Brothers, leading children's choirs. Some pedophiles may engage children whose gender is not their primary interest (for example, a homosexual pedophile has contact with pre-pubescent females) for similar reasons; that is, pre-pubescent males and females have not sexually differentiated enough to have created a clear boundary of preference for some pedophiles.

e) Incest Offenders vs. Pedophiles

Some pedophiles limit their offending behaviour to children within their family structure. Others only victimize children outside their families. The distinction between incest offenders and pedophiles is addressed below.

AGAINST FEMALE CHILDREN

Only a small percentage (about 10–15 percent) of fathers and stepfathers who offend against daughters and stepdaughters, respectively, are pedophiles. Men who offend against female children in a familial context are often "sexually normal" (gynephilic); that is, they prefer adult females to children. Their victimization of a child within the family may be based on the use of that child as a surrogate for a spouse who has either failed to meet their needs, or whom they wish to punish for some perceived wrong.

Often, incest offences against daughters and step-daughters are opportunistic behaviours. The child/victim selected may be seen as special, and as someone with whom the offender can more easily cross a boundary to establish a dyadic relationship. In the case of a child used as a surrogate to punish an intimate partner, the child selected (for example, as amongst two or three potential female child victims) may be different from her female siblings; she may be more vulnerable to victimization.

AGAINST MALE CHILDREN

Fathers and stepfathers who offend against sons and stepsons are almost invariably pedophiles. The incest dynamic—sexual involvement with the daughter or step-daughter as a surrogate for an adult female partner because of a family/marital relationship issue(s)—is understandably absent when the victim(s) is/are male.

f) Female Pedophiles

While the vast majority of pedophiles are males, female pedophilia does exist. It is uncommonly reported, possibly because female affections towards a child are seen as maternal. In addition, male children have been socialized not to see sexual contact with adult females as problematic, and they consequently may not report the incident. A number of males report becoming engaged in sexual activity by late adolescent/early adult females who may have been introduced to them as family friends, neighbours, or babysitters, when the male victims were twelve years old or younger.

g)   No Evidence that Pedophilic Sexual Preference can be Significantly Altered

Pedophilia is generally thought of as an incurable condition. There is no evidence at this time that pedophilic sexual preference can be altered to an extent that would allow pedophiles to transform this aberrant sexual interest into a normal one. Non-exclusive types of pedophiles are fortunate in that they have an interest in both minor and adult females — they have the ability to achieve sexual gratification with age appropriate partners.

2)   Hebephilia

Hebephilia, defined as an erotic preference for children in the pubertal age range (12–14), is a useful term in clinical practice as it helps to distinguish this group from pedophiles. The distinction has not, however, been included in the DSM IV-TR. The line of demarcation between pedophilia and hebephilia can be unclear; pedophiles and hebephiles may prefer prepubescent and post-pubescent children, respectively, and yet have interests and experiences with the other age group. This probably, in part, has to do with the limited degree of sexual differentiation between some pre-pubescent and peri-pubescent children.

3)   Exhibitionism

The core erotic experience for exhibitionists involves sexually arousing fantasies and urges to expose their genitals — and many frequently act on these urges — to unsuspecting strangers. Surprising or shocking the victim is often a component of the exhibitionist's fantasies, as is the hope that the victim will herself become sexually aroused by the act.

- Masturbation frequently accompanies exhibitionistic behaviour.
- The prevalence of exhibitionism is unclear, but current estimates are that exhibitionists comprise about one third of sex offenders seen in clinical practice.

- The onset of the disorder usually occurs by late adolescence. It is said to decline by about the fourth decade of life.
- Unlike other sex offenders, exhibitionists often have adult sexual partners. The latter's availability does not, however, evidently eliminate or obviate the fantasies and urges the offender feels in relation to exposing himself to strangers.

For example, a thirty-seven year old married male with two children was arrested and charged with public indecency after passersby complained that they had seen him masturbating in his car in the parking lot of a shopping centre. The accused initially stated that the behaviour represented a one-time aberrant act. In-depth discussions during the course of the assessment disclosed, however, that he had masturbated in his car (sometimes while driving) on a number of occasions. Although he at first conceived of the behaviour as a private act not intended for public viewing, he conceded that there was always a reasonable prospect that females who were invariably within his sight might take notice of his actions.

Exhibitionists or "flashers" were, up until fairly recently, thought of more as "nuisance-offenders." It was (incorrectly) assumed that the scope of their injurious behaviour was limited to the deleterious effects that exposing one's genitals could have on an unsuspecting stranger/victim. A significant number of exhibitionists have concurrent paraphilic interests and behaviours, however, including pedophilia, voyeurism, frotteurism, and telephone scatologia. A study conducted by Abel *et al.*[11] demonstrated that some paraphiliacs had engaged in as many as ten types of deviant behaviours. A number of rapists and child molesters, in fact, provide a sexual history which includes exhibitionism.

Freund *et al.*[12] elaborated the concept of "courtship disorders" —a group of paraphilic behaviours and conditions, often co-occurring, that represent anomalies in the progression of heterosexual adjustment and maturation through pre-coital courtship stages up until intercourse. The paraphiliac with one or more courtship disorder interests/behaviours (exhibitionism, voyeurism, frotteurism, toucheurism, telephone scatologia, and some preferential rape patters) is presumed to have gotten stuck (fixated) at one or more stages

---

11   G.G. Abel, J.V. Becker, J. Cunningham-Rathner, M. Mittleman, & J-L. Rouleau, "Multiple Paraphilic Diagnoses Among Sex Offenders" (1988) 16 Bulletin of American Academy of Psychiatry and Law 153.

12   K. Freund, H. Scher, & S. Hucker, "The Courtship Disorders" (1983) 12 Archives of Sexual Behavior 369.

of normal male reproductive behaviour that gives the impression of being an exaggeration of that stage. Thus voyeurism is a distortion of the first phase of sexual interaction—positively appraising and experiencing arousal at first sighting of a potential partner, exhibitionism is a distortion/exaggeration of normal pre-tactile interaction, and frotteurism-toucheurism is a fixation at the tactile phase.[13] A similar but considerably more elaborate theory was propounded by Money,[14] who coined the term "lovemap" to reflect the complex and often circuitous process of erotic differentiation during successive early life developmental stages. A lovemap—a person's unique pattern of inner erotic life and external sexual behaviour—is influenced by multiple personal, familial, social, and environmental variables.

The diagnostic criteria for exhibitionism are a) over a period of at least six months, recurrent, intense sexually arousing fantasies, sexual urges, or behaviours involving the exposure of one's genitals to an unsuspecting stranger; and b) the person has acted on these urges, or the sexual urges or fantasies cause marked distress or interpersonal difficulty.[15] DSM IV-TR[16] sets a temporal requirement of six months of symptoms or behaviours before a diagnosis can be made. Given the level of denial that these patients exhibit and the methods they employ to minimize the nature and impact of their behaviour (another example of cognitive distortions), it is often difficult to obtain precise information from them so as to ascertain that the time requirement has been met.

Telephone scatalogia (TS)—obscene phone calls for erotic purposes—is classified by DSM IV-TR[17] in the residual category of paraphilia not otherwise specified (NOS). TS, a fairly common behaviour, has also been seen as more of a nuisance offence, although, given its association with other paraphilic behaviours, sexual sadism being the most ominous in the group, it can hardly be thought of in that light. The different permutations and combinations of how different paraphilic behaviours associate with each other and whether it can truly be said that there is a spectrum with benign and malignant poles is a matter deserving of research.[18]

---

13   K. Freund & R.J. Watson, "Mapping the Boundaries of Courtship Disorder" (1990) 27 Journal of Sex Research 589.

14   J. Money, *Lovemaps* (New York: Irvington, 1986).

15   DSM IV-TR, above note 1 at 569.

16   *Ibid.*

17   *Ibid.* at 576.

18   M. Price, M. Kafka, M.L. Commons, T.G. Gutheil, & W. Simpson, "Telephone Scatalogia: Comorbidity with Other Paraphilias and Paraphilia-related Disorders" (2002) 25 International Journal of Law and Psychiatry 37.

4) Voyeurism

The erotic focus for voyeurs involves viewing unsuspecting individuals, usually strangers, who are either in the process of disrobing, or are naked, or engaged in sexual activity. Voyeurs frequently fantasize about having sex with the observed person, although that type of contact rarely occurs. The arousal is in the viewing, and not so much in the doing. Voyeuristic behaviour, which generally has its onset during middle-adolescence, may be chronic, episodic, or limited, such that an individual who has engaged in a few episodes of voyeuristic behaviour (peeping) may not again engage in that activity for years, if not for the rest of his or her life.

For example, a forty-six year old male was charged after he surreptitiously set up a camera designed to record a young adult female boarder getting undressed and/or engaging in self-stimulatory sexual activity in her room. The accused admitted to a history of voyeuristic behaviours, usually involving peering into windows from the street, or into office window buildings using binoculars, from his late-adolescence onwards. The activity went on unabated until the offence; the latter represented a clear escalation in the degree of intrusiveness used in order to gratify his voyeuristic fantasies and urges.

Like exhibitionism, voyeurism was earlier on regarded by the police and courts as more of a nuisance offence than one associated with harm to others. Voyeurism, too, is often not the only paraphilic inclination or behaviour in a paraphiliac's repertoire. Voyeurs have many associated paraphilic interests and practices, which may include pedophilia and sexual sadism. It is, in fact, rare for voyeurs to pursue just that interest.

The diagnostic criteria for voyeurism are a) over a period of at least six months, recurrent, intense sexually arousing fantasies, sexual urges, or behaviours involving the act of observing an unsuspecting person who is naked, in the process of disrobing, or engaging in sexual activity; and b) the person has acted on these urges, or the sexual urges or fantasies cause marked distress or interpersonal difficulty.[19]

5) Frotteurism and Toucherism

The paraphilic focus of frotteurism involves rubbing, usually the perpetrator's pelvic area (and often his erect clothed penis), against an unsuspecting and non-consenting person, usually a female stranger. The behaviour is accomplished using crowded environments (for example, public transit,

---

19   DSM IV-TR, above note 1 at 575.

shopping malls, busy sidewalks) in urban centres where the perpetrator can generally avoid detection. The "toucheristic" aspect involves touching a stranger's buttocks, breasts, or genitalia, again, in circumstances designed to avoid detection.

Consistent with other paraphilic diagnoses in DSM IV-TR,[20] the condition is only diagnosed if the frotteuristic and toucheristic fantasies have been experienced intensively and on a recurrent basis for at least six months, or when the individual has acted-out those behaviours on a recurrent basis over that time frame. Frotteurism and toucherism are also associated with other paraphilic pursuits, such as exhibitionism, pedophilia, voyeurism, and sadism.

Akin to other paraphilias, a diagnosis of frotteurism can only be posited if the fantasies or behaviours lead to clinically significant distress or impairment. Most individuals with this (and other paraphilic) condition(s) do not experience their aberrant sexual proclivities or interests as alien or problematic. For diagnostic purposes, however, their impairment can be said to arise from the obligatory nature of the paraphilic fantasy or behaviour, from the resultant sexual dysfunction in other ("normal") spheres, because it requires participation of non-consenting individuals, because it interferes with social and personal relationships, or because it leads to legal complications.

The diagnostic criteria for frotteurism are a) over a period of at least six months, recurrent, intense sexually arousing fantasies, sexual urges, or behaviours involving touching and rubbing against a non-consenting person; and b) the person has acted on these urges, or the sexual urges or fantasies cause marked distress or interpersonal difficulty.[21]

6) Fetishism

Individuals with fetishes derive their principal erotic gratification through use of a non-living object ("fetish"). Common fetish objects include women's shoes, stockings, bras, underpants, boots, or other apparel. The fetishist usually masturbates while touching, smelling, or rubbing the fetish object, or he may ask a sexual partner to wear the object during sexual involvement. Individuals with fetishes rarely come into conflict with the criminal justice system as a result of their fetish. Fetishists do not ordinarily experience their fetishistic interests as distressing, nor do they generally lead to impaired functioning. Fetishists, consequently, rarely seek treatment and are infrequently seen in clinical practice.

---

20   *Ibid.* at 570.
21   *Ibid.*

For example, a forty-two year old correctional officer charged with a very serious non-sexual violent offence against a female was the subject of a court ordered search of his home. Apart from evidence relating to the crime in question, the authorities discovered a large cache of pornographic video-tapes, the bulk of which centred on a leather fetish. Videotape participants wore leather extensively and used leather masks, bridles, and other objects in various sexual scenarios. The subject's garage contained more than thirty pairs of women's high heeled leather and patent leather boots, as well as other leather paraphernalia.

Fetishism often has its antecedents in childhood/early adolescence. There is, in fact, an extensive early psychoanalytic literature regarding the early life psychological underpinnings of a number of fetishes. Fetishes may be associated with other paraphilic interests, including transvestism, sado-masochism, and pedophilia. Partialism is a variant of fetishism, although it involves animate versus inanimate objects. Partialists are sexually aroused by specific areas of the body, such as feet or pubic hair. Membership in fetish-istic organizations allows fetishists to indulge their interests in the company of similarly minded individuals, acquire partners, obtain paraphernalia, etc.

The diagnostic criteria for fetishism are a) over a period of at least six months, recurrent, intense sexually arousing fantasies, sexual urges, or be-haviours involving the use of non-living objects (for example, female under-garments); b) the fantasies, sexual urges, or behaviours cause clinically significant distress or impairment in social, occupational, or other import-ant areas of functioning; and c) the fetish objects are not limited to articles of female clothing used in cross-dressing (as in transvestic fetishism) or de-vices designed for the purpose of tactile genital stimulation (for example, a vibrator).[22] The demarcation line for DSM IV-TR's[23] diagnostic purposes is met when the fetish becomes either obligatory or strongly preferred in order to achieve sexual excitement, such that erectile dysfunction in males may ensue absent the object. Fetishists may occasionally get into difficulty when the fetish object has been stolen.

7) Transvestic Fetishism

In transvestic fetishism (TF), the (almost invariably heterosexual) male de-rives erotic gratification from wearing female clothing, more often than not, undergarments for arousal and orgasm. Often, the subject is aroused to

---

22   *Ibid.*
23   *Ibid.*

thoughts of himself as a female (autogynephilia). TF is not diagnosed when the cross-dressing occurs in the context of gender identity disorder. The disorder generally begins in childhood and persists into adulthood, although, later on in adulthood, the erotic dimension may recede into the background to be replaced by cross-dressing for the purpose of alleviating depression and anxiety, sometimes associated with emerging gender identity dysphoria.

The incidence and prevalence of TF is unknown. A recent Swedish population study found that of 2,450 eighteen to sixty-year olds, almost 3 percent of men and 0.5 percent of women had engaged in at least one episode of cross-dressing for fetishistic purposes. A correlation (noted earlier on in the scientific literature and observed in clinical practice) between voyeurism, exhibitionism, and sexual masochism and a positive attitude towards TF was noted.[24]

The diagnostic criteria for transvestic fetishism are a) over a period of at least six months, in a heterosexual male, recurrent, intense sexually arousing fantasies, sexual urges, or behaviours involving cross-dressing; and b) the fantasies, sexual urges, or behaviours cause clinically significant distress or impairment in social, occupational, or other important areas of functioning. (With gender dysphoria, specify if the person has persistent discomfort with gender role or identity.)[25]

8) Sexual Sadism

The essential feature of sexual sadism involves recurrent and intense sexually arousing fantasies, urges, or behaviours involving actual acts during which the sadist is sexually aroused by a victim's physical or psychological suffering or humiliation. Individuals at the benign end of the sadism spectrum are able to gratify their sadistic fantasies and needs through consensual enactments, sometimes of a reciprocal nature—as sadists are sometimes gratified by engaging in the masochistic role. Sexual sadists with psychopathic personalities or anti-social personality disorder occupy the more malignant end of the spectrum. This group is associated with predatory victimization of the public, rape, and in some rarer instances, lust murder.

The diagnostic criteria, according to DSM IV-TR, for sexual sadism are a) over a period of at least six months, recurrent, intense sexually arousing fantasies, sexual urges, or behaviours involving acts (real, not simulated) in

---

24   N. Långström & K.J. Zucker, "Transvestic Fetishism in the General Population: Prudence and Correlates" (2005) 31 Journal of Sex and Marital Therapy 87.

25   DSM IV-TR, above note 1 at 575.

which the psychological or physical suffering (including humiliation) of the victim is sexually exciting to the person; and b) the person has acted on these urges with a non-consenting person, or the sexual urges or fantasies cause marked distress or interpersonal difficulty.[26]

9) Sexual Masochism

Sexual masochists are aroused by fantasies or acts that involve being made to physically or psychologically suffer, or by being humiliated. Again, there is a certain degree of non-exclusivity in both sadists and masochists. It is estimated that a third of masochists have engaged in sadistic behaviour. In the more benign scenario, sadists and masochists have an affinity for each other. A masochist and sadist might engage in enactments that are erotically stimulating to both; for example, master-slave, bondage and discipline, and teacher-pupil scenarios. Paraphernalia is often involved and can include handcuffs, electric shocks, clamps, blindfolds, or enemas. The masochist may revel in being defiled by being urinated or defecated upon.

The diagnostic criteria, according to DSM IV-TR, for sexual masochism are a) over a period of at least six months, recurrent, intense sexually arousing fantasies, sexual urges, or behaviours involving the act (real, not simulated) of being humiliated, beaten, bound, or otherwise made to suffer; and b) the fantasies, sexual urges, or behaviours cause clinically significant distress or impairment in social, occupational, or other important areas of functioning.[27]

10) Paraphilia Not Otherwise Specified (NOS)

According to DSM IV-TR, paraphilia not otherwise specified (NOS) is included for coding paraphilias that do not meet the criteria for any of the specific categories. Examples include, but are not limited to, telephone scatologia (see Section C.3, above), necrophilia (corpses), partialism (see Section C.6, above), zoophilia (animals), coprophilia (feces), klismaphilia (enemas), and urophilia (urine).[28]

---

26   *Ibid.* at 574.
27   *Ibid.* at 573.
28   *Ibid.* at 576.

D. PARAPHILIAS IN THE LEGAL DOMAIN—SEXUAL OFFENDERS

1) In General

The public often lumps child molesters, sex offenders and pedophiles into a single group, as if they were synonymous. This is not the case. The term "sex offender" is more of a legal and correctional designation. It refers to an individual who has been convicted of a sexual offence.

2) Age of Majority, Age Differentials and Sexual Offences

The age of majority in Canada is fourteen years. Criminal offences such as sexual interference (section 151) and invitation to sexual touching (section 152) are committed when the victim is under the age of fourteen. The following *Criminal Code*[29] provisions clarify the role of consent, and what the requisite age differential between victim and perpetrator must be in order to constitute an offence.

Consent no defence

150.1 (1) Where an accused is charged with an offence under section 151 or 152 or subsection 153(1), 160(3) or 173(2) or is charged with an offence under section 271, 272 or 273 in respect of a complainant under the age of fourteen years, it is not a defence that the complainant consented to the activity that forms the subject-matter of the charge.

Exception

(2) Notwithstanding subsection (1), where an accused is charged with an offence under section 151 or 152, subsection 173(2) or section 271 in respect of a complainant who is twelve years of age or more but under the age of fourteen years, it is not a defence that the complainant consented to the activity that forms the subject-matter of the charge unless the accused

(a) is twelve years of age or more but under the age of sixteen years;

(b) is less than two years older than the complainant; and

(c) is not in a position of trust or authority towards the complainant, is not a person with whom the complainant is in a relationship of dependency and is not in a relationship with the complainant that is exploitative of the complainant.

Exemption for accused aged twelve or thirteen

(3) No person aged twelve or thirteen years shall be tried for an offence under section 151 or 152 or subsection 173(2) unless the person is in a position

---

29   R.S.C. 1985, c. C-46.

of trust or authority towards the complainant, is a person with whom the complainant is in a relationship of dependency or is in a relationship with the complainant that is exploitative of the complainant.

Mistake of age

(4) It is not a defence to a charge under section 151 or 152, subsection 160(3) or 173(2), or section 271, 272 or 273 that the accused believed that the complainant was fourteen years of age or more at the time the offence is alleged to have been committed unless the accused took all reasonable steps to ascertain the age of the complainant.

(5) It is not a defence to a charge under section 153, 159, 170, 171 or 172 or subsection 212(2) or (4) that the accused believed that the complainant was eighteen years of age or more at the time the offence is alleged to have been committed unless the accused took all reasonable steps to ascertain the age of the complainant.

3) Motivation for Sexual Offending

A perpetrator may sexually offend for a variety of reasons. It should not automatically be assumed that he suffers from a sexual disorder. The motivation underlying, and psychopathology driving, a sexual offence has implications for the perpetrator's risk for recidivism. Some of the more common motives for a sexual offense are set out below. Note that the list is not an exhaustive one. Potential motivations for sexual offending include:

- gratification of deviant sexual arousal, interests, and urges (that is, a paraphilia);
- assertion of power and control;
- punishment of a victim;
- inducement of fear;
- retribution; and
- intellectual limitation (especially in an adolescent male who has emerging strong hormone-based urges, but lacks the skills and opportunity to engage females appropriately).

4) Psychopathology Associated with Sexual Offending

Even when psychopathology (psychiatric symptoms, conditions, or psychological disturbances) is associated with sexual offending, it is not necessarily paraphilic in nature. Sexual offenders may infrequently be diagnosed with one or more non-paraphilic psychiatric disturbances or with a non-paraphilic mental illness concurrently with a paraphilia. Diagnoses associated with sexual offending are provided below (see Chapter 1 for definitions):

- paraphilias;
- hypomania;
- delusional disorder;
- schizophrenia;
- organic mental disorder;
- mental retardation;
- alcohol abuse;
- fetal alcohol effect;
- street drug abuse;
- antisocial personality disorder;
- narcissistic personality disorder; and
- borderline personality disorder.

Antisocial personality disorder is perhaps the most common comorbid disorder contributing to the commission of a sexual offence. Current estimates suggest that 30 to 40 percent of incarcerated sex offenders have a co-occurring diagnosis of antisocial personality disorder.[30]

Sexual offences committed by severely mentally disordered patients often have a psychotic basis to them. For example, a twenty-five-year-old single male with a primary diagnosis of schizophrenia was found not criminally responsible on account of mental disorder for sexually assaulting an elderly demented female resident of the psychiatric hospital which he attended as an outpatient. The accused was experiencing both visual hallucinations and delusions. Apart from believing that the victim had consented to intercourse, he saw her as being an attractive young woman who was attempting to seduce him. In cases where the offender was psychotic at the time of commission of a sexual offence, the behaviour is likely to flow from a distorted belief, misperception, misapprehension, or confusion. Some potential psychotic scenarios are set out below:

- the false belief that the victim is in love with the perpetrator (this is an example of an erotomanic delusion that may be found in schizophrenia, mania, or delusional disorder);

---

30   H.E. Barbaree & D.M. Greenberg, "Overview of Sex Offenders and the Paraphilias" in H. Bloom, R.D. Schneider, & S.J. Hucker, eds., *Handbook of Psychiatry and the Law* (Toronto: Centre for Addiction and Mental Health and Irwin Law, forthcoming).

- the belief/misperception that the victim is someone other than who he or she is (misidentification);
- the false belief (that is, delusion) that the victim has consented;
- disinhibition due to alcohol or drug intoxication, hypomania, an organic brain injury, (especially frontal lobe pathology), a dementive condition, or schizophrenia;
- confusion (due to an organic brain syndrome like a dementive condition, or alcohol or drug intoxication or withdrawal); and
- impaired judgment (due to mania, substance abuse, schizophrenia, or an organic brain syndrome).

5) Child Molesters

Child molesters can be subcategorized according to the nature of their motivation and the psychopathology driving their actions, and by their choice of victims. "Child molester" is not a specific psychiatric term. It is used to denote a perpetrator whose sexual offence has been against a person below the legal age of consent. "Pedophile," on the other hand, has little to do with age and everything to do with the stage of psychosexual development of the victim. Offences by fathers and step-fathers against daughters, step-daughters and the daughters of common-law partners fall into the incest category. Incest perpetrators are unlikely to be pedophiles (see discussion in Section C.1(e), above).

6) Rapists

Rapists are men who have committed sexual assaults against women who are above the age of consent. Sexual sadism and rape are not synonymous. A percentage (between 5 and 45 percent) of rapists has been identified as being sexually sadistic. Rape is for the most part non-paraphilic (that is, the sexual act is not an expression of the individual's primary erotic interests) and generally reflects the perpetrator's wish for dominance and control over the victim. The rapist may use the victim as a receptacle for his long-standing anger and retributive and/or misogynistic feelings towards a specific woman or women in general.

Rapists present a fairly heterogeneous group. The group includes men with paraphilias; men who are angry (as noted above); inadequate men with poor social skills; men with limited psychosexual experience and aggressive tendencies; and personality disordered men whose sexual assaults on women are both opportunistic and a reflection of their sense of entitlement.

In their rapist taxonomy, Knight and Prentky[31] provide a general classification of male offenders based on four primary motivations for raping, as
detailed below:

- *Opportunistic rapists*, whose sexual offences are one of many unsocial-
  ized behaviours, often exhibit poor impulse control. The degree of
  violence used is commensurate with what is required to manage resistance. They are not angry or gratuitously violent. If harm occurs,
  they are indifferent to it.
- *Pervasively angry rapists* experience generalized anger. Women are not
  an exclusive target. The anger they experience, and violence they inflict, sometimes resulting in serious injury and death, are not the specific motivation for the sexual offence, nor are they associated with
  sexual arousal.
- *Sexually-motivated rapists* are motivated by their sexual fantasies, urges,
  and preoccupations. This category can be further subdivided into the
  sadist, who merges anger and aggression with sexual needs, and non-
  sadistic sexual types.
- *Vindictive rapists* employ verbal abuse and physical violence, and sometimes degradation and humiliation, as a part of the sexual assault.
  Their anger is exclusively directed at women.

Rape is generally an opportunistic crime committed by younger men, often
between their late teens to early- to mid-thirties. Rapists have varied criminal
backgrounds and may have offences on their records that include break and
enter and assault. A number of rapists begin their history of criminal offending fairly early in life. Some, who started their career by breaking into the
homes of others, may have moved on to consider and then enact rape, titillated
by the notion of having control over a woman whose home he has invaded.

Self-report studies of sex offenders (which are, for the most part, considered unreliable because of their transparency) have revealed a number of
cognitive distortions and skewed attitudes that help sexually aggressive men
justify their actions. A fair number of sexually aggressive men rationalize
their actions by characterizing females as unworthy of trust, or by otherwise
demonizing them, or by suggesting that rape scenarios are part of the sex-

---

31   Adapted from R.A. Knight & R.A. Prentky, "Classifying Sexual Offenders: The Devel-
      opment on Corroboration of Taxonomic Models" in W.L. Marshall, D.R. Laws, & H.E.
      Barbaree, eds., *Handbook of Sexual Assault: Issues, Theories, and Treatment of the Offenders*
      (New York: Plenum Press, 1990) at 44–45.

ual fantasy repertoire many women hold. A number of sex offenders will also endorse the notion that women have the ability to say "no" and resist a rape if they choose to do that. Minimization and denial are related findings, and at times represent willful untruthfulness on the offender's part, and at other times are the result of distorted thinking, misattribution, rationalization, and psychological denial in the interest of maintaining self-esteem.[32] These two constructs, in particular, have implications for an offender's treatability and prognosis. Some treatment programs will reject offenders who enlist and maintain these thought processes. Clinicians are best advised to manage these concerns by firstly maintaining a high index of suspicion, and secondly, ensuring that an official version of the events is available.

7) Sexual/Lust Murder

Sexual murders are quite rare, although they attract considerable public attention, and are the material of crime novels and thriller movies. There is no consensus, as yet, in the scientific literature, that sexual or lust murderers are an appropriate category unto themselves. Rather than being uniquely paraphilic, murders committed in a course of a sexual assault may well be underpinned by hostility and aggression, or be ancillary to the primary sexual assault, and not so much a function of paraphilic proclivities.

E. EVALUATION OF SEX OFFENDERS

1) Generally

The overriding considerations here, as would be the case in the evaluation of any offender who is at risk for causing harm to the public, is that the assessment be thorough and multi-disciplinary, that it identifies all relevant risks, and that it provides meaningful recommendations regarding the elimination/reduction of each and every identified risk factor. There is no standard format for the evaluation of sex offenders. A comprehensive evaluation and expert report is likely to include data subsumed by the subheadings that follow. A deliberate, focused, and methodical approach can often be facilitated or ensured by reliance on one or more of the various sexual and violence recidivism assessment schemes outlined at the conclusion of this chapter. If nothing else, formal risk assessment schemes (whether actuarial, clinical,

---

32   Barbaree & Greenberg, "Overview of Sex Offenders," above note 30.

or hybrid in nature — see Chapter 8) ensure that information relevant to the analysis has been considered.

2) Reviewing the Offender's Background and Historical Information

Of note here, and frequently found in the backgrounds of many sex offenders (and many offenders in general), is a history of child abuse and neglect, attention deficit hyperactivity disorder, parental separation, academic failure and learning disorders, conduct disorder, and early sexualization, etc.

The evaluation should carefully review the offender's past history of sexual transgressions, and from the clinician's perspective, the review should also cover sexually offensive behaviours for which the offender was never charged. A general history of criminal and antisocial behaviours, and the offender's ability to abide by supervision orders and other restrictions is also of importance. As much relevant collateral background information as is reasonable in the circumstances should be pursued. This would include all health care records (medical and mental health), educational and employment records, criminal and probation records, and records referable to military service.

3) The Clinical Assessment

Clinical assessment of offenders, apart from gathering relevant historical information, involves careful review of their sexual history, sexual functioning, sexual and masturbatory fantasies, capacity to control impulses, use/abuse of substances, problems with anger and aggression, capacity for empathy, attitude towards others, insight, motivation for treatment, ability to form a therapeutic relationship or alliance, and preparedness to abide by any conditions imposed on them. The clinical evaluation must necessarily include a detailed mental status examination (that is, evaluation of sensorium, perception, thought content, etc.).

As noted above, apart from behaviours that have attracted the attention of the authorities and led to criminal prosecution, paraphilic interests are disclosed by the sexual and masturbatory fantasies sex offence perpetrators and paraphiliacs (especially this latter category, by definition) harbour. Extracting a truthful representation of his sexual and masturbatory fantasy life from an offender is often an arduous task, met with considerable resistance, denial, distortion, and outright untruthfulness. A denial of sexual and masturbatory fantasies involving children by an individual who has, over the course of his adult life, been convicted of successive sexual offences against male minors is highly suspect (especially if his phallometric test results support a pedophilic diagnosis). The centrality of sexual and masturbatory fantasies was recognized early, and is captured by the following historical extract from Hühner:

> The masturbatory act supposes a much greater activity of the imagination; the immediate erotic impressions and sensations, which come spontaneously in coitus, must be replaced in masturbation by increased mechanical stimuli and by excessive demands upon the erotic conceptions. All these powerful accessories to sexual activity, which we receive in normal cohabitation from visual impressions, tactile sensations, kissing, sensations of smell (perfume) and of hearing, all these immediate perceptions must be replaced with the manual masturbator by the power of the imagination—truly an excess of mental effort, a waste of valuable nervous substance.[33]

The clinical assessment necessarily involves a detailed review of the index offence(s) with emphasis on motivation, victim selection, emotional and psychological stressors, and precipitants. It is important for the clinician to elicit the offender's longitudinal patterns and proclivities. She may be aided in that regard by using questionnaires and inventories such as the Derogatis Sexual Functioning Inventory,[34] the Multiphasic Sex Inventory,[35] and the Clarke Sexual History Questionnaire.[36] Apart from creating an inventory of the subject's sexual practices, historical behaviours, interests and fantasies, these tools also pick up on sexual attitudes and cognitive distortions. The clinical assessment often includes adjunctive psychological assessment and testing. See Chapter 1, Section C.3 for a list of commonly-used, albeit purpose-specific psychological tests.

a) Phallometric Testing

Phallometric testing, otherwise referred to as penile plethysmography, is a physiologic test of sexual arousal. It measures an individual's arousal, through either volumetric or circumferential apparatus, by looking at even

---

33   M. Hühner, *Disorders of The Sexual Function in the Male and Female* (Philadelphia: F.A. Davis, 1922) at 19–20.

34   L. Derogatis, *Derogatis Sexual Functioning Inventory* (Baltimore: Clinical Psychometric Research, 1975) [DSFI].

35   H.R. Nichols & I. Molinder, *The Multiphasic Sex Inventory Manual* (Tacoma, WA: Nichols & Molinder, 1984).

36   D. Paitich *et al.*, "The Clarke SHQ: A Clinical Sex History Questionnaire for Males" (1977) 6 Archives of Sexual Behavior 421.

minute changes in penile responses to a number of visual and/or auditory stimuli that he is presented with in the test procedure. Phallometric testing evaluates an individual's sexual preferences in hierarchy. Phallometric testing may be most useful for developing individualized treatment plans for sexual offenders, for helping offenders navigate their way to the truth about their sexual deviancy (by confronting them with physiologic evidence that runs contrary to their disclaimers of a sexual problem), and in this way, therapeutic gains may be fostered through this intervention.

There are appropriate and inappropriate uses of phallometric testing. Above all, the test ought not to be used to appraise the truthfulness of an offender's denial of having committed the sexual offence for which he is charged, nor should it be used to define sexual deviancy for which phallometric testing has not been proven to be efficacious. Following a review of the literature, with special reference to Murphy's and Barbaree's work,[37] Laws defines a number of "appropriate uses" and "inappropriate uses" for phallometric testing.[38] They are reviewed below.

- Appropriate uses of phallometric testing
  - to determine what impact certain stimuli have on a physiologic measure of sexual arousal;
  - to help classify research subjects into various groups based on their sexual responding to various types of stimuli, from a research perspective;
  - to identify deviant sexual arousal for the purpose of defining a treatment program; and
  - to confront test subjects who have denied deviant interests with their responses to the contrary.

- Inappropriate uses of phallometric testing
  - use of the subject's response as the sole criterion for entry into, or exit from, a treatment program, or to alter his level of security;
  - to determine ultimate issues in a legal proceeding; for example, whether a father should have access and/or custody rights to a child he has alleged to have sexually victimized, or whether someone al-

---

37   W.D. Murphy & H.E. Barbaree, *Assessment of Sex Offenders by Measures of Erectile Response: Psychometric Properties and Decision Making* (Brandon, VT: Safer Society Press, 1994).

38   D.R. Laws, "Penile Plethysmography: Will We Ever Get it Right?" in T. Ward, D.R. Laws, & S.M. Hudson, eds., *Sexual Deviance: Issues and Controversies* (Thousand Oaks, CA: Sage Publications, 2003).

leged to have committed a specific sexual offence fits the profile of the perpetrator of that offence; and

▷ as a screening measure in the general population to weed out sexual offenders.[39]

The hypothesized disorder (that is, pedophilia or rape/sadistic proclivities) dictates the nature of the visual and or auditory sexual stimuli presented to the test subject. The age preference test, for example, includes slide and film depictions, with accompanying audiotape scenarios involving children and adolescents. Many sex offenders exhibit disordered sexual arousal. Deviant sexual preference determined through phallometric testing is, in fact, one of the risk indicators on several sexual recidivism risk assessment tools (see below).

As helpful as phallometric testing is in defining age preference, its utility in discriminating between individuals with and without rape, coercive, or sadistic proclivities remains contentious. Phallometric testing was recently rejected as a reliable scientific test or procedure by the Supreme Court of Canada in *R. v. J-L.J.*[40] In that case, an experienced sexologist concluded that the accused was unlikely to have committed the series of child molestations he was charged with in light of his negative phallometric test results. Speaking on behalf of a unanimous court, Justice Binnie expressed concerns about "the possibility that such evidence—cloaked under the mystique of science—would distort the fact finding process ..."[41] Justice Binnie went on to say that although the technique (phallometric testing) was not novel, the expert in the instant case was proposing to use that test for a "novel purpose";[42] that is, to supplant the role of the trier of fact by making a pronouncement on the ultimate issue of the accused's culpability.

Although phallometric testing is a clinically useful test and should invariably be included in the clinical domain—that is, for diagnostic, therapeutic, and risk assessment and risk management purposes—it remains highly controversial, and continues to be the subject of much criticism, some of which is reviewed below:

---

39 Adapted from Murphy & Barbaree, "Assessment of Sex Offenders," above note 37 at 85, and Laws, *ibid.* at 98.

40 *R. v. J-L.J.*, [2000] 2 S.C.R. 600.

41 *Ibid.* at 627.

42 *Ibid.* at 617.

- There is a lack of standardization with respect to the training of individuals and the centres who carry out this test and with the materials used (different centres use different materials to elicit responses).[43]
- Even in the scientific community, there are no agreed upon cut-off points as to what defines normal and deviant responses.
- Normative data that defines the difference between sexually anomalous interest and normal sexual interest in the general population is lacking, which makes interpretation of deviancy difficult. Research indicates that normal heterosexual males respond to aberrant stimuli, especially rape scenario stimuli, albeit not nearly to the same degree as paraphiliacs do.[44]
- There are numerous ways in which phallometric test results can be manipulated, although various methods of avoidance and faking have been identified and addressed in the literature.[45] Some of the methods of manipulation/feigning in phallometric testing are
  - ▷ aversion of gays to the materials on screen (this is obviously more difficult to do with auditory stimuli);
  - ▷ masturbating or having intercourse just prior to the test;
  - ▷ thinking about neutral or aversive things in order to dampen responding;
  - ▷ rhythmic contractions of gluteal muscles (pumping) in order to increase output to normal stimuli;
  - ▷ manipulating perineal muscles to decrease penile reaction to anomalous stimuli;[46] and
  - ▷ use of intoxicants or medication to dampen responses.
- Retesting to assess therapeutic gains is highly suspect as test subjects may learn to manipulate the results (as described above) through knowledge and experience gained from having taken the test before.

---

43 Laws, "Penile Plethysmography," above note 38; W.D. Murphy & J.M. Peters, "Profiling Child Sexual Abusers: Psychological Considerations" (1992) 19 Criminal Justice and Behavior 24; W.T. Simon & P.G.W. Schouten, "Plethysmography in the Assessment and Treatment of Sexual Deviance: An Overview" (1991) 20 Archives of Sexual Behavior 75.

44 K. Freund & R.J. Watson, "Assessment of the Sensitivity and Specificity of a Phallometric Test: An Update of Phallometric Diagnosis of Pedophilia" (1991) 3 Psychological Assessment: A Journal of Consulting and Clinical Psychology 254.

45 K. Freund, R. Watson, & D. Rienzo, "Signs of Feigning in the Phallometric Test" (1988) 26 Behavior Research and Therapy 105; R. Langevin, *Sexual Preference Testing: A Brief Guide* (Toronto, ON: Juniper Press, 1989).

46 Langevin, *ibid.*

- Use of the phallometric test for the purpose of proving guilt or bolstering innocence is beyond the scope of the test's validity and neither meets the test for being a reliable scientific test[47] nor the U.S. test set out in *Daubert v. Merrell Dow Pharmaceuticals.*[48]

b) Biochemical/Hormonal Assessment

A detailed assessment often involves assessing medical status and biological parameters, including carrying out a physical examination, a CT scan of the head, and blood tests, particularly a screen of the offender's sex hormone status through evaluation of his hypothalamic-pituitary-gonadal axis.

The hypothalamic-pituitary-gonadal axis is the interactive system of glands that regulates the synthesis and action of testosterone, the male hormone responsible for sex drive. Some evidence indicates that over-activity in this system, and, particularly, an excessive amount of testosterone (or greater sensitivity to a normal amount of testosterone) is associated with high sex drive, sexual deviancy, and aggression. There is similarly evidence that reduction of serum testosterone, or interference with its action, reduces sex drive, deviant fantasy and impulses, and, therefore, the propensity to act out sexually.

c) Sexual Risk Appraisal Instruments

Assessors are wise to avail themselves of the focused approach offered by use of sexual recidivism risk appraisal tools (see Chapter 8 for a detailed discussion of risk assessment approaches and tools).

Examples of some of the more commonly used sexual recidivism risk appraisal tools are provided below.

THE SEXUAL OFFENDER RISK APPRAISAL GUIDE (SORAG)[49]

The SORAG is an actuarial instrument based on the VRAG specifically designed to predict sexual recidivism. The SORAG items are as follows:

- Hare Psychopathy Checklist—Revised (PCL-R) score;
- elementary school maladjustment score (up to and includes grade eight);

---

47 *R. v. J-L.J.*, above note 40; *Frye v. United States*, 293 F. 1013 (D.C. Cir. 1923).

48 *Daubert v. Merrell Dow Pharmaceuticals*, 43 F.3d 1311 (9th Cir. 1995).

49 V.L. Quinsey, G.T. Harris, M.E. Rice, & C. Cormier, *Violent Offenders: Appraising and Managing Risk.* (Washington, DC: American Psychological Association, 1998) at 157.

- lived with biological parents to age sixteen (except for separation caused by death; if separated at birth, code as No);
- Cormier-Lang score for non-violent offences prior to index offence;
- Cormier-Lang score for violent offence predating index offence;
- number of convictions for sexual offences prior to index offence;
- history of sexual offences against female children only (includes index offence);
- marital status;
- age at index offence (as of last birthday before);
- failure on conditional release prior to index offence (charges, parole revocation, probation breach, failure to comply, including bail and fail to attend, etc.);
- meets DSM III criteria for any personality disorder;
- meets DSM III criteria for schizophrenia;
- history of alcohol problem; and
- deviant sexual preferences on phallometric testing.

THE SEXUAL VIOLENCE RISK-20 (SVR-20)[50]

The Sexual Violence Risk-20 (SVR-20) isolates twenty key historic and dynamic risk factors for sexual offence recidivism. It considers the nature of the offence, frequency of offending behaviour and severity and likelihood of sexual violence in the future. The SVR-20 items are

- Psychosocial adjustment:
  - sexual deviation;
  - victim of child abuse;
  - psychopathy;
  - major mental illness;
  - substance use problems;
  - suicidal/homicidal ideation;
  - relationship problems;
  - employment problems;
  - past non-sexual violent offences;
  - past violent offences; and
  - past supervision failure.
- Sexual offences:
  - high-density sex offences;

---

50   Adapted from H.S. Boer, P.R. Kropp, & C. Webster, *Sexual Violence Risk-20* (Burnaby, BC: Mental Health, Law and Policy Institute, Simon Fraser University, 1997) at 15.

  ▷ multiple sex offence types;
  ▷ physical harm to victim(s) in sex offences;
  ▷ escalation in frequency or severity of sexual offences;
  ▷ uses weapons or threats of death in sex offences;
  ▷ extreme minimization or denial of sex offences; and
  ▷ attitudes that support or condone sex offences.
 ◆ Future plans:
  ▷ lacks realistic plans; and
  ▷ negative attitude towards intervention.

STATIC-99/STATIC-2002[51]

The Static is an easy-to-score brief measure of sex offence recidivism risk. It is intended to assess long-term potential for sexual and violence recidivism based on actuarial, objective, and easy to obtain information. The Static-2002 is intended for offenders who have an index sexual offence and who are in a position to reoffend by virtue of having received a community sentence or through release from a custodial disposition. The predecessor version, Static-99, was principally used in the correctional system. The Static-2002 items are reproduced below.[52]

 ◆ age at release
 ◆ persistence of sexual offending
  ▷ sentencing occasions for sexual offences
  ▷ juvenile arrest for a sexual offence (and convicted as an adult for a separate offence)
  ▷ high rate of sexual offending
 ◆ deviant sexual interests
  ▷ any convictions for non-contact sex offences
  ▷ any male victims
  ▷ two or more victims under twelve years, one unrelated
 ◆ relationship to victims
 ◆ general criminality
  ▷ arrest/sentencing occasions
  ▷ any breach of conditional release

---

51 R.K. Hanson, *Development of a Brief Actuarial Risk Scale for Sexual Offence Recidivism* (User Report No. 1997-04) (Ottawa: Department of the Solicitor General of Canada, Public Works and Government Services Canada, 1997); R.K. Hanson & D. Thornton, *Notes on the Development of Static-2002* (User Report No. 2003-01). (Ottawa: Department of the Solicitor General of Canada, Public Works and Government Services Canada, 2002).

52 Adapted from Static-2002, *ibid.*, Coding Form.

F. SENTENCING CONSIDERATIONS

Critical to the court's considerations is a detailed psychosexual evaluation and risk assessment, as outlined above, to assist the court in fashioning the most appropriate sentence. Risk assessments need to consider and make recommendations to remediate co-morbid conditions, such as substance abuse, anger management problems, impulsivity, anxiety disorders, or any other conditions relevant to the offender's risk for recidivism.

Psychiatric recommendations for rehabilitation are likely to involve a multi-modal treatment program that includes interventions such as cognitive therapy, empathy training, relapse prevention, social skills training, psychopharmacologic interventions, and in this regard, more specifically the use of anti-androgens (sex drive reducing medications — see Chapter 1).

CHAPTER EIGHT

Violence Risk Assessment Overview

A. INTRODUCTION

Evaluating an individual's risk for violence has always been an important task in the field of psychiatry, although it was only recently recognized as such. As Mossman puts it, psychiatrists "make predictions all the time, but usually without realizing it."[1] Mossman goes on to describe how predictions of one form or another of self-injurious or dangerous behaviour are unavoidable in psychiatry "because dozens of common clinical actions require implicit judgments about the violence potential of a patient or evaluee."[2] Beyond the domain of a general psychiatrist, assessing risk for future violence is a core component of forensic and correctional psychiatry.

Violence risk assessment is by its very nature a prospective inquiry. It considers the potential for an adverse aggressive event to occur within a wide temporal range that includes the immediate (seconds, minutes, a few hours), the foreseeable (days, a few weeks, perhaps up to a year), and the distant (several years) future.[3] Assessing imminent risk for violence, in particular, is precisely within the domain of the general psychiatrist, especially when the potential actor is either intoxicated or suffering from a severe mental disorder, or both (as opposed to being more from the criminal domain). Clinicians working in psychiatric hospitals, particularly those who assess pa-

---

1   D. Mossman, "Understanding Prediction Instruments" in R.I. Simon and L.H. Gold, eds., *Textbook of Forensic Psychiatry* (Washington, DC: American Psychiatric Publishing, Inc., 2004) at 501.

2   *Ibid.*

3   See H. Bloom & C.D. Webster, "Assessing Imminent Risk" in H. Bloom, R.D. Schneider, S.J. Hucker, eds., *Handbook of Psychiatry and the Law in Canada* (Toronto: Centre for Addiction and Mental Health and Irwin Law, forthcoming).

tients in the emergency room, must make moment-to-moment clinical judgments about a patient's risk for harm to himself or to others, if not for the benefit of those potentially in harm's way, then to ensure that the clinician is meeting her statutory obligations (for example, provincial and territorial civil commitment legislation) and common law obligations (for example, the duty to warn[4]).

The current debate in the field of violence risk assessment epitomizes the long-standing uncertain relationship between the courts and mental health experts. The law would prefer, understandably, a greater degree of certainty with regard to violence prediction than is possible, given the state of the art in the behavioural sciences. Risk assessment/violence prediction is essentially a fledgling (though rapidly and incrementally progressing) field. Over the thirty or so years that the subject of risk assessment and violence prediction has been a focus of formal clinical interest and scientific research, there have been marked oscillations in the perspective mental health experts have taken, and in their level of optimism about the extent to which an individual's future risk for violence can be defined. The expanding need for violence risk assessment in various legal, administrative, and clinical situations (see Section C below) speaks to the need for a focused approach to many situations where risk must be identified and quantified, and then eliminated or reduced (to the extent possible).

For the purpose of this chapter, *violence* may be defined as behaviour that causes physical or psychological harm to people and/or damages or destroys inanimate objects, while *aggression* characterizes the emotional and psychological state of a person who, through verbal or physical displays, signals that violence may occur as a manifestation of what that person is thinking and feeling.[5] Perhaps the most useful definition of risk assessment is that provided by Stephen Hart. He defines risk assessment as "a contingency-based action plan for what should be done in the future, not a quantitative statement of fact of what will occur in the future."[6] The declaration that an individual represents a risk for dangerous conduct in the community does not necessarily say anything about the precise nature of the risk, when it will manifest, the degree to which it will manifest, exactly who it will affect, and whether it will be isolated in its expression (that is, occur once or more than

---

4   See *Smith v. Jones*, [1999] 1 S.C.R. 455 [*Smith*].

5   See H. Bloom & C.D. Webster, above note 3.

6   S.D. Hart, "Complexity, Uncertainty, and the Reconceptualization of Violence Risk Assessment," keynote address at the Annual Meeting of the European Association of Psychology and Law (Lisbon, Portugal, 8 June 2001, unpublished). Reprinted with permission.

once). It also says nothing about any variables, either previously identified or currently unknown, which, if present, could modify (that is, increase or decrease) or avert the expression of the risk. Because of risk assessment's inherent human dimensions—written about a human, for humans to read—Hart suggests that risk assessment could be expressed in linguistic (storytelling) rather than quantitative terms. He refers to this (telling of a story) approach as the "anchored narrative approach," which he describes in the following way:

> The story must have key elements, including description of important events in the past and identification of key motivations in the present. But it must go beyond that to foreshadow how the person, in light of past and present circumstances, may act in response to possible futures. It is important to recognize that the story is fictional, insofar as no one *knows* what will happen; it is simply an educated guess. But if the story is conveyed well—if it includes elements that seem important, if the inferences about motivations are well illustrated, if the speculations about future conditions are reasonable—then readers will accept the verisimilitude of the story and act accordingly. If, on the other hand, the story lacks important detail, includes irrelevant detail, contains weak inferences about motivation, or speculates too wildly about the future, it will be—and, I think, should be—disbelieved.[7]

B.   MENTAL HEALTH CLINICIANS AND VIOLENCE RISK ASSESSMENT

It has been difficult to foster any significant degree of comfort in clinicians faced with the need to evaluate an individual's risk for engaging in violence at some point in the future, even though clinicians regularly engage in "predictions" of this kind, in one way or another, as a part of the everyday practice of psychiatry. Some aspects of psychiatry admittedly lend themselves more to the need for this type of exercise. Mossman makes the point that psychiatrists cannot, in any event, avoid making predictions about violence given the extent to which day-to-day clinical decision-making incorporates judgments about a patient's or evaluee's violence potential.[8] As much as it is part of the job of managing offenders in both the criminal justice and mental health systems, Hanson aptly points out that it has never been easy.[9]

---

7   *Ibid.* Reprinted with permission.
8   D. Mossman, above note 1.
9   R.K. Hanson, *The Validity of Static-99 with Older Sexual Offenders*, Report No. 2005-01 (Ottawa: Minister of Public Safety and Emergency Preparedness of Canada, 2005).

The American Psychiatric Association submitted an *amicus* brief in *Tarasoff v. Regents of University of California*,[10] contending that psychiatrists were unable to accurately predict violence. The court's reply was that therapists were not required to perform perfectly, "but only to exercise that reasonable degree of skill and care ordinarily possessed by members of their profession (in circumstances where a patient had the potential to actualize a violent fantasy or thought)."[11]

It appears that no matter how much experts sought (more so historically than currently) to disavow expertise in predicting violence, their continuing involvement in legal matters, both criminal and civil, both of which draw on as yet imperfect technology in assessing violence risk, is a testament of the extent to which risk assessment/violence prediction is needed by the courts.

C. THE NEED FOR, SCOPE, AND USES OF VIOLENCE RISK ASSESSMENT

Experts in the behavioural sciences tend to become involved with risk assessment:

1. when they themselves need to make urgent decisions about imminent risk on an emergency basis;
2. in their capacity as consultant to defence counsel, prosecutors, courts, and various other tribunals, professional regulatory bodies, and employers (for example, on the issue of workplace violence); and
3. as members of specially constituted boards whose mandate centres on risk assignment and management issues (for example, review boards constituted under the *Criminal Code*[12] and provincial and territorial mental health, consent, and capacity boards).

Psychiatrists and other mental health consultants often provide opinions about an ever-increasing number of risk-based scenarios within both the civil and criminal spheres. Pronouncements concerning an individual's certifiability pursuant to provincial civil commitment legislation is perhaps the best known example from the civil arena, whereas evaluating an offender's candidacy for the designation dangerous or long-term offender is a well-known example from the criminal arena. As early as 1978, Shah identified fifteen areas in which a mental health professional could become involved

---

10   *Tarasoff v. Regents of University of California*, 17 Cal. 3d. 425, 551 P.2d 334 (Cal. 1976).

11   *Ibid.* at 345 (cited to P.2d).

12   *Criminal Code*, R.S.C. 1985, c. C-46.

in assessing risk for violence.[13] In a more recent review, Hall and Ebert cited twenty-seven situations that required mental health professionals to assess potential dangerousness.[14]

Webster and Dassinger provide a review of the various criminal, civil, and other contexts for which violence risk assessment may be of value:[15]

1. Criminal
   (a) Sentencing
       (i) Sentencing process: treatability/rehabilitation vs. incapacitation
       (ii) Dangerous and long-term offender proceedings
   (b) Parole Decisions
       (i) Community management
   (c) Part XX.I *Criminal Code*—Post-NCR ("not criminally responsible")[16]
       (i) Threshold jurisdictional issue: accuseds are absolutely discharged if they are no longer a "significant threat to the safety of the public"
       (ii) Management of NCR and unfit accused persons in the least onerous and least restrictive manner
       (iii) Transfer to appropriate level of security
       (iv) Assessing whether a permanently unfit accused is a significant threat to the safety of the public for the purpose of a possible stay of the proceedings pursuant to 672.851 of the *Criminal Code*
   (d) Judicial interim release (bail)
       (i) Principally in relation to the secondary grounds for detention: the risk the accused would present to the public (and the likelihood of repeat criminal behaviour) if released.
2. Civil
   (a) Civil commitment
       (i) Involuntary detention is almost always predicated on a dangerousness standard, although there is some variation amongst the various provincial and territorial jurisdictions.

---

13 See S. Shah, "Dangerousness: A Paradigm for Exploring Some Issues in Law and Psychology" (1978) 33 American Psychologist 224.

14 See H.V. Hall & R.S. Ebert, *Violence Prediction: Guidelines for the Forensic Practitioner*, 2d ed. (Springfield, IL: Charles C. Thomas Publisher Ltd., 2002).

15 Adapted from C.D. Webster & C. Dassinger, "The Systematic Assessment of Risk for Aggressive and Violent Behaviour against Others" in H. Bloom, R.D. Schneider, & S.J. Hucker, eds., *Handbook of Psychiatry and the Law* (Toronto: Centre for Addiction and Mental Health and Irwin Law, forthcoming). Reprinted with permission.

16 Bill C-30 introduced some changes to the language in Part XX.I of the *Criminal Code*. The term "not guilty by reason of insanity" has been changed to "not criminally responsible" (NCR) on account of mental disorder.

      (ii) Psychiatric "gating"/predator laws: civil commitment legislation is sometimes used to continue the post-sentence detention of dangerous "mentally ill" offenders

  (b) Psychiatric practice and malpractice

      (i) Violence risk assessments are the basis for clinical decisions by mental health practitioners concerning the extent to which a given patient might cause harm to others — specific others, or more generally, to the public at large. The result of a risk appraisal could compel a clinician to disclose confidential patient information to the authorities, in the interest of third party safety.[17]

      (ii) Physicians may be liable for failing to assess competently the risk their patients represent for violence to third parties.

  (c) Custody and Access

      (i) Risk of physical or psychological harm towards child by custodial or accessing parent

3. National Security

  (a) Terrorism

      (i) With the recognition of terrorism as a national concern, the *Anti-terrorism Act*[18] includes measures to assess the risk of individuals posing threats; to use expertise and systematic methods to identify, prosecute, convict, and punish terrorists.

  (b) Immigration and deportation hearings

      (i) Allowing into or excluding from Canada in accordance with "maintaining the security of Canadian society"; that is, to deny access to "persons who are criminals or security risks"[19]

4. Private Sector

  (a) Workplace violence

      (i) The assessment of risk for workplace aggression in an identified employee, former employee, disgruntled customer, etc.

  (b) Schoolplace Violence

      (i) The evaluation of students prone to engage in violence at school (bullying behaviour, threats, targeted or random shootings at school)

---

17 For a discussion of public safety exception to the solicitor-client privilege and/or doctor-patient confidentiality, see *Smith*, above note 4. In essence, the exception is made when there is clear *risk* to an identifiable person or group, when the risk is of *serious bodily harm or death*, and when there is *imminent* danger.

18 *Anti-terrorism Act*, S.C. 2001, c. 41.

19 *Immigration and Refugee Protection Act*, S.C. 2001, c. 27.

5. Clinical and Other
    (a) Clinical
        (i) Quantify and characterize the scope of potential behavioural psychopathology (has implications for both diagnosis and management)
        (ii) Achievement of relevant, accurate, and useful judgments about risk (has implications for patient care/management)
    (b) Public Awareness
        (i) Risk assessment addresses the public's increasing awareness of and concern about dangerous individuals and its need to know if high-risk individuals are in its midst.

A key point clinicians need to bear in mind is that risk assessments carried out for any court, tribunal, or legal purpose are inextricably tied to the legal standard or test for which the risk assessment was sought in the first place. Psychiatric and psychological appraisals are of little use to lawyers and judges unless the assessor has borne the legal standard in mind prior to, and over the course of, the risk assessment, and then drafted his opinions with that in mind.

D. HISTORY AND EVOLUTION OF RISK ASSESSMENT

The burgeoning field of violence risk assessment owes its expansion to at least two key factors. The first has to do with a mid-1970s shift in the standard or test for civil commitment, first in the U.S. and then in Canada, away from a paternalistic concern for people in need of treatment to a dangerousness standard. Another key factor has to do with the demonstration, some thirty years ago by Steadman and Cocozza,[20] that clinicians err considerably in favour of over-predicting violence. Steadman and Cocozza's work represents a first-of-its-kind outcome study of patients released by order of the U.S. Supreme Court from Dannemora State Hospital for the Criminally Insane in New York State.[21] Although it was postulated that these individuals, previously considered dangerous, would soon enact their dangerousness in the community, very few of the cohort of patients released as a result of the *Baxstrom* decision acted out violently once in the community. The *Bax-*

---

20   See H.J. Steadman & J.J. Cocozza, *Careers of the Criminally Insane: Excessive Social Control of Deviance* (Lexington, MA: Lexington Book, 1974).
21   *Baxstrom v. Herold*, 383 U.S. 107 (1966) [*Baxstrom*].

strom results were replicated several years later in *Dixon v. Attorney General of the Commonwealth of Pennsylvania*.[22] As noted by Webster and Hucker, the *Baxstrom* and *Dixon* decisions had the effect of "galvanizing research into violence prediction, assessment and management"[23] and significantly influenced Monahan's classic text, *Predicting Violent Behaviour: An Assessment of Clinical Techniques* (1981).[24]

Using a simple two-by-two table, Monahan poignantly demonstrated some of the inherent shortcomings in violence prediction.[25] The table (reproduced below) shows that apart from two accurate types of predictions (a true negative: no violence was predicted and none occurred; and a true positive: violence was predicted and did occur), there are two possible inaccurate predictions (a false negative: violence was not predicted and did occur; and a false positive: violence was predicted and did not occur). A false positive, if accepted in situations where an individual's civil liberties and freedom hang in the balance, can result in serious infringements of those rights, whereas a false negative can result in a tragedy. The understandable wish to avoid false negative predictions drives the long-recognized tendency toward over-prediction of violence.

Outcome (Violence)

	Low Risk	TRUE NEGATIVE	FALSE NEGATIVE
Prediction			
	High Risk	FALSE POSITIVE	TRUE POSITIVE

Reflecting the above discussion back to the *Baxstrom* case, the greater number of the patients released from hospital were true negatives (fifty-nine of the ninety-eight patients), in that they were not considered violent, and did not commit violence upon release. Eleven of the ninety-eight patients were true positives; that is, they were predicted to be violent, and did engage in violence in the community. Only three of the ninety-eight patients who were

---

22   *Dixon v. Attorney General of the Commonwealth of Pennsylvania*, 325 F.Supp. 966 (M.D. Pa. 1971) [*Dixon*].

23   C.D. Webster & S.J. Hucker, *Release Decision Making: Assessing Violent Risk in Mental Health, Forensic, and Correctional Settings* (Hamilton, ON: St. Joseph's Healthcare, 2003) at 25.

24   J. Monahan, *Predicting Violent Behaviour: An Assessment of Clinical Techniques* (Beverly Hills, CA: Sage Publications, 1981).

25   *Ibid.*

predicted non-violent, in fact, engaged in violence in the community over the four-year study, and they were consequently false negatives. The false positive category involved twenty-five patients who were rated as likely to be violent, but who did not, in fact, engage in violence.[26]

Risk assessment is an evolving science and technology. Below is an overview, perhaps unduly simplified, of the progression and direction of violence risk assessment.

FIRST GENERATION RISK ASSESSMENT: CLINICAL JUDGMENT

- based on file review and interviews
- "in my professional opinion"
- can be based on personal bias ("gut feelings" and intuition)
- can overlook important information
- can overemphasize unimportant information

SECOND GENERATION RISK ASSESSMENT: ACTUARIAL ASSESSMENT

- based on static historical factors (for example, criminal charges, age at first conviction, etc.)
- is more objective, empirically-based, and validated
- has higher degree of predictive validity than clinical decision making
- has clear rules

THIRD GENERATION RISK ASSESSMENT: ACTUARIAL AND DYNAMIC

- combines information from actuarial-based instruments with professional judgments based on fact
- assesses a wider range of variables
- is sensitive to change as a result of maturation, the effects of treatment, and environmental manipulation

FOURTH GENERATION RISK ASSESSMENT: ACTUARIAL AND EMPIRICALLY-BASED FACTORS

- considers empirically validated/theoretically relevant factors specific to type of risk assessment (for example, sexual recidivism)
- strengthens value of clinical/dynamic factors by ensuring empirically relevant
- considers the role of protective factors

---

26 For an interesting and thorough review of the history of dangerousness (as a topic of scientific and clinical interest) and risk assessment, see C.D. Webster & G. Bailes, "Assessing Violence Risk in Mentally and Personality Disordered Individuals" in C.R. Hollin, ed., *The Essential Handbook of Offender Assessment and Treatment* (Chichester; NY: John Wiley and Sons Ltd., 2004) c. 2.

Canadian researchers and mental health clinicians have played and continue to play a prominent role in risk assessment research and literature. Years ago, John Monahan, an American psychologist and pivotal figure in the field, noted the "remarkably strong international presence of Canada in forensic psychology and psychiatry."[27]

E. MENTAL DISORDER AND RISK FOR VIOLENCE

Much of the general public, in part owing to the way mental illness has been portrayed in the media, has concluded that violence and mental illness are inevitably connected.[28] The relationship, in reality, is not nearly so close, nor so clear. The evidence over the last number of years has, in fact, demonstrated that the more specific relationship is the one that exists between symptoms and violence, not mental disorder *per se* and violence,[29] and that treating the symptoms has a greater impact on reducing violence than does managing the disorder more generally.[30] This approach accords with the more current emphasis on isolating individual risk factors and managing them accordingly. In this regard, and strictly with respect to personality variables, Nestor[31] has identified four variables which, in differing configurations and degrees, mediate the expression of violence. The four variables are impulse control, affect regulation, narcissism, and paranoid personality style. Nestor points out that, from a practical perspective, paying close attention to these variables and measuring them objectively (to the extent possible) could have "potentially incalculable benefits" for the safety and security of potential victims.[32]

---

27   J. Monahan, "Foreword" in C.D. Webster, M.A. Jackson *et al.*, eds., *Impulsivity: Theory, Assessment, and Treatment* (New York: Guilford Press, 1997) at x. For a review of Canada's contribution to the field, see H. Bloom, C.D. Webster *et al.*, "The Canadian Contribution to Violence Risk Assessment: History and Implications for Current Psychiatric Practice" (2005) 50 Canadian Journal of Psychiatry 3 ["The Canadian Contribution"].

28   See B.G. Link & A. Stueve, "Psychotic Symptoms and the Violent Illegal Behavior of Mental Patients Compared to Community Controls" in J. Monahan & H.J. Steadman, eds., *Violence and Mental Disorder: Developments in Risk Assessment* (Chicago: University of Chicago Press, 1994) 137; C. Stark, B. Paterson *et al.*, "Newspaper Coverage of a Violent Assault by a Mentally Ill Person" (2004) 11 Journal of Psychiatric and Mental Health Nursing 635.

29   See P.J. Taylor, M. Leese *et al.*, "Mental Disorder and Violence: A Special (High Security) Hospital Study" (1998) 172 British Journal of Psychiatry 218.

30   See K. Tardiff, P.M. Marzuk *et al.*, "A Prospective Study of Violence by Psychiatric Patients after Hospital Discharge" (1997) 48 Psychiatric Services 678.

31   P.G. Nestor, "Mental Disorder and Violence: Personality Dimensions and Clinical Features" (2002) 159 American Journal of Psychiatry 1973.

32   *Ibid.* at 1977.

Violence almost never takes place in a vacuum. It almost always requires the intersection of two or more factors. If the formula for an occurrence of violence could be rendered to an equation, it would like something like this:

Predisposed Individual + Susceptible Victim + Enabling Environment + Situational Spark = Violent Occurrence

A more detailed schematic representation of those factors that interact to result in violence is shown in the figure below.[33]

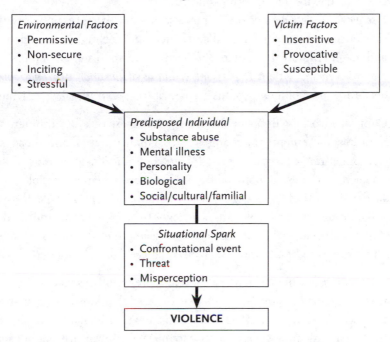

Comorbid conditions, particularly substance abuse, substantially increase violence risk in mentally accused.[34] Medication non-compliance together with substance abuse in a mentally disordered individual further potentiates the risk.[35] Bloom and Webster identify some of the key intoxicants associated

---

33   H. Bloom & C.D. Webster, above note 3. Reprinted with permission.

34   See J.W. Swanson, C.E. Holzer *et al.*, "Violence and Psychiatric Disorder in the Community: Evidence from the Epidemiological Catchment Area Surveys" (1990) 41 Hospital and Community Psychiatry 761; H.J. Steadman, E.P. Mulvey *et al.* "Violence by People Discharged from Acute Psychiatric Inpatient Facilities and by Others in the Same Neighbourhoods" (1998) 55 Archives of General Psychiatry 393.

35   See M.S. Swartz, J.W. Swanson *et al.*, "Violence and Severe Mental Illness: The Effects of Substance Abuse and NonAdherence to Medication" (1998) 155 American Journal of Psychiatry 226.

with violence and describe the particular mechanism or effect in the direction of violence associated with the substance:[36]

1. *Alcohol*: disinhibition, emotional lability, impaired judgment
2. *Cocaine (especially crack)*: irritability and agitation, mood swings, paranoid ideation ▸ psychosis and reduced control over aggressive impulses or delirium
3. *Phencyclidine (PCP)*: disorganized psychosis and bizarre behaviour associated with extreme aggression and suicide
4. *Lysergic Acid Diethylamide (LSD)*: not associated with aggression *per se*, but can cause extreme perceptual disturbances and feelings of omnipotence and invulnerability that can lead to harm or death to self and others
5. *Central Nervous System Depressant Withdrawal (alcohol, benzodiazepines, opiates)*: 1) irritability ▸ psychosis ▸ delirium; 2) extreme drug craving

Clinicians working in the field—those who assess risk for imminent violence in hospital emergency rooms and psychiatric wards, and those who provide longer range forecasts of risk for violence in forensic settings—often have a keen awareness of both subtle and overt propensities for violence associated with some of the major clinical conditions seen in the field of psychiatry. Bloom and Webster provide a review of the psychiatric and medical conditions associated with the risk for violence and the circumstances under which violence might manifest as a consequence of the condition:[37]

1. *Schizophrenia*: Violence may manifest as a pre-emptive strike by a patient with hallucinations or delusions and the fear that she will be attacked. It may also result from psychotic disorganization or akathisia. Violence may occur precipitously in response to internal stimuli and without signs of impending aggression.
2. *Mania*: Violence may occur in the context of an acute manic state (agitation, delusions, hallucinations, impulsivity) or as a form of resistance to being contained, limited, or interfered with while in an irritated/expansive state.
3. *Depression*: Violence may be the result of nihilistic delusions associated with suicide that may include other persons. In addition, interfered-with suicidality may involve others.
4. *Antisocial Personality Disorder*: If not utilitarian, violence can result from low frustration tolerance or the inability to contain anger.

---

36   H. Bloom & C.D. Webster, above note 3. Reprinted with permission.
37   *Ibid.* Reprinted with permission.

5. *Borderline Personality Disorder*: Violence may result from intense anger, impulsivity, and substance abuse. The context is often rage related to actual or threatened loss, triggered by projective identification, or caused by transient psychosis.

6. *Narcissistic Personality Disorder*: Violence is uncommon, but most likely to occur in the context of severe shame and ensuing narcissistic rage.

7. *Intermittent Explosive Disorder*: Impulse control disorder in which aggression is out of proportion to stimulus.

8. *Organic Brain Disorders*: These disorders include temporal lobe epilepsy, grand mal epilepsy (violence may manifest as disorganized violence in the ictal or interictal phase), delirium, and dementia (including Alzheimer's, Huntington's, Pick's, and Wilson's diseases), as well as strokes, head trauma, temporal and frontal lobe tumors, and infections (syphilis, viral encephalitis). The context may be misperception or disorganization. Another disorder in this category is that of mental retardation. With this condition, violence is usually in response to frustration and anger.

9. *Medical Conditions such as Hypoglycaemia, Hyperthyroidism, and Hyperadrenocorticism (Cushing's Disease)*: The violence mechanism for these conditions is usually delirium and agitation.

The intense focus over the last thirty years or so on variables associated with violence has yielded a sizeable list. A number of factors posited over the course of time have been put to the test of focused consideration, dialogue, and, above all, research, much of which has been distilled down to form the content of actuarial and structured professional judgment risk assessment guides (see Section F.1, below).

The symptoms, conditions, and demographic and other circumstances associated with risk for future violence are described briefly in Section E.1, and following, and represent the authors' efforts to compile a list of factors most deserving of consideration.

The most recent research into the strength and validity of some of the factors described below was carried out by the MacArthur Violence Risk Assessment Study,[38] without a doubt the largest and most extensive study of violence in released U.S. psychiatric patients. The multi-site project involved the systematic study of over 1,000 psychiatric patients released from psychiatric facilities in several U.S. states, who were followed-up closely over the course of the year.

---

38   J. Monahan, H.J. Steadman *et al.*, *Rethinking Risk Assessment: The MacArthur Study of Mental Disorder and Violence* (Oxford; NY: Oxford University Press, 2001) [*Rethinking Risk Assessment*].

The purpose of the MacArthur Study, the research methods employed, and the findings of the study are set out in the study's executive summary, which appears on the MacArthur Foundation's website and is summarized below.[39]

PURPOSE

Beliefs about the causes of mental disorder have shifted over the centuries, but the belief that mental disorder predisposes many of those suffering from it to behave violently has endured. Indeed, this belief appears to have increased in intensity in the past several decades, despite many educational campaigns designed to allay public apprehension.

These perceptions are reflected both in formal policies toward people with mental disorders and in the public's expectations about the role of mental health professionals in ensuring the safety of the community. Violence risk assessment now is widely assumed by policy makers and the public to be a core skill of the mental health professions and plays a pivotal role in mental health law throughout the world. "Dangerousness to others" is now a principal standard for inpatient commitment, outpatient commitment, and commitment to a forensic hospital. The imposition of tort liability on mental health professionals who negligently fail to anticipate and avert a patient's violence to others has become commonplace.

Despite the pervasiveness of violence risk assessment in mental health law, research continues to indicate that the unaided abilities of mental health professionals to perform this task are modest at best. Many have suggested that making available to clinicians statistical (actuarial) information on the empirical relationships between various risk factors and subsequent violent behaviour is the only way to reduce the disconnect between what the law demands and what clinicians currently are able to provide.

RESEARCH METHODS

Three sources of information were used to ascertain the occurrence and details of a violent incident in the community. Interviews with patients, interviews with collateral individuals (that is, persons named by the patient as those who would know what was going on in his life), and official sources of information (arrest and hospital records) were all coded and compared. For the analyses reported here, the patients and collaterals were interviewed twice (every ten weeks) over the first twenty weeks—approximately four to five months—from the date of hospital discharge. Violence to others was

---

39   Adapted from the executive summary of the MacArthur Violence Risk Assessment Study, online: www.macarthur.virginia.edu/risk.html.

defined to included acts of battery that resulted in physical injury, sexual assaults, assaultive acts that involved the use of a weapon, or threats made with a weapon in hand.

RESULTS

At least one violent act during the first twenty weeks after discharge from the hospital was committed by 18.7 percent of the patients we studied. Of the 134 risk factors we measured in the hospital, approximately half (70) had a statistically significant bivariate relationship with later violence in the community ($p < 0.05$). Below are some examples of specific risk factors that were — or were not — significantly related to violence.

- *Gender*: Men were somewhat more likely than women to be violent, but the difference was not large. Violence by women was more likely than violence by men to be directed against family members and to occur at home, and less likely to result in medical treatment or arrest.
- *Prior violence*: All measures of prior violence — self-report, arrest records, and hospital records — were strongly related to future violence.
- *Childhood experiences*: The seriousness and frequency of having been physically abused as a child predicted subsequent violent behaviour, as did having a parent — particularly a father — who was a substance abuser or a criminal.
- *Neighbourhood and race*: While there was an overall association between race and violence, African Americans and whites who lived in comparably disadvantaged neighbourhoods had the same rates of violence.
- *Diagnosis*: A diagnosis of a major mental disorder — especially a diagnosis of schizophrenia — was associated with a lower rate of violence than a diagnosis of a personality or adjustment disorder. A co-occurring diagnosis of substance abuse was strongly predictive of violence.
- *Psychopathy*: Psychopathy, as measured by a screening version of the Hare Psychopathy Checklist, was more strongly associated with violence than any other risk factor we studied. The "antisocial behaviour" component of psychopathy, rather than the "emotional detachment" component, accounted for most of this relationship.
- *Delusions*: The presence of delusions — or the type of delusions or the content of delusions — was not associated with violence. A generally "suspicious" attitude toward others was related to later violence.
- *Hallucinations*: Neither hallucinations in general, nor "command" hallucinations *per se*, elevated the risk of violence. If voices specifically commanded a violent act, however, the likelihood of violence was increased.

◆ *Violent thoughts*: Thinking or daydreaming about harming others was associated with violence, particularly if the thoughts or daydreams were persistent.

◆ *Anger*. The higher a patient scored on the Novaco Anger Scale in the hospital, the more likely she was to be violent later in the community.

1) Demographic Factors Associated with Increased Risk

In this category, younger males, especially with regard to violent crime, are better represented, as are those who are unemployed and of low socio-economic status. Low educational achievement, learning disorders, and attention deficit/hyperactivity disorder correlate to violence later in life.

2) Past History of Violence

There is no doubt that a past history of violence is one of the most powerful predictors of future potential for violence.

3) Substance Abuse

Drug and alcohol abuse and dependence are significant contributors to violence in both non-mentally disordered and mentally disordered offenders. Substance abuse is more prevalent in mentally disordered offenders than in the general population. Substance abuse doubles the lifetime risk of violence in severely mentally disordered accused, particularly if the substance abuse began early in life.

4) Psychiatric Diagnosis and Risk for Violence

The risk for violence is several times greater in individuals suffering from psychosis than occurs in the general population. Earlier studies regarding the relationship between schizophrenia and violence were equivocal. As noted, the relationship is a function of psychiatric symptoms and their intensity more so than the actual diagnosis.

5) Acute Psychiatric Symptoms

a) Mania and Violence

See the definition of a manic episode in Chapter 1. Mania, which is characterized by either an irritable or elevated mood and a sense of grandiosity as well as psychomotor activation, can result in threatening and assaultive behaviour. Violence can occur as the result of an anticipatory assault by a paranoid manic patient, or when there is interference with his grandiose scheme.

b) Depression and Violence

See the definition of a depressive episode in Chapter 1. Patients who are significantly depressed may be suicidal. Suicide is an ambivalent act frequently associated with oscillating intention. Self-loathing can cause the patient to direct the aggression towards himself, but in an instant, that self-loathing can become redirected towards others (towards whom the patient harbours ill-will, and of which she may or may not be aware of at a conscious level) and result in marked violence.

Depression is occasionally severe enough to lead to psychosis. The depressed individual may suffer delusions with implications for the safety of others, particularly family members. For example, a depressed patient might develop the delusional notion that a family member is seriously ill and headed towards a painful death. The individual may then feel justified in taking that family member's life (and potentially his own life, as well as those of other family members) to spare both the victim and family members a worse fate.

c) Delusions and Violence

Please note the definition for delusion in Chapter 1. Delusions that are particularly relevant here are those of being threatened by others, which may be associated with an attendant need to strike out pre-emptively. In the category of delusions, certain specific and well-known delusional syndromes that lead to stalking behaviour are associated with a high risk for violence.

Stalking is sometimes associated with delusional ideation. In the typology of stalkers, the most common type is the rejected partner who simply cannot take "no" for an answer. Although that subtype of stalker often exhibits personality pathology, he is unlikely to be psychotic. There are several subtypes of stalkers who are, however, psychotic, most notably the erotomanic (that is, delusional disorder — erotomanic subtype). These stalkers believe that an individual, often someone outside their social or economic sphere, is in love with them and sending them (often telepathic) messages encouraging a relationship. Other subtypes of stalkers include those who perceive the victim as the best match for them (pathological love), and those who suffer from pathological jealousy. This latter state can be lethal to a victim if the perpetrator develops the view that if he can't have the victim, then no one else will.

d) Hallucinations and Violence

Of greatest concern here are command voices directing the accused to engage in dangerous behaviour. Some studies have indicated that individuals who hear command auditory hallucinations act on them in 40 percent of cases. The risk of violence is evidently greater when the voice is familiar to the accused (for example, his mother).

6) Violent Fantasies

Violent fantasies or homicidal thoughts of one kind or another, at one time or another, occur fairly commonly in the general male population (about 70 percent have had them). Persistent violent thoughts, however, are worrisome, and are associated with violence, especially in patients with severe substance abuse. These individuals are more dangerous than acutely psychotic individuals.

7) Severe Personality Pathology

The most notable personality pathology associated with criminality and violence are antisocial personality disorder (ASPD) and psychopathic personality. The diagnostic entities psychopathy and ASPD are often used synonymously in error. Although there is a measure of (behavioural) similarity between the two, they are distinct diagnostic entities. In the interest of greater diagnostic certainty, the American Psychiatric Association, in the third edition of the *Diagnostic and Statistical Manual of Mental Disorders*, recast an earlier description of psychopathic personality as the behavioural syndrome that became to be known as ASPD.[40]

a) Antisocial Personality Disorder

Of four seemingly synonymous concepts (psychopathy, sociopathy, habitual criminal, and ASPD), ASPD is the only category represented as a discrete diagnosis in the fourth edition of the *Diagnostic and Statistical Manual of Mental Disorders*.[41] The diagnostic criteria for ASPD are as follows:

---

40   *Diagnostic and Statistical Manual of Mental Disorders*, 3d ed. (Washington, DC: American Psychiatric Association, 1980) [DSM III].

41   *Diagnostic and Statistical Manual of Mental Disorders*, 4th ed., Text Revision (Washington, DC: American Psychiatric Association, 2000) [DSM IV-TR].

1. There is a pervasive pattern of disregard for and violation of the rights of others occurring since age fifteen years, as indicated by three (or more) of the following:

    (a) failure to conform to social norms with respect to lawful behaviours as indicated by repeatedly performing acts that are grounds for arrest;

    (b) deceitfulness, as indicated by repeated lying, using of aliases, or conning others for personal profit or pleasure;

    (c) impulsivity or failure to plan ahead;

    (d) irritability and aggressiveness, as indicated by repeated physical fights or assaults;

    (e) reckless disregard for safety or self or others;

    (f) consistent irresponsibility, as indicated by repeated failure to sustain consistent work behaviour or honour financial obligations;

    (g) lack of remorse, as indicated by being indifferent to or rationalizing having hurt, mistreated, or stolen from another.

2. The individual is at least age eighteen years.

3. There is evidence of conduct disorder with onset before age fifteen years.

4. The occurrence of antisocial behaviour is not exclusively during the course of schizophrenia or a manic episode.[42]

DSM IV-TR continues to set out a predominantly behavioural syndrome in describing the features of ASPD, and implies that it is synonymous with psychopathy. Under the heading "Associated Features and Disorders," DSM IV-TR mentions some of the core psychopathic features: "They may have an inflated and arrogant self-appraisal (e.g. feel that ordinary work is beneath them ...) and may be excessively opinionated, self-assured or cocky. They may display a glib or superficial charm, and can be quite voluble and verbally facile ..."[43]

ASPD is highly represented in the severely mentally ill population and in prisons (50–70 percent). It correlates strongly with substance abuse, and is a strong predictor of criminal recidivism, particularly violent recidivism.

b) Psychopathy

The designation (psychopath) defines a personality construct that has frequently been considered as synonymous with sociopath, habitual criminal, and antisocial personality. Psychopathic personalities frequently subsume

---

42   *Ibid.* at 706. Reprinted with the permission of the American Psychiatric Association. © 2000.

43   *Ibid.* at 703.

the unempathic, aloof, grandiose, and interpersonally exploitative style of narcissistic personalities and the behavioural, impulsive, and lifelong criminal lifestyle characteristics of antisocial personalities. Clinicians and researchers frequently rely on the *Hare Psychopathy Checklist — Revised*[44] as a means of defining the extent to which an individual qualifies for the clinical construct "psychopath." High scores are consistently correlated to violence in both forensic patients and incarcerated offenders. The MacArthur Study confirms that the construct of psychopathy, as measured by the twelve-item *Hare Psychopathy Checklist: Screening Version,*[45] has particularly robust predictive abilities compared to many of the other risk factors that are often considered.[46] Psychopathy is a centre-stage concept when it comes to assessing risk for violence to others. This may in part be due to the fact that each of the twenty items on the Hare PCL-R has been carefully defined.[47]

8) The Role of Organic Factors and Learning Disorders

Prominent here are seizure disorders: epilepsy (see Chapter 5, Section H.2(a)) and attention deficit/hyperactivity disorder (ADHD) (see definition in Chapter 1). ADHD in childhood is associated with childhood aggression, conduct disorder behaviour, and criminality later in life.

9) Biological Factors and Risk for Violence

This group consists of either congenital or acquired brain abnormalities. Genetic defects are characteristic of the first group, whereas perinatal neurological damage, frontal lobe injury or atrophy, brain trauma, or other neuropsychiatric disorders are characteristic of the acquired brain abnormality category.

10) Attachment Disorders, Early Childhood Learning, and Criminality and Relationship to Victim

Apart from biological predisposition, children learn the rules of the world through key relationships and through close interaction and intimacy with

---

44   R. Hare, *The Hare Psychopathy Checklist-Revised* (Toronto: Multi-Health Systems, 1991) [PCL-R]. See Chapter 1, Section C.4.

45   S.D. Hart, D. Cox *et al.*, *The Hare Psychopathy Checklist: Screening Version* (Toronto: Multi-Health Systems, Inc., 1995) [PCL:SV].

46   See J. Monahan, H.J. Steadman *et al.*, *Rethinking Risk Assessment*, above note 38.

47   See C.D. Webster & C. Dassinger, above note 15.

primary caregivers. The absence of key relationships or disruption of these attachments can lead to significant psychopathology and criminality in some individuals later on life.

The precise relationship between early childhood adverse experiences such as abuse or neglect and criminality and violence has yet to be fully elucidated, but it appears that there is such a relationship, and likely a fairly a significant one.

11) Adverse Early Life Experiences, and Their Relationship to Mental Disorder and Violence

There is some evidence, albeit incomplete, of a relationship between negative early life experiences and subsequent criminality and violence.[48]

F. THE COMPREHENSIVE VIOLENCE RISK EVALUATION

A comprehensive violence (and sexual recidivism) risk assessment requires a thorough investigative approach carried out by a specifically trained consultant. Even a cursory glance at the figure that follows (see Section F.3, below) demonstrates the breadth and scope of information required to do a thorough and proper risk assessment, and further leaves the impression that the amount of information to be synthesized before an opinion can be given is, at a minimum, a daunting task. A non-exhaustive list of key areas to be considered and reported in respect of a risk assessment are reviewed below.

1) Documentary Information

The subject's complete medical and psychiatric histories must be obtained and reviewed. In the case of the subject's psychiatric history, examiners must obtain as much detail as possible about medication compliance and the factors, stressors, and environments that either promote decompensation or foster stability.

Clinicians must obtain detailed documentary information, to the extent possible, about the subject's history of psychoactive substance use. The inquiry should look into use of substances such as alcohol, street drugs, prescription medications, or abuse of over-the-counter medications. This review

---

48 For a more detailed review of the issues covered in Chapter 8, Section E: Mental Disorder and Risk for Violence, see S.J. Hucker, *Psychiatric Aspects of Risk Assessment* (2003), online: www.forensicpsychiatry.ca.

is particularly important given the well-known association between psycho-active substance use and crime, particularly violent crime. Records should be obtained from any alcohol or drug rehabilitation programs to determine what inroads the subject made in resolving any substance abuse problems. One often finds that individuals with substance abuse problems who engage in criminality are unable to endure the program's duration. Records referable to criminal and violence histories often provide details about the circumstances, victim variables, and psychological and emotional correlates of the offending behaviour. Records should be obtained that provide observations about the individual's functioning in a variety of settings, such as school, work, or the military, while subject to probation and other supervision orders.

2) Collateral Interviews

Individuals who have known the subject in a variety of settings, such as family members, spouses, probation officers, etc., should be interviewed. Although experts (and others) are often cautious about potentially re-traumatizing victims by interviewing them, victims should be interviewed if collateral documentation fails to provide information relevant to offending behaviour.

3) Clinical Assessment

Psychiatric evaluations should focus on all aspects of the individual's history, with special emphasis on criminality, violence, substance abuse, sexual history, relationships, life stressors, and a detailed evaluation of the accused's mental state. Apart from serving as a method of gathering information that may not be available in the documentation and providing an opportunity to test the quality and veracity of the subject's report as against documented fact, the clinical assessment creates an opportunity to evaluate a number of potentially important and changeable clinical variables associated with risk. In this regard, Douglas and Skeem emphasize the importance of assessing *risk state*—a dynamic and more fluid dimension of an individual's potential for violence, impacted over time in response to interventions—as opposed to their *risk status*, which is more of an unchanging estimate based on an appraisal of the individual's risk assessed at a single point in time.[49]

---

49   See K.S. Douglas & J.L. Skeem, "Violence Risk Assessment: Getting Specific About Being Dynamic" (2005) 11 Psychology, Public Policy, and Law 347.

Psychological assessment plays an important role in appraising risk. Apart from standard psychological testing (see the figure below) that provides valuable measures of personality, authenticity, amenability to treatment, motivation, impression management, and experience and expression of anger, psychologists are often more adept at appraising and scoring subjects on the various (particularly actuarial) violence risk appraisal tools discussed in Section F.4, below.

The Comprehensive Violence and Sexual Violence Risk Appraisal

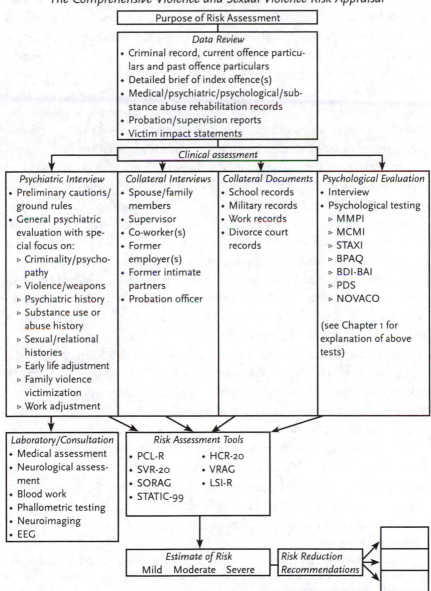

4) Actuarial Prediction vs. Structured Clinical Approach

Work over the last twenty years has resulted in the creation of a number of schemes designed to assess risk for violence. While most clinicians and workers in the field concede that it is not possible to predict violence with unequivocal accuracy, the various tools (described below) have significantly improved predictive abilities in this area. There is an ongoing debate as to which method—actuarial or clinical prediction—is best in relation to assessing risk in mentally disordered patients and persons accused or convicted of violence. The debate need not be entirely resolved, particularly given limitations inherent in either method. The debate regarding which is the preferred approach—actuarial assessment or structured clinical guide—is a fruitless one. A prudent clinician will harness the value of both actuarial and structured clinical approaches in the interest of doing the most thorough evaluation possible.[50] Mossman points out that if the choice were between using actuarial measures or unaided clinical judgment, then the actuarial method is arguably the preferred approach.[51] Clinical judgment alone (that is, unaided and unstructured) is a thing of the past. Most current clinicians, even those predisposed to a clinical approach, tend to rely on clinical aids and tools that incorporate actuarial elements, as well as dynamic risk factors that have been extracted from clinical practice and the scientific literature only following a process of careful critical appraisal and selection (and more recently, research).

Lawyers, judges and clinicians are invited to consider a hybrid but eminently sensible position; that is, one that suggests that both clinical and actuarial risk projections (and the tools used in each approach) are important in assessing an individual's potential for future violence. The more important and more encompassing issue is what kinds of credible information has the risk assessor/violence predictor considered in formulating an individual's risk for violence, and can each contributing piece of information be substantiated as a variable deserving of consideration?

A number of Ontario's provincial psychiatric hospitals (which appraise risk for violence for various reasons, most notably with respect to the detention and conditions of detention of patients found NCR and held subject to a provincial or territorial review board) take the sensible approach of assessing subjects using a variety of risk appraisal tools (both actuarial and clinical) and then reconciling any discrepancy between the scores of one tool and another.

---

50   See C.D. Webster, S.J. Hucker *et al.*, "Transcending the Actuarial Versus Clinical Polemic in Assessing Risk for Violence" (2002) 29 Criminal Justice and Behavior 659.

51   See D. Mossman, above note 1.

Judges should have a high index of suspicion when it comes to considering the evidence of experts who purport to define a person's future risk for violence by reference to a specific numeric figure—although in circles where the actuarial approach is preferred, a numeric range of probability is commonly provided. Violence risk assessment is inherently complex and uncertain, and does not lend itself to precise and accurate quantification.

a) Actuarial Tools

Actuarial tools approach violence prediction much in the way actuaries in the insurance industry approach appraising the cost of insurance for an individual whose demographic, historical, and other factors correlate, based on extensive research, with a specific and quantifiable degree of risk. The creators of actuarial instruments accord different but specific statistical weighting to different variables extracted from an individual's history. By their very nature, actuarial factors are fixed in time and unchangeable. Research prior to the creation of these tools involved careful and detailed follow-up of large numbers of patients over a time frame of many years. Those factors that subsequently correlated to a risk of recidivism were isolated and form the nucleus of actuarial tools. Mossman notes that it is easy to underestimate both the value of actuarial instruments and the advantages they afford over the old way of doing things. It is also easy to attribute more significance to results produced by actuarial measures than the developers of these measures intended.[52]

Best known amongst the various actuarial tools currently available is the *Violence Risk Appraisal Guide* (VRAG).[53] This instrument was created by drawing on data of mentally disordered offenders who were detained at the Oakridge/Penetanguishene maximum security psychiatric facility between 1965 and 1980. The VRAG is an actuarial tool that draws principally on the individual's PCL-R score and on a collection of other historic factors in order to forecast the individual's risk of violent recidivism within a circumscribed period of time (that is, seven to ten years). The VRAG items are as follows:

- Hare Psychopathy Checklist-Revised (PCL-R) score;
- elementary school maladjustment score (up to and includes grade eight);
- meets DSM III criteria for any personality disorder;

---

52   *Ibid.*
53   V.L. Quinsey, G.T. Harris *et al.*, *Violent Offenders: Appraising and Managing Risk* (Washington, DC: American Psychological Association, 1998).

- lived with both biological parents to age sixteen;
- failure on conditional release prior to index offence (charges, parole revocation, probation breach, failure to comply, including bail and failure to attend, etc.);
- Cormier-Lang score for juvenile and adult non-violent offence(s) predating index offence(s);
- marital status;
- meets DSM III criteria for schizophrenia (negatively related);
- victim injury (most serious) for index offence (negatively related);
- history of alcohol problem;
- age at index offence (as of last birthday before it); and
- female victim (negatively related).[54]

As noted earlier, the Hare PCL-R does a good deal of the VRAG's predictive work. The items of the Hare PCL-R are set out as follows:

- glibness/superficial charm;
- grandiose sense of self worth;
- need for stimulation/proneness to boredom;
- pathological lying;
- conning/manipulative;
- lack of remorse or guilt;
- shallow affect;
- callous/lack of empathy;
- parasitic lifestyle;
- poor behavioural controls;
- promiscuous sexual contacts;
- early behaviour problems;
- lack of realistic, long-term goals;
- impulsivity;
- irresponsibility;
- failure to accept responsibility for own actions;
- many short-term marital relationships;
- juvenile delinquency;
- revocation of conditional release; and
- criminal versatility.[55]

---

54   *Ibid.* at 237–39 (adapted).
55   PCL-R, above note 44 at 1.

b) Structured Clinical Guides/Structured Professional Judgment

Structured clinical guides, or structured professional judgment (SPJ) as it is called more recently,[56] focus clinicians' attention on variables that have been established over the years (through research and clinical practice) when clinicians conduct risk assessment on correctional, forensic, or mental health populations. These guides are sometimes referred to as "decision enhancing" procedures or "best practice" guidelines. The Hare PCL-R[57] is one example of such a guide, as is the HCR-20,[58] the name of which is an acronym for its ten Historical items, five Clinical items, and five Risk Management items. Mossman characterizes the HCR-20 as an easy to understand device.[59] The HCR-20 manual clearly and succinctly describes published research data that supports the inclusion of the particular item.

The HCR-20 scheme is set out below. Each item is scored as either not present (o), possibly present (1), or definitely present (2), to yield a potential score of 40. Use of the scheme involves melding historical and dynamic risk factors in order to come up with a broad estimation of risk, expressed as low, moderate, or high risk for violent recidivism. Webster *et al.* organize the HCR-20 items as follows:[60]

HISTORICAL ITEMS

    (H1)   Previous Violence

    (H2)   Young Age at First Violent Incident

    (H3)   Relationship Instability

    (H4)   Employment Problems

    (H5)   Alcohol or Drug Abuse

    (H6)   Mental Disorder

    (H7)   Psychopathy

    (H8)   Early Maladjustment

    (H9)   Personality Disorder

    (H10) Prior Release or Detention Failure

---

56   C.D. Webster & C. Dassinger, above note 15.

57   PCL-R, above note 44.

58   See C.D. Webster, D. Eaves *et al.*, *The HCR-20 Scheme: The Assessment of Dangerousness and Risk* (Vancouver: Simon Fraser University and Forensic Psychiatric Services Commission of British Columbia, 1995); C.D. Webster, K.S. Douglas *et al.*, *The HCR-20: Assessing the Risk for Violence, Version 2.* (Burnaby, BC: Mental Health, Law, and Policy Institute, Simon Fraser University, 1997).

59   D. Mossman, above note 1.

60   Adapted from C.D. Webster, D. Eaves *et al.*, above note 58 at 11.

CLINICAL ITEMS

(C1) Lack of Insight

(C2) Negative Attitudes

(C3) Active Symptoms of Major Mental Illness

(C4) Impulsivity

(C5) Unresponsive to Treatment

RISK MANAGEMENT ITEMS

(R1) Plans Lack Feasibility

(R2) Exposure to Destabilizers

(R3) Lack of Personal Support

(R4) Non-compliance with Remediation Attempts

(R5) Stress

A variety of tools have been developed over the last number of years specific to different types of risk (for example, domestic and workplace violence), specific offence categories (criminal recidivism, violence, or sexual recidivism), and age groups (children, youth, and adults). The PCL-R and HCR-20, in particular, have spawned a number of population-specific risk assessment guides, intended as aids for clinicians and other service providers in evaluating risk for aggression in specific groups and to serve as a foundation for making meaningful recommendations for intervention. A representative number of these various population-specific and purpose-specific tools are set out below.

Domestic Violence: The Spousal Assault Risk Assessment (SARA)[61]

The SARA, a twenty-item clinical checklist of risk factors for spousal assault, was developed to address a rising concern about the pervasiveness of relational violence. Its principal purpose is to assess and consequently evaluate an individual's risk for future spousal violence. The SARA's twenty items were selected following an extensive review of the empirical literature on spousal assaults/domestic violence, and by a review of clinical articles authored by clinicians with extensive experience in evaluating men who have abused their partners. The SARA is not a psychological test in the usual sense. It need not be administered by a psychologist or credentialed individual. Its purpose is to assist any stakeholder in relational violence to arrive at a considered view of an individual's level of risk through the use of aided guidelines and judgment.

---

61 Adapted from P.R. Kropp, S.D. Hart *et al.*, *Manual for the Spousal Assault Risk Assessment Guide* (Toronto: Multi-Health Systems, Inc., 1999) at 29–49.

Evaluations of risk for relational violence are important in a number of contexts, including

- an alleged offender's candidacy for bail;
- sentencing;
- suitability for treatment in correctional contexts;
- parole or released decision-making;
- suitability for community treatment;
- family law matters, custody and access in particular; and
- a duty to warn the authorities about an individual's risk for harm to an intimate partner.

For example, a forty-two-year-old separated man with three young children was due to be released from custody after serving eighteen months for a number of serious charges involving threatening and aggressive behaviour towards a spouse who had rejected him. A marginal character at best, the offender could think about little else beyond violent retribution against his ex-wife, and potentially anyone who stood in the way of him gaining access to his children. His open and ongoing declaration of his fantasy and oscillating intention to commit this harm created the imminent serious physical and/or psychological danger to an identifiable victim or pool of victims that compels disclosure of otherwise confidential medical information to the authorities.[62]

An evaluation of an individual's risk for future spousal abuse must consider information from collateral information sources, such as criminal records, victim impact statements, probation reports, interviews with victims and family members, and not just from the subject of the assessment.

The SARA elaborates ten factors generally associated with the risk for violence and ten factors specific to spousal violence. The ten factors dealing with violence more generally include

1) past assault of family members;
2) past assault of strangers or acquaintances;
3) past violation of conditional release or community supervision;
4) recent relationship problems;
5) recent employment problems;
6) victim of and/or witness to family violence;
7) recent substance abuse/dependence;
8) recent suicidal or homicidal ideation/intent;

---

62   For a detailed discussion of the duty to disclose confidential information, see *Smith*, above note 4. See also Section C, above.

9) recent psychotic and/or manic symptoms; and

10) personality disorder with anger, impulsivity, or behavioural instability.

The ten factors dealing with spousal violence include:

1) past physical assault;

2) past sexual assault or sexual jealousy;

3) past use of weapons or credible threats to death;

4) recent escalation in severity or frequency of spousal assault;

5) past violation of no-contact orders;

6) extreme minimization or denial of spousal assault; and

7) attitudes that support or condone spousal assault.

Of these ten factors, three concern most recent incident:

8) severe or sexual assault;

9) use of weapons or credible threats of death; and

10) violation of no-contact orders.

The individual's risk is ultimately expressed in crude terms by rating it as low, moderate, or high.

Children and Youth: The Early Assessment of Risk List for Boys (EARL-20B),[63] *The Early Assessment of Risk List for Girls* (EARL-21G),[64] *and the Manual for the Structured Assessment of Violence Risk in Youth* (SAVRY)[65]

The EARL-20B is a twenty-item scheme designed to be used by trained clinicians, educators, and professionals experienced in working with high-risk boys under the age of twelve, considered to be demonstrating evidence of severe emotional and behavioural difficulties. The EARL-21G deals with the same age group and concerns, but in relation to girls. The SAVRY is the most recent addition in this genre of violence and aggression risk appraisal schemes. The SAVRY was specifically created to assess risk in adolescents between the ages of twelve and eighteen, and is applicable to both male and female adolescents. The SAVRY considers ten historical risk factors, six so-cial/contextual risk factors, and eight individual risk factors. The SAVRY is

---

63 L. Augimeri, C. Koegl *et al.*, *The Early Assessment of Risk List for Boys*, Version 2 (Toronto: Earlscourt Child and Family Centre, 2001) [EARL-20B].

64 K.S. Levene, L.K.Augimeri *et al.*, *The Early Assessment of Risk List for Girls*, Version 1, Consultation Edition (Toronto: Earlscourt Child and Family Centre, 2001) [EARL-21G].

65 R. Borum, P. Bartel *et al.*, *A Manual for the Structured Assessment of Violence Risk in Youth*, Version 1.1 (Tampa, FL: University of South Florida, 2002) [SAVRY].

otherwise unique in its innovation of specific consideration of six resiliency or protective factors.

Sexual Offenders: See Chapter 7.

Workplace Violence: *The Workplace Risk Assessment* (WRA-20)[66] and *The Employee Risk Assessment* (ERA-20)[67]

The WRA-20 is designed to evaluate organizational risk factors. Use of the WRA-20 compels the evaluator to focus on and consider risk factors for violence intrinsic to the workplace. All of the items listed in the WRA-20 are known to be associated with violent behaviour in both "blue collar" and "white collar" private and public sector work settings, including educational, religious, and recreational organizations. The twenty WRA items are organized under five headings: status, prevention, communication, responsiveness, and environment. The WRA-20 has as its goal to make organizational personnel, particularly management, more aware of deficiencies in the organization that may create or augment a risk for violence in the workplace.

The ERA-20 is a workplace violence assessment tool used by professionals to assist in carrying out a focused risk evaluation. It is based on the best known scientifically grounded and clinically-relevant risk factors. Systematic use of the ERA-20 by experienced and trained personnel can help them reach a judgment as to whether the subject is at low, medium, or high risk of perpetrating particular forms of violence in the workplace. It also allows for identification of interventions designed to reduce risk.

5) Risk Assessment Conclusions

The conclusions should detail the rationale behind the appraisal of risk. Risk assessments should make recommendations as to how risk could be reduced and, in the course of doing so, explain the relationship between the recommendation and its impact on risk.

G. ORDERING A RISK ASSESSMENT

There are no provisions in the *Criminal Code* specifically providing for the order of a "risk assessment." There are, however, a number of instances where

---

66 H. Bloom, R.S. Eisen *et al.*, *The Workplace Risk Assessment*, Version 1a (Toronto: workplace.calm, inc., 2002) [WRA-20].

67 H. Bloom, C.D. Webster *et al.*, *The Employee Risk Assessment* (Toronto: workplace.calm, inc., 2002) [ERA-20].

risk assessment will form a significant part of the more broadly framed assessment, as outlined below.

1) Assessments ordered pursuant to provincial legislation in relation to judicial interim release (see Chapter 4, Section A) or sentencing (see Chapter 9).

2) Assessments ordered pursuant to section 672.11(d) to determine the least onerous and least restrictive disposition in respect of accused found to be either unfit to stand trial or not criminally responsible on account of mental disorder (see Chapter 9).

3) Assessments ordered pursuant to the provisions of section 752.1(1) in respect of applications to have an accused declared a dangerous or long-term offender (see Chapter 10).

H. CONCLUSION: PRINCIPLES OF RISK ASSESSMENT AND MANAGEMENT

Risk assessment is a complex and evolving discipline that has, over the last thirty years, increasingly drawn on scientific advances in order to underpin that discipline. A number of uniquely helpful guidelines and schemes concerning the way risk assessment should be carried out are the results of those efforts. Key amongst these guidelines is that assessments of a matter as weighty as an individual's future risk (and all attendant implications, depending on the legal context) must be carried out having regard to some form of structure that, if nothing else, ensures that important information is not overlooked, and unimportant information is not relied upon. This is best accomplished by seeing to it that the most relevant data is obtained through the medium of risk assessment schemes that consider actuarial risk and SPJ. If an analogy is appropriate, then the authors prefer the model of the pre-flight checklist that pilots unwaveringly carry out to ensure that any potential risk factor associated with the intended flight has been deliberately addressed before anyone is put at risk.

Our conclusions, which we believe apply to all risk contexts—civil, criminal, correctional, the workplace, and national security—are succinctly summarized in the various points made below:

- The purpose of the risk assessment must be absolutely clear and specific to the legal issues that lead to the assessment.
- Experts must concede the appreciable limitations to their approach, whether they incline towards an actuarial or structured clinical meth-

odology, given inherent limitations in the discipline of violence risk assessment. Experts should also acknowledge any shortcomings in their approach, or in the comprehensiveness of their data.

- Risk assessments are not fishing expeditions. The legal pronouncements that can be made as a result of a risk assessment are almost invariably weighty and involve restriction of liberty and privileges. In the criminal arena, risk assessments are specifically tied to the legal test or standard that is the subject matter of the particular case (for example, long-term and dangerous offender proceedings, release under the *Corrections and Conditional Release Act*,[68] release or de-restriction from the jurisdiction of a provincial or territorial review board, and in the civil context, civil commitment, etc.). Risk assessments are particularly problematic when the behaviour or contingency that is the subject of concern occurs so infrequently in society (that is, has a low base rate), that few, if any, generalizations or predictions can be made about its likelihood to recur.

- Members of any potential victim pool must be identified.

- The actuarial versus SPJ approach to risk assessment debate need not be resolved. Clinicians should invariably obtain actuarial data in order to focus and strengthen risk assessment,[69] and to incorporate it into an overall appraisal of the subject's risk that includes other relevant factors such as current clinical state, future plans, victim and environmental variables, etc. The Hare PCL-R,[70] which is already a key component of several violence risk appraisal schemes, can reasonably be seen as the backbone of violence risk assessment.

- The risk management plan that follows as a consequence of the assessment should be specifically designed for the subject of the assessment.

- Risk assessments must be thorough and consider both the subject's longitudinal and cross-sectional histories. Current best practices require risk assessors to incorporate as much accurate and objective data as is available in the case.

- The potential severity of the outcome is a factor to be considered, even when other variables favour de-restriction or release. In other words, even a relatively small risk of an absolutely heinous or catas-

---

68 S.C. 1992, c. 20.
69 H. Bloom, C.D. Webster *et al.*, "The Canadian Contribution," above note 27.
70 PCL-R, above note 44.

trophic outcome may skew favourable factors on the risk assessment in the direction of either ongoing detention or a more conservative approach to de-restriction. A gradual approach to releasing a mentally disordered offender is not only safest, but guards against the risk of potential errors due to inherent limitations in risk appraisal methods and technology.

- The conclusions and recommendations of a risk assessment should be expressed in clear and intelligible terms. They should identify and substantiate the risk factors, outline the variables that increase or decrease risk, as well as the interventions that will eliminate or modify risk.

- The best means of expressing the reality, limitations, and contingencies of a risk assessment are expressed by appropriately filling in the blanks of the following statement:

  ▷ This accused is at (what degree of) risk for (what harm(s)) through (what means) towards (whom) within (what time frame).

- Risk assessment evidence, if accepted by the trier of fact, often plays an important role both in according an accused the maximum amount of liberty, de-restriction, and privileges he or she is entitled to by law, and protecting society from dangerous people. With respect to accused being held under the jurisdiction of a provincial or territorial review board, case law makes it abundantly clear that every factor permissive of de-restricting an accused ought to be taken into consideration in order to fashion the least onerous and least restrictive alternative.[71]

Carefully and thoroughly conducted and thoughtfully presented risk assessments are complex exercises that allow mental health professionals to participate in some of the most challenging decisions a clinician (and more importantly a court) can make concerning an individual's fate and society's protection.

---

71   See *Winko v. British Columbia (Forensic Psychiatric Institute)*, [1999] 2 S.C.R. 625; *Regina v. Pinet* (1995), 23 O.R. (3d) 97 (C.A.); and *Penetanguishene Mental Health Centre v. Ontario (Attorney General)*, [2001] O.J. No. 2016 (C.A.) [*Tulikorpi*].

CHAPTER NINE

Disposition and Sentencing

A. INTRODUCTION

This chapters deals with the mentally disordered accused following the rendering of a verdict. After a verdict of unfit to stand trial, or NCR, a "disposition" must be rendered, whereas after a finding of guilt and/or a conviction the accused must be sentenced. To paraphrase Plato: injustice may result when two accused are dealt with in a different manner; greater injustice may result when two accused are dealt with in the same manner.

B. DISPOSITIONS

1) The NCR Accused

The disposition-making provisions of Part XX.1 are set out in section 672.54 of the *Criminal Code*.[1] An accused must be discharged absolutely unless the court (at first instance) or review board is able to find affirmatively that the accused is a significant threat to the safety of the public.[2] Where this has been found, the accused may be either discharged from hospital subject to conditions, or detained in the custody of a hospital subject to conditions. The accused must receive the least onerous and least restrictive disposition after considering 1) the need to protect the public from dangerous persons; 2) the mental condition of the accused; 3) the reintegration of the accused into society; and 4) the other needs of the accused.

---

1   R.S.C. 1985, c. C-46.
2   See *Winko v. British Columbia (Forensic Psychiatric Institute)*, [1999] 2 S.C.R. 625 [*Winko*].

"Significant threat" means a real risk of physical or psychological harm. As noted in Chapter 3, Section N.3:

1. there is to be no presumption that the mentally disordered accused poses a significant threat to the safety of the public;

2. the accused is never in a position of having to disprove dangerousness—the accused is therefore relieved of any legal or evidentiary burden—the accused need do nothing (unless, of course, dangerousness is otherwise established);

3. this tactical incentive to adduce evidence is not properly described as a shifting of the legal or evidentiary burden to the accused;

4. if the court or review board is unable to conclude that the accused constitutes a significant threat to the safety of the public, the accused must be absolutely discharged;

5. jurisdiction over the accused cannot be maintained where there is doubt regarding dangerousness, continued jurisdiction requires an affirmative finding of significant threat;

6. the threat posed must be more than speculative in nature; it must be supported by the evidence;

7. the threat must also be "significant," both in the sense that there must be a real risk of physical or psychological harm occurring to individuals in the community and in the sense that this potential harm be serious. A miniscule risk of a grave harm will not suffice. Similarly, a high risk of trivial harm will not meet the threshold;

8. the conduct or activity creating the harm must be criminal in nature; and

9. finally, it is up to the court or review board to ensure that it has sufficient information in order to make the determination.[3]

"Significant threat" clearly contemplates a prospective inquiry.[4] The least onerous and least restrictive standard must be applied to not only the type of disposition imposed (that is, discharge, discharge subject to conditions, or detention subject to conditions) but to the particular conditions themselves.[5]

---

3   *R. v. Kearly*, [2005] O.J. No. 5394 (Ct. J.).
4   *Ibid.*
5   *Penetanguishene Mental Health Centre v. Ontario (Attorney General)* (2003), [2004] 1 S.C.R. 498 [*Tulikorpi*].

2) The Unfit Accused

While a treatment order is also defined as a disposition, here, we are assuming that a treatment order has either not been made or was unsuccessful and, therefore, the accused remains unfit. We are also assuming that the court has been satisfied with respect to the provisions of section 672.45 of the *Criminal Code* concerning disposition hearings:

> *Hearing to be held by a court*
>
> 672.45 (1) Where a verdict of not criminally responsible on account of mental disorder or unfit to stand trial is rendered in respect of an accused, the court may of its own motion, and shall on application by the accused or the prosecutor, hold a disposition hearing.

> *Transmittal of transcript to Review Board*
>
> (1.1) If the court does not hold a hearing under subsection (1), it shall send without delay, following the verdict, in original or copied form, any transcript of the court proceedings in respect of the accused, any other document or information related to the proceedings, and all exhibits filed with it, to the Review Board that has jurisdiction in respect of the matter, if the transcript, document, information or exhibits are in its possession.

> *Disposition to be made*
>
> (2) At a disposition hearing, the court shall make a disposition in respect of the accused, if it is satisfied that it can readily do so and that a disposition should be made without delay.

That, first of all, a disposition hearing has been held; and secondly, that the court can readily make a disposition, and that one should be made without delay.

The disposition-making provisions of Part XX.1 are set out in section 672.54. The options for the unfit accused are exactly the same as for the NCR accused, except that an unfit accused may *not* be discharged absolutely. That is because an unfit accused is, while subject to the terms of a disposition, also subject to the jurisdiction of the court where the information or indictment remains. Subsection 672.54(a), if invoked, terminates the accused's matter and would therefore be inconsistent with the notion that an unfit accused returns to court if and when the accused becomes fit.

However, the Supreme Court of Canada has recently found that the failure of parliament to provide for the possibility of an absolute discharge for an accused who is permanently unfit and not dangerous violates provisions of the *Charter* and therefore sent the legislation back to parliament for revision.[6] The result is section 672.851 which is set out in its entirety and discussed in Chapter 3, Section N. The new provisions permit a judicial stay of proceedings where certain conditions are satisfied, including that the accused is permanently unfit to stand trial, is not likely to ever become fit, and is not a significant threat to the safety of the public.

a)   Discharge Subject to Conditions

Principally, this means that the accused is discharged from hospital.[7] Therefore, the court (or review board) cannot discharge an accused and then make it a term that the accused reside at a hospital.

b)   Detention Hospital

While not explicitly stated, "detention in hospital" has by convention been taken to encompass a wide range of dispositions from detention in a maximum security facility with no privileges to detention in minimum security with a "privilege," to be exercised by the administrator, to live in the community. There are a range of options in between these two extremes. Any term which is relevant to the provisions of section 672.54 may be included; however, there must be a rational connection between the restriction of liberty and the threat the accused poses. "Hospital" is defined in section 672.1 and means a hospital designated by the minister of health for the province (see Chapter 3).

c)   Counsel

While the accused's fitness is in issue or the accused has a verdict of unfit to stand trial, it is mandatory that the accused be represented by counsel (section 672.24). Where the accused is not represented by counsel, the court shall order that the accused be represented by counsel. Counsel should be appointed prior to the making of an assessment order.

> *Counsel*
>
> 672.24 (1) Where the court has reasonable grounds to believe that an accused is unfit to stand trial and the accused is not represented by counsel, the court shall order that the accused be represented by counsel.

---

6   *R. v. Demers,* [2004] 2 S.C.R. 489.

7   *British Columbia (Forensic Psychiatric Institute) v. Johnson,* [1995] B.C.J. No. 2247 (C.A.).

Counsel fees and disbursements

(2) Where counsel is assigned pursuant to subsection (1) and legal aid is not granted to the accused pursuant to a provincial legal aid program, the fees and disbursements of counsel shall be paid by the Attorney General to the extent that the accused is unable to pay them.

Taxation of fees and disbursements

(3) Where counsel and the Attorney General cannot agree on the fees or disbursements of counsel, the Attorney General or the counsel may apply to the registrar of the court and the registrar may tax the disputed fees and disbursements.

i) Assessment Orders

Where the court has reasonable grounds to believe that further information is needed to make a disposition or hold a hearing, the court may order an assessment pursuant to the provisions of subsection 672.11(d).

With the proclamation of Bill C-10 on 19 May 2005, the review boards were, for the first time, given statutory authority to order assessments of the accused. Arguably, one can find common law authority for such a power in *Winko* given the review board's obligation to obtain sufficient information to make a disposition.

Review Board may order assessment

672.121 The Review Board that has jurisdiction over an accused found not criminally responsible on account of mental disorder or unfit to stand trial may order an assessment of the mental condition of the accused of its own motion or on application of the prosecutor or the accused, if it has reasonable grounds to believe that such evidence is necessary to

(a) make a recommendation to the court under subsection 672.851(1); or

(b) make a disposition under section 672.54 in one of the following circumstances:

(i) no assessment report on the mental condition of the accused is available,

(ii) no assessment of the mental condition of the accused has been conducted in the last twelve months, or

(iii) the accused has been transferred from another province under section 672.86.

The apparent restriction contained in subsection 672.121(b)(i) can be diluted considerably. An "assessment report" must be read to be a *relevant* report. In that most reports which are available at this juncture will have had a focus other than recommendations under section 672.851, in most cases there will be no (relevant) report available, and therefore, an assessment order can be made notwithstanding a fresh/recent report on some other issue (for example, fitness).

For the same reasons as above, the apparent restriction in subsection 672.121(b)(ii) should generally not preclude a new assessment order from being made. Again, "assessment" must be read to mean assessment in respect of an issue before the court/board. Generally, assessments made within the past twelve months will not be relevant and should not be considered a limitation within the meaning of this provision.

With respect to subsection 672.121(b)(iii), where the accused has just arrived from another jurisdiction by way of interprovincial transfer (section 672.86), an assessment would typically be warranted in that "least onerous, least restrictive" must be assessed relative to the resources and in the context of where the accused will be living.

ii) Assessment
Assessment means an assessment by a medical practitioner (section 672.1). Form 48 is used in the making of the order by the court, whereas a Form 48.1 is used by the review board. While the above provisions pertain to the making of a court ordered assessment, any witness who is able to give relevant information may be called at the actual trial of the issue. Mental health practitioners such as psychologists may be particularly appropriate.

iii) Who May Request that an Assessment be Ordered?
Either party may request an assessment, or it may be ordered upon the court's own motion.

iv) Custody
It is presumed that all assessments will take place out of custody, with certain exceptions imported from subsection 515(10) (section 672.16).

v) Duration of the Assessment
An assessment order shall be in force for no more than thirty days or, in compelling circumstances, sixty days (section 672.14).

vi) Variation of Assessment Orders
This may be made upon application (section 672.18).

vii) Treatment of an Accused During an Assessment

An assessment order shall not direct an accused to receive or submit to treatment (section 672.19).

viii) Bail Hearings

No order for the release or detention of an accused shall be made while an assessment order is in force (section 672.17).

ix) Reports

An assessment order may direct the assessor to submit an assessment report (section 672.2(1)). Where a report is ordered it shall be filed with the court as directed (section 672.2(2)). It shall be provided to the prosecutor, the accused, and counsel for the accused (section 672.2(4)).

x) Disposition Information

Subject to the provisions of section 672.51, the court or review board shall consider assessment reports and any other written information about the accused that is relevant to making a disposition.

3) Disposition Hearings

Disposition hearings may be held in as informal a manner as is appropriate in the circumstances (section 672.5(1)). Evidence need not be taken under oath.

a) Terms of Disposition

Virtually any term that is logically connected to the accused's needs and risk may be included in either of the above dispositions with the exception of treatment, which may only be ordered with the accused's consent (section 672.55(1)).

b) Review of Court's Disposition

Where the court makes a disposition, it shall be reviewed by the review board within ninety days (subsection 672.47(3)). Where the court elects not to make a disposition, the review board shall hold a hearing and make a disposition within forty-five days (subsection 672.47(1)).

c) Reasons for Disposition

The court or review board shall state its reasons for making a disposition in the record of the proceedings and shall provide every party with a copy of the disposition and those reasons (section 672.52(3)).

C. SENTENCING

A just sentence must fit the offender as well as the offence. "The determination of a just and appropriate sentence is a delicate art which attempts to balance carefully the societal goals of sentencing against the moral blameworthiness of the offender and the circumstances of the offence, while at all times taking into account the needs and current conditions of and in the community."[8]

1) Mental disorder may have been operative in the commission of the offence but not to an extent sufficient to have an impact upon the verdict, or
2) The accused may have quite rationally elected not to raise the issue during the course of the trial notwithstanding the potential success of the defence,
3) The court must nevertheless take into consideration evidence of mental disorder during the sentencing process.

1) Particular Sentencing Considerations

Generally, mental disorder is seen as a factor in mitigation for the following reasons:

* The accused is viewed as less reprehensible.[9]
* The accused copes poorly in prison.[10]
* A reduced sentence may ensure that an accused receives needed psychiatric treatment.[11]
* The principle of general deterrence is not relevant.[12]
* The principle of specific deterrence is not relevant.[13]
* Sentences must not be made longer in order to facilitate treatment.[14] This is to be contrasted with the previously mentioned principle that an otherwise appropriate sentence may be reduced in order to facilitate treatment.

---

8   *R. v. C.A.M.*, [1996] 1 S.C.R. 500 at para. 91, Lamer C.J.C.
9   *R. v. Pegg* (1987), 24 O.A.C. 74 (C.A.); *R. v. Barker*, [1995] M.J. No. 154 (Prov. Ct.).
10   *R. v. Brown* (1972), 8 C.C.C. (2d) 13 (Ont. C.A.); *R. v. Shahnawaz* (2000), 40 C.R. (5th) 195 (Ont. C.A.).
11   *R. v. Wallace* (1973), 11 C.C.C. (2d) 95 (Ont. C.A.).
12   *R. v. Robinson* (1974), 19 C.C.C. (2d) 193 (Ont. C.A.); *R. v. Hynes* (1991), 64 C.C.C. (3d) 421 (Nfld. C.A.); *R. v. Peters*, [2000] N.J. No. 287 (C.A.).
13   *R. v. Valiquette* (1990), 60 C.C.C. (3d) 325 (Que. C.A.); *R. v. Hynes, ibid.*; *R. v. Peters, ibid.*
14   *R. v. Luther* (1971), 5 C.C.C. (2d) 354 (Ont. C.A.); *R. v. Lee*, [1985] N.S.J. No. 421 (C.A.).

- Sentences for mentally disordered accused must not exceed the tariff which would otherwise fit the offence.[15]
- A court has no jurisdiction to order that an accused serve his sentence in a psychiatric hospital.[16] However, where the accused and a hospital agree, it may be possible to accomplish a hospital stay within the terms of a conditional sentence.[17]

2) Assessments

Section 723(3) provides a means whereby the court may, on its own motion after hearing argument from the prosecutor and the offender, require the production of evidence that would assist it in determining the appropriate sentence.

Production of evidence

(3) The court may, on its own motion, after hearing argument from the prosecutor and the offender, require the production of evidence that would assist it in determining the appropriate sentence.

3) Consider Any Relevant Information

Section 726.1 requires the sentencing court to consider any relevant information placed before it, including representations or submissions made by or on behalf of the prosecutor or offender.

Relevant information

726.1 In determining the sentence, a court shall consider any relevant information placed before it, including any representations or submissions made by or on behalf of the prosecutor or the offender.

4) Report of Probation Officer

Section 721 provides for a report by a probation officer once a finding of guilt has been made.

Report by probation officer

721. (1) Subject to regulations made under subsection (2), where an accused, other than an organization, pleads guilty to or is found guilty of an

---

15   *R. v. Keefe* (1979), 44 C.C.C. (2d) 193 (Ont. C.A.); *R. v. Lyons*, [1987] 2 S.C.R. 309; *R. v. Hynes*, above note 12.
16   *R. v. Deans* (1977), 37 C.C.C. (2d) 221 (Ont. C.A.).
17   See also *R. v. Jacobish*, [1997] N.J. No. 225 (C.A.); *R. v. McCullough*, [1983] A.J. No. 858 (C.A.).

offence, a probation officer shall, if required to do so by a court, prepare and file with the court a report in writing relating to the accused for the purpose of assisting the court in imposing a sentence or in determining whether the accused should be discharged under section 730.

Provincial regulations

(2) The lieutenant governor in council of a province may make regulations respecting the types of offences for which a court may require a report, and respecting the content and form of the report.

Content of report

(3) Unless otherwise specified by the court, the report must, wherever possible, contain information on the following matters:

(a) the offender's age, maturity, character, behaviour, attitude and willingness to make amends;

(b) subject to subsection 119(2) of the *Youth Criminal Justice Act*, the history of previous dispositions under the *Young Offenders Act*, chapter Y-1 of the Revised Statutes of Canada, 1985, the history of previous sentences under the *Youth Criminal Justice Act*, and of previous findings of guilt under this Act and any other Act of Parliament;

(c) the history of any alternative measures used to deal with the offender, and the offender's response to those measures; and

(d) any matter required, by any regulation made under subsection (2), to be included in the report.

(4) The report must also contain information on any other matter required by the court, after hearing argument from the prosecutor and the offender, to be included in the report, subject to any contrary regulation made under subsection (2).

Copy of report

(5) The clerk of the court shall provide a copy of the report, as soon as practicable after filing, to the offender or counsel for the offender, as directed by the court, and to the prosecutor.

5) Psychiatric Assessments

Curiously, section 672.11, the general provisions with respect to assessments in Part XX.1 of the *Criminal Code*, do not provide for psychiatric assessments for the purposes of assisting the court with either judicial interim release or sentencing.

a) Assessments Pursuant to Civil Legislation

Sections 21 and 22 (for out-of-custody and in-custody, respectively) of the *Mental Health Act*,[18] however, may be used for the purpose of obtaining a psychiatric assessment in Ontario.[19] In other provinces, the civil mental health legislation may be relied upon to fill the gap in section 672.11 where the provisions permit. In Ontario these orders may be made on Forms 6 and 8, respectively (see Appendices H and I). Note that where legislation outside of the *Criminal Code* is relied upon to obtain psychiatric assessments, the array of protective provisions attached to section 672.11 (see section 21 of the *Criminal Code*) do not apply. It is recommended that the court make similar conditions as part of any order made outside of the *Criminal Code*.

6) Credit For Time Spent in Pre-Trial Custody

Although, as a matter of convention, courts have recognized the discretion to give an accused "enhanced" credit for time spent in pre-trial custody,[20] recently, courts have been giving a greater enhanced credit due to the substandard conditions (for example, overcrowding) at various remand centres. It may be that the courts will be confronted with the argument that greater enhanced credit should be given because of the accused's mental disorder and the consequent hardship resulting from a reduced ability to cope.

7) Terms Which May be of Assistance

While there is no ability to order that an accused submit to treatment other than under the exceptional circumstances set out in section 672.58, with the proclamation of Bill C-41, a court may direct the accused to rehabilitative programs which may mitigate the risk the accused poses to the community:

- within the context of a probation order "if the offender agrees and subject to the program director's acceptance of the offender, participate in a treatment program approved by the province" (clause 732.1(3)(g)).
- there may be much greater latitude to order hospitalization where the accused advocates such a term and the hospital agrees to admit the accused.[21]

---

18   R.S.O. 1990, c. M.7.
19   *R. v. Lenart* (1998), 123 C.C.C. (3d) 353 (Ont. C.A.).
20   *R. v. Wust* (2000), 143 C.C.C. (3d) 129 (S.C.C.); *R. v. Jabbour*, [2001] O.J. No. 3820 (S.C.J.); *R. v. Legere* (1995), 22 O.R. (3d) 89 (C.A.).
21   See *R. v. Knoblauch* (2000), 149 C.C.C. (3d) 1 (S.C.C.).

Optional conditions of probation order

(3) The court may prescribe, as additional conditions of a probation order, that the offender do one or more of the following:

(a) report to a probation officer

(i)   within two working days, or such longer period as the court directs, after the making of the probation order, and

(ii) thereafter, when required by the probation officer and in the manner directed by the probation officer;

(b) remain within the jurisdiction of the court unless written permission to go outside that jurisdiction is obtained from the court or the probation officer;

(c) abstain from

(i)   the consumption of alcohol or other intoxicating substances, or

(ii) the consumption of drugs except in accordance with a medical prescription;

(d) abstain from owning, possessing or carrying a weapon;

(e) provide for the support or care of dependants;

(f) perform up to 240 hours of community service over a period not exceeding eighteen months;

(g) if the offender agrees, and subject to the program director's acceptance of the offender, participate actively in a treatment program approved by the province;

(g.1) where the lieutenant governor in council of the province in which the probation order is made has established a program for curative treatment in relation to the consumption of alcohol or drugs, attend at a treatment facility, designated by the lieutenant governor in council of the province, for assessment and curative treatment in relation to the consumption by the offender of alcohol or drugs that is recommended pursuant to the program;

(g.2) where the lieutenant governor in council of the province in which the probation order is made has established a program governing the use of an alcohol ignition interlock device by an offender and if the offender agrees to participate in the program, comply with the program; and

(h) comply with such other reasonable conditions as the court considers desirable, subject to any regulations made under subsection 738(2), for protecting society and for facilitating the offender's successful reintegration into the community.

- comply with such other reasonable conditions as the court considers desirable, subject to any regulations made under subsection 738(2), for protecting society and for facilitating the offender's successful re-integration into the community (subsection 732.1(h).
- within the context of a conditional sentence "attend a treatment program approved by the Province" (clause 742.3(2)(e)). This is also arguably the accused's "option" in that declining the conditional sentence containing the offensive term is the accused's prerogative. There may be much greater latitude to order hospitalization where the accused is advocating for such a term and the hospital agrees to admit the accused.[22]

Optional conditions of conditional sentence order

(2) The court may prescribe, as additional conditions of a conditional sentence order, that the offender do one or more of the following:

(a) abstain from

    (i) the consumption of alcohol or other intoxicating substances, or

    (ii) the consumption of drugs except in accordance with a medical prescription;

(b) abstain from owning, possessing or carrying a weapon;

(c) provide for the support or care of dependants;

(d) perform up to 240 hours of community service over a period not exceeding eighteen months;

(e) attend a treatment program approved by the province; and

(f) comply with such other reasonable conditions as the court considers desirable, subject to any regulations made under subsection 738(2), for securing the good conduct of the offender and for preventing a repetition by the offender of the same offence or the commission of other offences.

The real value in having an accused attend at the offices of a mental health practitioner or facility lies not so much in having the accused submit to treatment as it does in having the accused *monitored regularly* so that if the accused does decompensate, the civil legislation can be employed to treat or hospitalize.

---

22   *Ibid.*

8) Delay in Sentencing

Section 720 provides that an accused shall be sentenced as soon as practicable after a finding of guilt. This should not be delayed to see how the accused behaves or responds to an interim treatment program.[23]

> *Sentencing proceedings*
>
> 720. A court shall, as soon as practicable after an offender has been found guilty, conduct proceedings to determine the appropriate sentence to be imposed.

---

23   *R. v. Cardin* (1990), 58 C.C.C. (3d) 221 (Que. C.A.).

CHAPTER TEN

Dangerous and Long-Term Offenders

A. INTRODUCTION

In Canada, and most other parts of the world, significant concerns in relation to high-risk violent offenders have been well documented in the media and have been the focus of high-profile inquests resulting in legislative amendments. Governments have employed a number of different methods in acting to protect society against the risk of violence posed by such offenders. Canada has had legislation focused on the high-risk offender since 1947, which was re-written in 1997. Part XXIV of the *Criminal Code*[1] provides for the category of long-term offender in addition to the classification of dangerous offender. Now, for the first time, a mechanism allows for supervision in the community for a limited period of time after a determinate sentence.

The number of offenders designated as dangerous offenders has increased over the last number of years as illustrated below in Figure 10.1.[2]

- As of 24 September 2000, there were 276 active dangerous offenders (DOs), representing approximately 2 percent of the total federal inmate population. Of these, 268 are incarcerated, 1 has been deported and 7 are being supervised in the community.
- Of the 276 DOs, 11 offenders have determinate sentences, whereas 265 have indeterminate sentences.
- The majority of DOs were designated in Ontario and British Columbia.
- There are currently no female DOs.

---

1   R.S.C. 1985, c. C-46.
2   Solicitor General of Canada, *High Risk Offenders: A Handbook for Criminal Justice Professionals* (Ottawa: Solicitor General of Canada, 2001) at 139 [*High Risk Offenders*].

Figure 10.1: *Number of Dangerous Offenders Declared per Year*

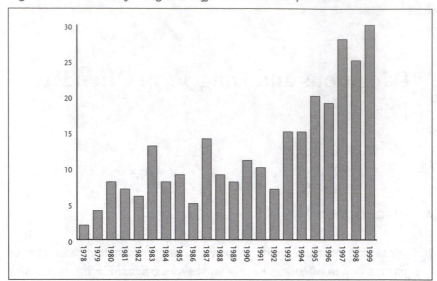

- ◆ Aboriginal offenders account for 17.4 percent of DOs and 17 percent of the total inmate population.

Note that in addition to the DOs, there remain within federal jurisdiction fifty-two dangerous sexual offenders and eight habitual offenders at the time of writing.[3]

B. STATUTORY PROVISIONS FOR DANGEROUS AND LONG-TERM OFFENDERS

1) Application for a Finding that an Offender is a Dangerous Offender

Clauses 753(1)(a) and (b) of the *Criminal Code*:

> 753. (1) The court may, on application made under this Part following the filing of an assessment report under subsection 752.1(2), find the offender to be a dangerous offender if it is satisfied
>
> (a) that the offence for which the offender has been convicted is a serious personal injury offence described in paragraph (a) of the definition of that expression in section 752 and the offender constitutes a threat to the

---

3   *Ibid.*

life, safety or physical or mental well-being of other persons on the basis of evidence establishing

(i) a pattern of repetitive behaviour by the offender, of which the offence for which he or she has been convicted forms a part, showing a failure to restrain his or her behaviour and a likelihood of causing death or injury to other persons, or inflicting severe psychological damage on other persons, through failure in the future to restrain his or her behaviour,

(ii) a pattern of persistent aggressive behaviour by the offender, of which the offence for which he or she has been convicted forms a part, showing a substantial degree of indifference on the part of the offender respecting the reasonably foreseeable consequences to other persons of his or her behaviour, or

(iii) any behaviour by the offender, associated with the offence for which he or she has been convicted, that is of such a brutal nature as to compel the conclusion that the offender's behaviour in the future is unlikely to be inhibited by normal standards of behavioural restraint; or that the offence for which the offender has been convicted is a serious personal injury offence described in paragraph (b) of the definition of that expression in section 752 and the offender, by his or her conduct in any sexual matter including that involved in the commission of the offence for which he or she has been convicted, has shown a failure to control his or her sexual impulses and a likelihood of causing injury, pain or other evil to other persons through failure in the future to control his or her sexual impulses.

2) Time for Making Application

Subsection 753(2) of the *Criminal Code*:

732 (2) An application under subsection (1) must be made before sentence is imposed on the offender unless

(a) before the imposition of sentence, the prosecution gives notice to the offender of a possible intention to make an application under section 752.1 and an application under subsection (1) not later than six months after that imposition; and (b) at the time of the application under subsection (1) that is not later than six months after the imposition of sentence, it is shown that relevant evidence that was not reasonably available to the prosecution at the time of the imposition of sentence became available in the interim.

3) Application for Remand for Assessment after Imposition of Sentence

Subsection 753(3) of the *Criminal Code*:

> 753 (3) Notwithstanding subsection 752.1(1), an application under that subsection may be made after the imposition of sentence or after an offender begins to serve the sentence in a case to which paragraphs (2)(a) and (b) apply.

4) If Offender Found to be Dangerous Offender

Subsection 753 (4) of the *Criminal Code*:

> (4) If the court finds an offender to be a dangerous offender, it shall impose a sentence of detention in a penitentiary for an indeterminate period.

5) If Application Made after Sentencing

Subsection 753(4.1) of the *Criminal Code*:

> (4.1) If the application was made after the offender begins to serve the sentence in a case to which paragraphs (2)(a) and (b) apply, the sentence of detention in a penitentiary for an indeterminate period referred to in subsection (4) replaces the sentence that was imposed for the offence for which the offender was convicted.

6) If Offender Not Found to be Dangerous Offender

Subsection 753(5) of the *Criminal Code*:

> (5) If the court does not find an offender to be a dangerous offender,
> (a) the court may treat the application as an application to find the offender to be a long-term offender, section 753.1 applies to the application and the court may either find that the offender is a long-term offender or hold another hearing for that purpose; or
> (b) the court may impose sentence for the offence for which the offender has been convicted.

7) Victim Evidence

Subsection 753(6) of the *Criminal Code*:

> (6) Any evidence given during the hearing of an application made under subsection (1) by a victim of an offence for which the offender was convicted

is deemed also to have been given during any hearing under paragraph (5)(a) held with respect to the offender.

C. APPLICATION FOR FINDING THAT AN OFFENDER IS A LONG-TERM OFFENDER

Subsection 753.1(1) of the *Criminal Code*:

753.1 (1) The court may, on application made under this Part following the filing of an assessment report under subsection 752.1(2), find an offender to be a long-term offender if it is satisfied that

(a) it would be appropriate to impose a sentence of imprisonment of two years or more for the offence for which the offender has been convicted;

(b) there is a substantial risk that the offender will reoffend; and

(c) there is a reasonable possibility of eventual control of the risk in the community.

1) Substantial Risk

Subsection 753.1(2) of the *Criminal Code*:

(2) The court shall be satisfied that there is a substantial risk that the offender will reoffend if

(a) the offender has been convicted of an offence under section 151 (sexual interference), 152 (invitation to sexual touching) or 153 (sexual exploitation), subsection 163.1(2) (making child pornography), subsection 163.1(3) (distribution, etc., of child pornography), subsection 163.1(4) (possession of child pornography), subsection 163.1(4.1) (accessing child pornography), section 172.1 (luring a child), subsection 173(2) (exposure) or section 271 (sexual assault), 272 (sexual assault with a weapon) or 273 (aggravated sexual assault), or has engaged in serious conduct of a sexual nature in the commission of another offence of which the offender has been convicted; and

(b) the offender

(i) has shown a pattern of repetitive behaviour, of which the offence for which he or she has been convicted forms a part, that shows a likelihood of the offender's causing death or injury to other persons or inflicting severe psychological damage on other persons, or

(ii) by conduct in any sexual matter including that involved in the commission of the offence for which the offender has been convicted, has shown a likelihood of causing injury, pain or other evil to other persons in the future through similar offences.

2) If Offender Found to be Long-Term Offender

Subsection 753.1(3) of the *Criminal Code*:

(3) Subject to subsections (3.1), (4) and (5), if the court finds an offender to be a long-term offender, it shall

(a) impose a sentence for the offence for which the offender has been convicted, which sentence must be a minimum punishment of imprisonment for a term of two years; and

(b) order the offender to be supervised in the community, for a period not exceeding ten years, in accordance with section 753.2 and the *Corrections and Conditional Release Act*.

3) Exception — If Application Made After Sentencing

Subsection 753.1(3.1) of the *Criminal Code*:

(3.1) The court may not impose a sentence under paragraph (3)(a) and the sentence that was imposed for the offence for which the offender was convicted stands despite the offender's being found to be a long-term offender, if the application was one that

(a) was made after the offender begins to serve the sentence in a case to which paragraphs 753(2)(a) and (b) apply; and

(b) was treated as an application under this section further to the court deciding to do so under paragraph 753(5)(a).

4) Exception — Life Sentence

Subsection 753.1(4) of the *Criminal Code*:

(4) The court shall not make an order under paragraph (3) (b) if the offender has been sentenced to life imprisonment.

5) Exception to Length of Supervison

Where new declaration. Subsection 753.1(5) of the *Criminal Code*:

(5) If the offender commits another offence while required to be supervised by an order made under paragraph (3)(b), and is thereby found to be a long-

term offender, the periods of supervision to which the offender is subject at any particular time must not total more than ten years.

6) If Offender Not Found to be Long-Term Offender

Subsection 753.1(6) of the *Criminal Code*:

(6) If the court does not find an offender to be a long-term offender, the court shall impose sentence for the offence for which the offender has been convicted.

7) Long-Term Supervision

Subsection 753.2(1) of the *Criminal Code*:

753.2 (1) Subject to subsection (2), an offender who is required to be supervised by an order made under paragraph 753.1(3)(b) shall be supervised in accordance with the *Corrections and Conditional Release Act* when the offender has finished serving

(a) the sentence for the offence for which the offender has been convicted; and

(b) all other sentences for offences for which the offender is convicted and for which sentence of a term of imprisonment is imposed on the offender, either before or after the conviction for the offence referred to in paragraph (a).

a) Authority to Impose Conditions of Release

Section 133(2) of the *Corrections and Conditional Release Act*[4] confers authority to impose standard conditions on all offenders. Section 133.1 provides for special authority to impose conditions for the release of long-term offenders.

Section 134.1(1) *CCRA* states that "every offender who is required to be supervised by a long-term supervision order is subject to the conditions prescribed by subsection 161(1) of the *Corrections and Conditional Release Regulations*[5] with such modifications as the circumstances require."[6]

8) Non-Carceral Sentences

Subsection 753.2(2) of the *Criminal Code*:

---

4   S.C. 1992, c. 20 [*CCRA*].
5   SOR/92-620 [*CCRR*].
6   *High Risk Offenders*, above note 2 at 151.

(2) A sentence imposed on an offender referred to in subsection (1), other than a sentence that requires imprisonment of the offender, is to be served concurrently with the long-term supervision ordered under paragraph 753.1(3)(b).

9) Application for Reduction in Period of Long-Term Supervision

Subsection 753.2(3) of the *Criminal Code*:

(3) An offender who is required to be supervised, a member of the National Parole Board, or, on approval of that Board, the parole supervisor, as that expression is defined in subsection 134.2(2) of the *Corrections and Conditional Release Act*, of the offender, may apply to a superior court of criminal jurisdiction for an order reducing the period of long-term supervision or terminating it on the ground that the offender no longer presents a substantial risk of reoffending and thereby being a danger to the community. The onus of proving that ground is on the applicant.

10) Notice to Attorney General

Subsection 753.2(4) of the *Criminal Code*:

(4) The applicant must give notice of an application under subsection (3) to the Attorney General at the time the application is made.

D. GENERAL DISCUSSION: APPLICATIONS FOR FINDING THAT AN OFFENDER IS A DANGEROUS OFFENDER UNDER SECTION 753 OF THE *CRIMINAL CODE*

Section 753 (see above) of the *Criminal Code* of Canada outlines the basis for an application for a finding of dangerous offender. An application is made following the conviction of a person for an offence but before the actual sentencing occurs. The Crown has the burden of showing beyond a reasonable doubt that the individual before the court has all the necessary elements present for the dangerous offender finding. The following conditions have to be met:

- The offence for which the offender has been convicted is a "serious personal injury offence" as defined in section 752 of the *Criminal Code* of Canada.
- In addition, the person before the court must constitute a threat to the life, safety, physical, or mental well-being of other persons on the basis

of evidence establishing that the person's behaviour comes within the categories of clause 753(1)(a)(i) to (iii) and (b) of the *Criminal Code* of Canada.

E. ASSESSMENTS UNDER SECTION 752.1 OF THE *CRIMINAL CODE*

Section 752.1(1) allows the court, if it is of the opinion there are reasonable grounds to believe the offender may be found a dangerous offender or long-term offender, to order the accused remanded for a period of not more than sixty days to the custody of a person the court directs who can perform an assessment or have one completed by experts. A report must be submitted not later than fifteen days after the end of the assessment period. A copy of the report is to be made available to both the prosecution and counsel for the offender. An assessment must, to be useful, address the above criteria.

Application for remand for assessment

752.1 (1) Where an offender is convicted of a serious personal injury offence or an offence referred to in paragraph 753.1(2)(a) and, before sentence is imposed on the offender, on application by the prosecution, the court is of the opinion that there are reasonable grounds to believe that the offender might be found to be a dangerous offender under section 753 or a long-term offender under section 753.1, the court may, by order in writing, remand the offender, for a period not exceeding sixty days, to the custody of the person that the court directs and who can perform an assessment, or can have an assessment performed by experts. The assessment is to be used as evidence in an application under section 753 or 753.1.

Report

(2) The person to whom the offender is remanded shall file a report of the assessment with the court not later than fifteen days after the end of the assessment period and make copies of it available to the prosecutor and counsel for the offender.

Note that in the past, the court had the discretion to declare a person a dangerous offender and, once that declaration was made, to impose a penitentiary term for an indeterminate period or, depending on the nature of the underlying offence, the court could impose a determinate sentence based on the likelihood of treatment being successful. Under Bill C-55,[7] this has now

---

7 S.C. 1997, c. 17.

changed. Where the court finds the accused to be a dangerous offender, an indeterminate sentence is the only option.

F. DISCRETION OF THE SENTENCING JUDGE

A sentencing court must take into consideration the long-term offender provisions prior to declaring an offender "dangerous" and imposing an indeterminate sentence. The language of subsection 753(1) of the *Criminal Code* indicates that a sentencing judge retains the discretion not to declare an offender dangerous even if the statutory criteria in paragraphs (a) or (b) are met.[8] The word "may" (in the phrase "may find the offender to be a dangerous offender") denotes a discretion. The proposition that a court is under a duty to declare an offender dangerous every time the statutory criteria are satisfied would introduce an unnecessary rigidity into the process and overshoot the public protection purpose.[9]

A judge's discretion as to whether to declare an offender dangerous must be guided by the relevant principles of sentencing contained in sections 718 to 718.2 of the *Criminal Code* which would include proportionality. A sentencing judge must also consider the possibility that a less restrictive sanction would attain the same sentencing objectives as one more restrictive. Therefore, if the sentencing options available under the long-term offender provisions are sufficient to reduce the threat to life, safety or physical or mental well-being of other persons to an acceptable level, the sentencing judge cannot properly declare an offender dangerous and thereupon impose an indeterminate sentence even if all the statutory criteria have been met. The imposition of an indeterminate sentence is justifiable only insofar as it actually serves the objective of protecting society. Prospective factors, including the possibility of eventual control of risk in the community, must thus be considered prior to a dangerous offender designation. Lastly, subsection 753(5) of the *Criminal Code* does not preclude a sentencing judge from considering the long-term offender provision until after she has already determined that the offender is not a dangerous offender.

Under subsection 753.1(3), if the court finds an offender to be a long-term offender, it shall: (a) impose a sentence for the offence for which the offender has been convicted, which sentence must be a minimum of punishment of

---

8   See *R. v. Johnson*, [2003] 2 S.C.R. 357.

9   *Ibid.*

two years; and (b) order the offender to be supervised in the community for a period not to exceed ten years.

G. DANGEROUS OFFENDER DESIGNATION

1) Conditions for Finding that an Offender is a Long-Term Offender

A dangerous offender designation will only be appropriate where the statutory criteria set out in subsection 753(1) have been met and a long-term offender designation cannot satisfy the sentencing principles.[10] The application for a finding that an offender is a long-term offender also requires an assessment report (section 752.1(1)). The court can find an offender to be a long-term offender if the court is satisfied that:

a) it would be appropriate to impose a sentence of imprisonment of two years or more for the offence for which the offender has been convicted;

b) there is a substantial risk that the offender will reoffend; and

c) there is a reasonable possibility of eventual control of risk in the community.

2) Meeting the "Substantial Risk that the Offender Will Reoffend" Test

The test that "there is a substantial risk that the offender will reoffend" contained in clause 753.1(1)(b) of the *Criminal Code* dealing with long-term offenders will be met if the following are found:

a) the offender has been convicted of an offence under sections 151 (sexual interference), 152 (invitation to sexual touching) or 153 (sexual exploitation), subsection 173(2) exposure or sections 271 (sexual assault), 272 (sexual assault with a weapon) or 273 (aggravated sexual assault) or has engaged in serious conduct of a sexual nature in the commission of another offence of which the offender has been convicted; and

b) the offender

   i) has shown a pattern of repetitive behaviour of which the offence for which he has been convicted forms a part that shows, a likelihood of the offender causing death or injury to other persons or inflicting severe psychological damage on other persons, or

   ii) by a conduct of any sexual matter including that involved in commission of the offence for which the offender has been convicted has

---

10   *Ibid.*

shown a likelihood of causing injury, pain, or evil to other persons in the future through similar offences.

If the individual is found to be a long-term offender the minimum period of incarceration imposed is two years and there must be an order for the offender to be supervised in the community for a period not to exceed ten years in accordance with section 753.2 of the *Criminal Code* and the *CCRA*.

H. CASE LAW

A considerable volume of decided cases are relevant to the above statutory provisions:

*   *R. v. Jackson*: The onus is on the prosecution to establish beyond a reasonable doubt all of the elements required to demonstrate that the accused is a dangerous offender.[11]
*   *R. v. Langevin*: The court held that the "pattern of repetitive behaviour" may be made out where there is only one other incident but both incidents display elements of similarity. With respect to the element of future conduct, the Crown need only establish an "existing likelihood."[12]
*   *R. v. Dawson*: The court found that "failure to control sexual impulses" required more than simply the proof of a conviction for a sexual offence. There has to be evidence of circumstances where there had clearly been a loss of control of sexual impulses and evidence to show such a problem. At the same time, the accused may call evidence to show that the conviction was not of a sexual nature or show that he had not failed to control his impulses.[13]
*   *R. v. George*: The pattern of "aggressive behaviour" must include a consideration of the social realities relevant to the accused. In this case, the accused's aboriginal status and disadvantaged background required a differentiation in considering childhood aggression as opposed to adult criminality for the purpose of determining the pattern of aggressive behaviour. Furthermore, the accused's "indifference" must include a consideration not only of the conduct at the time of the offence but also any genuine expressions of remorse after the crime.[14]

---

11   *R. v. Jackson* (1981), 23 C.R. (3d) 4 (N.S.S.C.A.D.).
12   *R. v. Langevin* (1984), 11 C.C.C. (3d) 336 (Ont. C.A.).
13   *R. v. Dawson*, [1970] 3 C.C.C. 212 (B.C.C.A.).
14   *R. v. George* (1998), 126 C.C.C. (3d) 384 (B.C.C.A.).

- *R. v. Neve*: A finding that one of the past conduct thresholds has been met does not automatically lead to a finding that the accused is a threat. The type of behaviour encompassed must involve some degree of actual or attempted violence or endangerment. "Repetitive behaviour" or "persistent behaviour" can be established by similarities either in the kind of offences or in the degree of violence or aggression inflicted.[15]

I.   ASSESSMENT CONSIDERATIONS

1)   General Principles

The most important consideration (as noted in Chapters 7 and 8) is that assessments of dangerousness and risk for violent and sexual recidivism be multidisciplinary and thorough in order that experts not miss any dimension of risk. As is the case with all medico-legal or psycho-legal evaluations, the assessment needs to concern itself with the legal standard enunciated in the relevant legislation or in case law. With respect to dangerous offender proceedings, the assessment team, psychiatrist and/psychologist will necessarily evaluate the psychological and psychiatric correlates of the legal test and components of the test enunciated in section 753. Consequently, it goes without saying that the criteria to be met by the legislation, for example, the "likelihood of causing death or injury to other persons, or inflicting severe psychological damage on other persons" contemplates some measure of forecasting an individual's future dangerousness. In this regard, experts need not opine that it is a foregone conclusion that an offender will recidivate. As Justice La Forest wrote for the majority of the Supreme Court of Canada in *R. v. Lyons*, "it is nowhere required that it be proved that the offender will act in a certain way. Indeed, inherent in the notion of dangerousness is the risk, not the certainty, of harm."[16]

Experts will similarly need to insure that areas explored in their assessment as well as their conclusions address other criteria of the legislative test; for example, "a pattern of repetitive behaviour," "a failure to restrain his or her behaviour" (section 753 (1)(a)(i)), or "or a pattern of persistent aggressive behaviour" (section 753(1)(a)(ii)), and "a substantial degree of indifference on the part of the offender" (section 753(1)(a)(ii)).

---

15   *R. v. Neve* (1999), 137 C.C.C. (3d) 97 (Alta. C.A.).
16   *R. v. Lyons* (1987), 37 C.C.C. (3d) 1 at 47 (S.C.C.).

2) Evaluations Carried Out at a Psychiatric Facility

Given what is at stake, Crown attorneys and defence counsel have generally gravitated to psychiatrists and psychologists with considerable expertise and experience in assessing risk for dangerousness. These clinicians are frequently, although not invariably, attached to university hospitals and/or forensic psychiatric facilities where multi-disciplinary teams, who generally possess greater expertise in this area, review, assess and then synthesize a detailed fund of information relevant to the task of assessing the offender's risk.

3) What a Court Will Want to Know

The court will want to know the following:

1) Does the accused constitute a threat to the life, safety or physical or mental well-being of other persons? (section 753(1)(a))
2) Is there a pattern of repetitive behaviour showing a failure to restrain his or her behaviour and a likelihood of causing death or injury to other persons, or inflicting severe psychological damage to other persons through failure to restrain his or her behaviour? (section 753(1)(a)(i))
3) Is there a pattern of aggressive behaviour showing a substantial degree of indifference respecting the reasonably foreseeable consequences of his or her behaviour? (section 753(1)(a)(ii))
4) Is there any behaviour that is of such a brutal nature as to compel the conclusion that the accused's behaviour is unlikely to be restrained by normal standards of behavioural restraint? (section 753(1)(a)(iii))
5) Has the accused shown a failure to control his or her sexual impulses and a likelihood of causing injury, pain or other evil to other persons through failure to control his or her sexual impulses? (section 753(1)(b))
6) Is there a substantial risk that the accused will reoffend? (section 753.1(1)(b))
7) Is there a reasonable possibility of eventual control of the risk posed in the community? (section 753.1(1)(c))

While the ultimate answer to these questions must be decided by the courts, it is at these junctures that the assessment will be of particular importance.

4) Twenty Points to Consider When Assessing Risk of Future Violence

Eaves *et al.*,[17] drawing on earlier work done by Webster *et al.*,[18] suggested twenty points that mental health experts should consider in their assessment of an accused's risk for future violence:

1. *Clarification of purpose.* Experts need to be fully conversant with the purpose and design of the relevant legislation.

2. *Adequate assessment circumstances must be sought out.* Evaluators require an environment as well as all the appropriate data in order to do their jobs properly.

3. *Assessor competence.* Apart from being well versed in psychiatric diagnosis, experts who engage in this kind of work must have specific training, expertise, and experience in violence risk assessment, and in the use and limitations of risk assessment tools.

4. *Acknowledgement of assessor bias.* As noted earlier in a detailed discussion of this issue (see Chapter 2, Sections B and H) it generally cannot be said that experts are without bias. The more appropriate reckoning of the issue is that every expert, like all people, has certain leanings. The issue is more whether the expert can hold his biases in check and prevent them from exerting any undue influence on the process of the assessment and its outcome. In certain instances, bias may preclude an assessor's involvement in a particular case (for example, if he has had therapeutic dealings with the subject of the assessment, or where an assessor and his family has been personally affected by the types of crimes or behaviours of which the accused has been accused of or convicted).

5. *Systematic analysis.* The serious nature of DO and LTO proceedings warrants a carefully considered approach to the pending assessment.

6. *Familiarity with files.* DO and LTO proceedings are often predicated on the availability of a well-researched and extensive fund of information about the offender's life, behaviours, psychopathology, etc. Experts will need to be very familiar with file data prior to getting into the clinical portion of the assessment.

---

17 D. Eaves, K.S. Douglas, C.D. Webster, J.R.P. Ogloff, & S.D. Hart, *Dangerous and Long Term Offenders: An Assessment Guide* (Burnaby, BC: The Mental Health, Law and Policy Institute. Simon Fraser University, 2000) at 5–16 (adapted below).

18 C.D. Webster, K.S. Douglas, D. Eaves, & S.D. Hart, *The HCR-20: Assessing the Risk for Violence*, Version 2 (Burnaby, BC: Mental Health, Law and Policy Institute, Simon Fraser University, 1997).

7. *Correctness of data.* File information invariably contains errors and inconsistencies, which, if undetected, could falsely skew actuarial and clinical measures in a direction that will misrepresent the offender's dangerousness.

8. *Actuarial emphasis.* Having regard to the literature, experts must concede the superior (that is, more accurate) nature of information gleaned from actuarial assessment (using actuarial risk assessment tools, such as the *Violence Risk Appraisal Guide*), compared to unstructured clinical assessment alone. What is particularly problematic here is clinical predictions and opinions which are not grounded in acceptable diagnostic procedures.

9. *Case-specific information.* Actuarial assessment alone, however, is insufficient. It should be complemented by a carefully carried out clinical evaluation that specifically enquires into the psychopathology and underpinnings of the offender's behaviour.

10. *Consideration of current symptomatology.* Diagnoses must be offered in a manner that clearly explains the current symptom profile, drawing on accepted diagnostic terminology, for example, the scheme contained in the DSM IV-TR,[19] or the International Classification of Diseases.[20]

11. *Situational emphasis.* As much as the offender is the central figure in the violent transaction that brings him or before the court, focus on his or her predisposition alone is often insufficient. A violent exchange is often, if not invariably, the result of several interactive variables, including the offender's predisposition, environmental variables, and a situational spark. It would be of great value, for the purposes of both defining and then managing the offender's risk, for the evaluator to elucidate the environmental conditions under which violence may or may not occur.

12. *Logic and relevance of information.* The risk factors the experts choose to consider in appraising an offender's dangerousness should be isolated as robust risk factors, that is, variables that have been empirically derived as having strong predictive value for the particular population to which that information is extrapolated. There may well be factors that are more

---

19   American Psychiatric Association, *Diagnostic and Statistical Manual of Mental Disorders*, 4th ed., Text Revision (Washington, DC: American Psychiatric Association, 2000) [DSM IV-TR].

20   World Health Organization, *ICD-10: International Statistical Classification of Diseases and Related Health Problems*, 10th revision (Geneva: World Health Organization, 1992) [ICD-10].

potent for particular populations, for example, mentally disordered of-fenders, personality disordered habitual criminals, etc.

13. *Consideration of risk management.* All evaluations of a subject's risk should be accompanied by meaningful risk reduction recommendations. It is ethically and professionally responsible for evaluators to provide recom-mendations that might remediate a risk factor, as opposed to just pointing it out and creating concern about it. That exercise also balances the role of mental health experts who participate in proceedings of this kind.

14. *Use of base rate statistics.* Behaviours that occur at a low to relatively low frequency are particularly difficult to predict. It is consequently impor-tant, wherever possible, to have as accurate an understanding of the fre-quency with which a particular behaviour occurs in the population (its base rate) as that determination has implications for making predictions. An understanding of the base rate of a number of offences has increased, in any event, in the last number of years as a result of scientific data de-rived from long-term follow up studies that have helped define types of subpopulations and types of risk.

15. *Predictions specificity.* The nature of the particular harm or harms contem-plated, which the assessment would have focused on, should be made impeccably clear during the course of the assessment and ultimately, in the report. A global appraisal of an individual's risk (without specifying the particular harm(s)) is no longer as acceptable as it was in the past.

16. *Justification of opinion.* No matter what method(s) is being employed in as-sessing the individual's risk, that is, an actuarial assessment, structured clinical assessment, or both, the expert should be prepared to justify rely-ing on the process that she employed.

17. *Use of second opinions.* There are many instances in which a second opin-ion, obtained from an experienced senior forensic clinician, would be of great value.

18. *Probabilistic reporting.* Experts provide their "predictions" in either actuarial (numeric) terms or probabilistic ones; for example, the accused is at "low," "moderate," or "high," risk for violence. None of these terms are used by the legislation. The test for maintaining jurisdiction over a mentally disordered accused under the review board's jurisdiction, for example, is whether he or she continues to represent "a significant threat" to the safety of the public. Under the long-term offender provisions a court must be satisfied, that "there is substantial risk that the offender will reoffend" amongst other factors. Some form of translation is required to make lan-guage from one domain or professional sphere meaningful to another.

19. *Relevant reporting.* Risk evaluations should pursue and then report information that is relevant to the task at hand. Experts should screen and limit superfluous information that could prove to be prejudicial.

20. *Use of outcome data.* Expert evaluators should be relying on published outcome data, on an ongoing basis, given the considerable flux and rapid expansion of knowledge in the field of violence risk assessment.

5) What a Final Assessment Report Should Include

The report in a typical dangerous offender or long-term offender assessment should include:[21]

Background of the referral: This section states where the referral came from, who initiated the assessment, and on what grounds.

Informed consent: This section would state that the offender had been fully and understandably informed as to the nature and purpose of this assessment. This section would also generally state that the offender has signed a statement indicating they have been informed of the purpose and nature of this assessment or a witnessed statement indicating the offender declined to give their consent to the assessment. When the offender is in a residential facility and the offender declines to be involved in the assessment, the assessment proceeds without consent. In cases where the offender declines to participate in the assessment process, the assessment is conducted primarily in form file review. In these cases observational information gained from front-line staff is even more important.

Demographics: This section would generally include the offender's date of birth, family information (or lack there of), marital status (including past marriages and involvements) vocational and schooling information and employment status at time of arrest.

List of tests used: This section of the report should list all psychological tests and assessments administered to the offender in the course of the assessment.

List of information provided: This section should list all papers and files reviewed by the assessor in preparation of the report. This is an essential check that the person giving an overall assessment of dangerousness has seen all relevant documentation.

---

21   *High Risk Offenders*, above note 2 at 144–46.

Review of the index offence: The index offence is the serious personal injury offence or set of defences that brought the offender for assessment; generally the set of offences for which the offender has just been found guilty. This section should compare and contrast the information received from the Crown, such as police incident reports and court transcripts, with the offender's verbal report of what happened.

Review of previous psychological/psychiatric assessments: Offenders who reach this level of intervention have usually been seen in the judicial or mental health system before. It is important to review previous reports to look for trends in psychological and behavioural functioning over time.

Standard behavioural observations: This section should include not only how the offender presented him/herself while in direct assessment by the principal assessor, but also staff reviews of the offender's behaviour as seen in the residential setting. The report of the principal assessor would review the presentation, attitude, and posture of the offender, their level of co-operation, and the rapport developed between the assessor and the offender during the assessment interview(s). Residential staff should be encouraged to comment upon how the offender interacts with their environment. This would include observations on any temperamental/ violent outbursts, how the offender interacted with staff and other residents and the degree to which this offender was a management concern while in remand. Emphasis should be placed upon the offender's ability to cope with her surroundings and the offender's problem resolution skills.

Test results: This section presents the results of the various tests used during the assessment. This section should include references to tests of cognitive ability and intelligence, a section devoted to tests of psychopathology, a personality assessment inventory, and tests of anxiety and depression, and tests of alcohol and drug use/dependency. This section would also include results of specific assessments of dangerousness, recidivism potential, and psychopathy.

Phallometric data: In cases where a sexual offence had been committed, phallometric testing may be useful. Phallometric testing assess the physiological response to pictures of sexual content or audiotaped descriptions of sexual activities. This test helps to determine the presence of sexual deviance, non-normative sexual attractions, and proclivities. It is important to remember that these tests, while helpful in outlining possible treatment targets, do not speak to the issue of guilt or innocence. Physiological sexual preference tests for female offenders are seldom used and remain at the experimental stage.

Clinical interview: A summary review of the interview is presented. This section deals more with impressions and opinions, as opposed to the section on behavioural observations. This would include a description of how the offender defines his or her problem and a description of what general areas of inquiry were covered during the clinical interview(s).

Summary and conclusions: This section should include prognostic statements concerning the offender and some direct statement concerning the offender's risk level. A statement about the offender's general psychological fitness, levels of sexual deviance, and the extent to which deviant behaviours appear to have been repeated or are persistent. This section should include a statement concerning the offender's attitude towards accepting treatment or willingness to participate in treatment. When the assessment is being used for a dangerous offender hearing, a statement should be included concerning the offender's potential for future dangerousness. When the assessment is being used for a long-term offender application, this section should include a statement giving an opinion on the possible eventual control of this offender in the community after a term of federal incarceration.

Potential treatment targets: Recommendations should be made considering needed treatment options for this offender. These might include sex offender treatment, social competencies training, or anger management.[22]

---

22   *R. v. A.N.*, [2002] O.T.C. 1032 at para. 249 (S.C.J):

Experts in dangerous offender proceedings must provide guidance to the Court on the likelihood of eventual control in the community. The experts must be conversant not only with actuarial studies and test methods to assess risk based upon a person's past, as well as the research literature, but must also be knowledgeable with respect to the practical aspects of risk management. This includes an understanding of the kind of programmes, treatment, and structure available in the correctional system, as well as the community.

Form 48: Assessment Order of the Court

This form is contained in the *Criminal Code*. It has been modified slightly in order to permit the administrator of the hospital to return the accused to court earlier than anticipated if the assessment is complete prior to the return date on the information.

When an accused is to be returned to court earlier than anticipated, the administrator issues a letter which authorizes the wagon to pick up the accused and take the accused to court. The administrator contacts the court clerk at court room 102, who adds the information to the list. Duty counsel will notify counsel if the accused has retained counsel or, alternatively, take instructions.

FORM 48
(Section 672.13)
ASSESSMENT ORDER OF THE COURT

Canada,
Province of
(*territorial division*)

Whereas I have reasonable grounds to believe that evidence of the mental condition of (name of accused), who has been charged with _____, may be necessary to determine*

- ☐ whether the accused is unfit to stand trial
- ☐ whether the accused suffered from a mental disorder so as to exempt the accused from criminal responsibility by virtue of subsection 16(1) of the *Criminal Code* at the time of the act or omission charged against the accused
- ☐ whether the balance of the mind of the accused was disturbed at the time of commission of the alleged offence, if the accused is a female person charged with an offence arising out of the death of her newly-born child
- ☐ if a verdict of unfit to stand trial or a verdict of not criminally responsible on account of mental disorder has been rendered in respect of the accused, the appropriate disposition to be made in respect of the accused pursuant to section 672.54 or 672.58 of the *Criminal Code*
- ☐ if a verdict of unfit to stand trial has been rendered in respect of the accused, whether the court should order a stay of proceedings under section 672.851 of the *Criminal Code*

I hereby order an assessment of the mental condition of (name of accused) to be conducted by/at (name of person or service by whom or place where assessment is to be made) for a period of ____ days.

This order is to be in force for a total of ____ days, including travelling time, during which time the accused is to remain*

- ☐ in custody at (*place where accused is to be detained*)
- ☐ out of custody, on the following conditions: (*set out conditions, if applicable*)

* Check applicable option.

Dated this _____ day of _____ A.D. _____, at _____ .

_____

(Signature of justice or judge or clerk of the court, as the case may be)

Form 48.1: Assessment Order of the Review Board

This form is contained in the *Criminal Code*. It appeared for the first time with the proclamation of Bill C-10. It may be used by the Review Board to order the assessment of the accused pursuant to the provisions of section 672.121 of the *Criminal Code*.

FORM 48.1
(Section 672.13)
ASSESSMENT ORDER OF THE REVIEW BOARD

Canada,
Province of
(*territorial division*)

Whereas I have reasonable grounds to believe that evidence of the mental condition of (*name of accused*), who has been charged with _____, may be necessary to*

- ☐ if a verdict of unfit to stand trial or a verdict of not criminally responsible on account of mental disorder has been rendered in respect of the accused, make a disposition under section 672.54 of the *Criminal Code*
- ☐ if a verdict of unfit to stand trial has been rendered in respect of the accused, determine whether the Review Board should make a recommendation to the court that has jurisdiction in respect of the offence charged against the accused to hold an inquiry to determine whether a stay of proceedings should be ordered in accordance with section 672.851 of the *Criminal Code*

I hereby order an assessment of the mental condition of (*name of accused*) to be conducted by/at (*name of person or service by whom or place where assessment is to be made*) for a period of _____ days.

This order is to be in force for a total of _____ days, including travelling time, during which time the accused is to remain*

- ☐ in custody at (*place where accused is to be detained*)
- ☐ out of custody, on the following conditions: (*set out conditions, if applicable*)

* Check applicable option.

Dated this _____ day of _____ A.D. ____ , at _____ .

_____
(Signature of Chairperson of the Review Board)

Treatment Order (Section 672.58)

This form is not contained in the *Criminal Code*. The following form is a creation of one of this book's authors, Richard Schneider. It is a modified version of a form produced the the Ontario Ministry of the Attorney General. It has been modified slightly in order to permit the administrator of the hospital to return the accused to court earlier than anticipated if the treatment has been successful, and the accused rendered fit, prior to the return date on the information.

When an accused is to be returned to court earlier than anticipated, the administrator issues a letter which authorizes the delivery of the accused back to court. The administrator contacts the court clerk at court room 102, who adds the information to the list. Duty counsel will notify counsel if the accused has retained counsel or, alternatively, take instructions.

TREATMENT ORDER
Ontario Court of Justice

CANADA   *Section 672.58*
PROVINCE OF ONTARIO
Toronto
(Region)

WHEREAS (hereinafter referred to as the "Accused") (*name of accused*) has been charged with the following offence(s) (*charges*)

AND WHEREAS the accused was found unfit to stand trial on (*today's date*) by (*name of Judge or Justice*)

AND WHEREAS the prosecutor has applied for a treatment order pursuant to section 672.58 of the *Criminal Code*

AND WHEREAS the Court is satisfied on the basis of testimony of a medical practitioner that:

i)   a specified treatment should be administered to the accused for the purpose of making the accused fit to stand trial within a period not to exceed 60 days;

ii) without the treatment the accused is likely to remain unfit to stand trial;

iii) the risk of harm to the accused from the treatment is not disproportionate to the benefit anticipated to be derived; and

iv) the treatment is the least restrictive and least intrusive that could be provided for the purpose.

AND WHEREAS the following person or persons have given their consent as required by s. 672.62:

☐   _____ the person in charge of the hospital where the accused is to be treated or

☐   _____ the person to whom responsibility for the treatment of the accused has been assigned by the court.

I HEREBY DIRECT the treatment of the accused is to be conducted by/at (*Name of person or service by whom or place where treatment is to be administered*) for a period of _____ days (*Not to exceed 60 days*)

I HEREBY DIRECT that the specific treatment to be administered to the accused be as follows:

I HEREBY DIRECT that during the time of the treatment the accused is to remain: (Check applicable option)

☐   in custody at _____ and shall return to 102 court (*place where accused to be detained*) on _____ at _____ or such earlier date specified by the Administrator of the hospital. (*return date*) (*time*)

☐   out of custody, on the following conditions: (*set out conditions, where applicable*)

Dated at the *City of Toronto* this _____ (today's date)

_____Signature of Judge or Justice as the case may be

"Keep Fit" Order (Section 672.29)

This form is not contained in the *Criminal Code*. It is the creation of one of this book's authors, Richard Schneider. It covers the provisions of section 672.29 of the *Criminal Code*, which allow for an accused who obtains a verdict of "fit to stand trial" to be hospitalized until the completion of his trial in order to preserve fitness. It is to be used to preserve fitness *only after the issue has been tried.*

CANADA   *Section 672.29*
PROVINCE OF ONTARIO
Toronto
(Region)

WARRANT OF COMMITTAL
Detention of Accused in Hospital Until Completion of Trial (672.29)

To the peace officers in the said region, and to the keeper (administrator, warden) of the _____ (prison, hospital or other appropriate place where the accused is currently detained)

This warrant is issued for the committal of: (hereinafter called the accused) (*accused name*)

Whereas the accused has been charged that (set out briefly the offence in respect of which the accused was charged)

And whereas the accused, upon a trial of the issue, has been found *FIT TO STAND TRIAL* and there are reasonable grounds to believe that the accused would become unfit to stand trial if released.

It is therefore Ordered, pursuant to the provisions of section 672.29 of the *Criminal Code of Canada*, that you, _____in her Majesty's name, take the accused in custody and convey the accused safely to the _____ (hospital) and there deliver the accused to the Administrator with the following precept:

I do therefore command you the said Administrator to receive the accused In your custody in the said hospital and to keep the accused safely there until the completion of the accused's trial or such earlier time as may be Ordered.

Dated at the _City of Toronto_ this _____ (today's date)

_____
Signature of Judge or Justice as the case may be

Hospital Pending Review Board
(Section 672.46(2))

This form is not contained in the *Criminal Code*. It is the creation of one of this book's authors, Richard Schneider. The following form covers the provisions of subsection 672.46(2) of the *Criminal Code*, which permit the court to place an accused, upon the verdict of either unfit or NCR, in hospital pending the accused's hearing before the Ontario Review Board, rather returning the accused to jail.

CANADA   *Section 672.46(2)*
PROVINCE OF ONTARIO
Toronto
(Region)

WARRANT OF COMMITTAL

Detention of Accused in Hospital Pending Disposition of the Ontario Review Board (672.46(2))

To the peace officers in the said region, and to the keeper (administrator, warden) of the (*prison, hospital or other appropriate place where the accused is currently detained*)

This warrant is issued for the committal of: (hereinafter called the accused) (*accused name*)

Whereas the accused has been charged that (*set out briefly the offence in respect of which the accused was charged*)

And whereas the accused, upon a trial of the issue, has been found

> *Check One*
>
> ☐   UNFIT TO STAND TRIAL
> ☐   NOT CRIMINALLY RESPONSIBLE ON ACCOUNT OF MENTAL DISORDER,
>
>   and a Disposition has not been held pursuant to the provisions of sections 672.54,

It is therefore Ordered, pursuant to the provisions of section 672.46(2) of the *Criminal Code of Canada*, that you, in her Majesty's name, take the accused in custody and convey the accused safely to the (*hospital*) and there deliver the accused to the Administrator with the following precept:

I do therefore command you the said Administrator to receive the accused in your custody in the said hospital and to keep the accused safely there until a hearing has been held by the Ontario Review Board and a Disposition made.

Dated at the *City of Toronto* this _____ (today's date)

_____
Signature of Judge or Justice as the case may be

Disposition: Detention in Hospital (Section 672.54(c))

FORM 49

This form is contained in the *Criminal Code*. It is used where the court makes a disposition (for either an unfit or an NCR) pursuant to the provisions of section 672.54(c). This form, along with a "New Accused Information Sheet" filled out by the Crown, is sent to the Review Board within forty-eight hours. Note that any disposition of the court (other than section 672.54(a)) is reviewed by the Review Board within ninety days.

FORM 49
(Section 672.57)
WARRANT OF COMMITTAL
DISPOSITION OF DETENTION

Canada,
Province of
(*territorial division*)

To the peace officers in the said (*territorial division*) and to the keeper (*administrator, warden*) of the (*prison, hospital or other appropriate place where the accused is detained*).

This warrant is issued for the committal of A.B., of _____, (*occupation*), hereinafter called the accused.

Whereas the accused has been charged that (*set out briefly the offence in respect of which the accused was charged*);

And whereas the accused was found*

- □ unfit to stand trial
- □ not criminally responsible on account of mental disorder

This is, therefore, to command you, in Her Majesty's name, to take the accused in custody and convey the accused safely to the (*prison, hospital or other appropriate place*) at _____, and there deliver the accused to the keeper (*administrator, warden*) with the following precept:

I do therefore command you the said keeper (*administrator, warden*) to receive the accused in your custody in the said (*prison, hospital or other appropriate place*) and to keep the accused safely there until the accused is delivered by due course of law.

The following are the conditions to which the accused shall be subject while in your (*prison, hospital or other appropriate place*):

The following are the powers regarding the restrictions (*and the limits and conditions on those restrictions*) on the liberty of the accused that are hereby delegated to you the said keeper (*administrator, warden*) of the said (*prison, hospital or other appropriate place*):

* Check applicable option.

Dated this _____ day of _____ A.D. _____, at _____ .

_____

(Signature of judge, clerk of the court, provincial court judge or chairperson of the Review Board)

Disposition: Discharge Subject to Conditions (Section 672.54(b))

DISPOSITION

This form is not contained in the *Criminal Code*. It is the creation of one of this book's authors, Richard Schneider. Parliament did not include a form for the making of a disposition where the disposition is not a custodial one. Where the accused is to be discharged absolutely (section 672.54(a)), no form is required; however, where the accused is to be discharged subject to conditions (section 672.54(b)), the following form may be used to record the disposition.

CANADA   *Section 672.54 (b)*
PROVINCE OF ONTARIO
Toronto
(Region)

DISPOSITION
Accused Out of Custody

WHEREAS (hereinafter referred to as the "Accused") (*name of accused*) has been
charged with (*set out briefly the offence in respect of which the accused was charged*)

And whereas the accused, upon a trial of the issue, has been found

Check One

☐ UNFIT TO STAND TRIAL
☐ NOT CRIMINALLY RESPONSIBLE ON ACCOUNT OF MENTAL DISORDER,

and a hearing has taken place pursuant to the provisions of section 672.47(1) of the
Criminal Code of Canada and it has been determined that the least onerous and least
restrictive Disposition is that the accused be discharged subject to conditions, it is
Ordered that: [*list terms of Discharge*]

THIS IS THEREFORE TO COMMAND you, _____, in Her Maj-
esty's name, to comply with the terms of this Disposition and, upon Notice, to appear
before the Ontario Review Board as directed.

Dated at the City of Toronto this _____ (today's date)

_____
Signature of Judge or Justice as the case may be

Hospital Assessment: Out of Custody

FORM 6: ASSESSMENT BY A HOSPITAL OF AN ACCUSED WHO IS OUT OF CUSTODY*

This form reflects the provisions of subsection 21(1) of the *Mental Health Act* of Ontario. These provisions allow for the assessment of an accused who appears before the court out of custody. Note that a precondition to the making of the order is the consent of the prospective assessing facility.

---

*   *Mental Health Act*, R.R.O. 1990, Reg. 741, Form 6.

Ministry of Health
Form 6

Mental Health Act

ORDER FOR ATTENDANCE FOR EXAMINATION

Subsection 21(1) of the Act

In the (*name of court*) held at (*address*)

TO (*name of psychiatric facility*)

WHEREAS (*name of person in full*) (*addresss*)

Strike out inapplicable words	☐ is charged with	
	☐ has been convicted of	(*offence*)

AND WHEREAS he/she has appeared before me and I have reason to believe that he/she suffers from mental disorder;

AND WHEREAS I have ascertained from (*name of senior physician, as defined in the Act*) the senior physician of (*name of psychiatric facility*) that the services of the said psychiatric facility are available to the above-named person;

I HEREBY ORDER that the above-named person attend, by appointment, the said psychiatric facility for examination;

_____ (Judge)

Date _____ (day / month / year)

Hospital Assessment: In Custody

FORM 8: ASSESSMENT BY A HOSPITAL OF AN ACCUSED WHO IS IN CUSTODY*

This form reflects the provisions of subsection 22(1) of the *Mental Health Act* of Ontario. These provisions allow for the assessment of an accused who appears before the court in custody. Note that a precondition to the making of the order is the consent of the prospective assessing facility.

---

*   *Mental Health Act*, R.R.O. 1990, Reg. 741, Form 8.

Ministry of Health
Form 8   *Mental Health Act*

ORDER FOR ADMISSION

Subsection 22(1) of the Act

In the (*name of court*) held at (*address*)

TO the Peace Officers in the _____ of _____

AND TO (*name of psychiatric facility*)

WHEREAS (*name of person in full*) (*address*) is a person charged with (*offence*) contrary to section _____ of the _____;

AND WHEREAS he/she has appeared before me and I have reason to believe that he/she suffers from mental disorder;

AND WHEREAS I have ascertained from (*name of senior physician, as defined in the Act*) the senior physician of (*name of psychiatric facility*) that the services of the said psychiatric facility are available to the above-named person;

I HEREBY ORDER that the above-named shall be remanded for admission as a patient to the said psychiatric facility for a period of not more than _____;

AND I FURTHER ORDER and direct you, the said Peace Officers, or any of you, to convey him/her to said psychiatric facility;

AND I AUTHORIZE you, the authorities of said psychiatric facility, to admit him/her in accordance with this order.

_____ (Judge)

Date _____ (day / month / year)

Bibliography

ABEL, G.G. *et al.*, "Multiple Paraphilic Diagnoses among Sex Offenders" (1988) 16 Bulletin of American Academy of Psychiatry and Law 153

ABEL, G.G. *et al.*, *The Treatment of Child Molesters* (B.M.L., Emory University, 1984)

AMERICAN PSYCHIATRIC ASSOCIATION, *Diagnostic and Statistical Manual of Mental Disorders*, 3d ed., Revised (Washington, DC: American Psychiatric Association, 1987)

AMERICAN PSYCHIATRIC ASSOCIATION, *Diagnostic and Statistical Manual of Mental Disorders*, 4th ed., Text Revision, (Washington, DC: American Psychiatric Association, 2000)

ANDREWS, L.B. & J.L. BONTA, *The Level of Service Inventory — Revised* (Toronto: Multi-Health Systems, Inc., 1998)

APPELBAUM, K.L., "Criminal Defendants Who Desire Punishment" (1990) 18 Bulletin of the American Academy of Psychiatry and the Law 385

ASHFORD, J.B. *et al.*, eds., *Treating Adult and Juvenile Offenders with Special Needs* (Washington, DC.: American Psychological Association, 2001)

AUGIMERI, L. *et al.*, *The Early Assessment of Risk List for Boys (EARL-20B)*, Version 2 (Toronto: Earlscourt Child and Family Centre, 2001)

BACH-Y-RITA, G. *et al.*, "Pathological Intoxication: Clinical and Electroencephalographic Studies" (1970) 127 American Journal of Psychiatry 698

BARBAREE, H.E. & D.M. GREENBERG, "Overview of Sex Offenders and the Paraphilias" in H. Bloom, R.D., Schneider, & S.J. Hucker, eds., *Handbook of Psychiatry and the Law* (Toronto: Centre for Addiction and Mental Health and Irwin Law, forthcoming)

BECK, A.T. & R.A. STEER, *Beck Anxiety Inventory* (San Antonio: PsychCorp, 1993)

BECK, A.T. *et al.*, *Beck Depression Inventory-II* (San Antonio: PsychCorp, 1996)

BLOOM, H.& M. BAY, eds., *A Practical Guide to Mental Health, Capacity, and Consent Law of Ontario* (Toronto: Carswell, 1996)

BLOOM, H. & B.T. BUTLER, *Defending Mentally Disordered Persons* (Toronto: Carswell, 1995)

Bloom, H. et al., *Workplace Risk Assessment (WRA-20)*, Version 1a (Toronto: workplace.calm, inc., 2002)

Bloom, H. & C.D. Webster, "Assessing Imminent Risk" in H. Bloom, R.D. Schneider, & S.J. Hucker, eds., *Handbook of Psychiatry and the Law* (Toronto: Centre for Addiction and Mental Health and Irwin Law, forthcoming)

Bloom, H. et al., *The Employee Risk Assessment (ERA-20)* (Toronto: workplace.calm, inc., 2002)

Bloom, H. et al., "The Canadian Contribution to Violence Risk Assessment: History and Implications for Current Psychiatric Practice" (2005) 50 Canadian Journal of Psychiatry 3

Boer, H.S. et al., *Sexual Violence Risk-20* (Vancouver: Mental Health, Law, and Policy Institute, Simon Fraser University, 1997)

Bonta, J. et al., *The Crown File Research Project: A Study of Dangerous Offenders* (Ottawa: Solicitor General of Canada, 1996)

Borum, R. et al., *A Manual for the Structured Assessment of Violence Risk in Youth, Version 1.1.* (Tampa, FL: University of South Florida, 2002)

Bradford, J.M.W. et al., "The Paraphilias: A Multiplicity of Deviant Behaviours" (1992) 37 Canadian Journal of Psychiatry 104

Bradford, J.M.W. et al., *The Bradford Sexual History Inventory* (unpublished research questionnaire, 1992)

Burt, M.R., Albin, R.S., "Rape Myths, Rape Definitions and Pprobability of Conviction" (1981) 11 Journal of Applied Social Psychology 212

Buss, A.H. & H. Durkee, "An Inventory for Assessing Different Kinds of Hostility" (1957) 21 Journal of Consulting & Clinical Psychology 343

Buss, A.H. & M. Perry, "The Aggression Questionnaire" (1992) 63 Journal of Personality and Social Psychology 452

Butcher, J.N. et al., *Minnesota Multiphasic Personality Inventory-2* (Minneapolis: University of Minnesota Press, 1989)

Clare, I.C. & G.H. Gudjonsson, "Interrogative Suggestibility in People with Mild Learning Disabilities (Mental Handicap): Implications for Reliability during Police Interrogations" (1993) 32 British Journal of Clinical Psychology 295

Curry, S., et al., *The Fantasy Checklist* (unpublished research questionnaire, 1992)

Daniel, A.E. et al., "Factors Correlated with Psychiatric Recommendations of Incompetency and Insanity" (1984) 12 Journal of Psychiatry and Law 527

Derogatis, L., *Derogatis Sexual Functioning Inventory* (Baltimore: Clinical Psychometric Research, 1975)

Douglas, K.S. et al., eds., *HCR-20 Violence Risk Management Companion Guide* (Burnaby, BC: Mental Health, Law, and Policy Institute, Simon Fraser University, 2001)

Douglas, K.S. et al., "Evaluation of a Model of Violence Risk Assessment among Forensic Psychiatric Patients" (2003) 54 Psychiatric Services 1372

DOUGLAS, K.S. & J.L. SKEEM, "Violence Risk Assessment: Getting Specific about Being Dynamic" (2005) 11 Psychology, Public Policy, and Law 347

EAVES, D. *et al.*, *Dangerous and Long Term Offenders: An Assessment Guide* (Burnaby, BC: Mental Health, Law, and Policy Institute, Simon Fraser University, 2000)

EXNER, J.E., *The Rorschach: A Comprehensive System*, 2d ed., vol. 1 (New York: Wiley, 1986)

FINE, E., Alcohol Intoxication: Psychiatric, Psychological, Forensic Issues (Balboa Island, CA: ACFP Press, 1996)

FIRST, M.B. *et al.*, *Structured Clinical Interview for DSM IV Axis I Personality Disorders* (Washington, DC: American Psychiatric Publishing, Inc., 1997)

FIRST, M.B. *et al.*, *Structured Clinical Interview for DSM IV Axis II Personality Disorders* (Washington, DC: American Psychiatric Publishing, Inc., 1997)

FOA, E.B. *et al.*, "Reliability and Validity of a Brief Instrument Assessing Post-Traumatic Stress Disorder" (1993) 4 Journal of Traumatic Stress 459

FOA, E.B., *Post-Traumatic Stress Diagnostic Scale* (Bloomington, MN: Pearson Assessments, 1995)

FREEDMAN, M.I. *et al.*, *Clock Drawing: A Neuropsychological Analysis* (Oxford: Oxford University Press, 1994)

FREUND, K. & R. BLANCHARD, "The Concept of Courtship Disorder" (1986) 12 Journal of Sex and Marital Therapy 79

FREUND, K. *et al.*, "The Courtship Disorders" (1983) 12 Archives of Sexual Behavior 369

FREUND, K. & R.J. WATSON, "Mapping the Boundaries of Courtship Disorder" (1990) 27 Journal of Sex Research 589

FREUND, K. & R.J. WATSON, "Assessment of the Sensitivity and Specificity of a Phallometric Test: An Update of Phallometric Diagnosis of Pedophilia" (1991) 3 Psychological Assessment: A Journal of Consulting and Clinical Psychology 254

FREUND, K. *et al.*, "Signs of Feigning in the Phallometric Test" (1988) 26 Behaviour Research & Therapy 105

GOLD, A.D., "Effective Expert Evidence," presented at "Where Law and Science Meet," 46th Annual Conference of the Canadian Society of Forensic Science, Edmonton, AB, 18 November 1999

GOLD, A.D., *Expert Evidence in Criminal Law: The Scientific Approach* (Toronto: Irwin Law, 2003)

GUDJONSSON, G.H., *Gudjonsson Suggestibility Scales Manual* (Hove, UK: Psychology Press, 1997)

HALL, J., *Personal Reaction Index* (Waco, TX: Teleometrics International, 1971)

HALL, H.V. & R.S. EBERT, *Violence Prediction: Guidelines for the Forensic Practitioner*, 2d ed. (Springfield, IL: Charles C. Thomas Publisher, Ltd., 2002)

Hanson, R.K. & M. Bussiere, *Predictors of Sexual Recidivism: A Meta-Analysis* (Ottawa: Solicitor General of Canada, 1996)

Hanson, R.K., *Development of a Brief Actuarial Risk Scale for Sexual Offence Recidivism* (User Report No. 1997-04) (Ottawa: Department of the Solicitor General of Canada, Public Works and Government Services Canada, 1997)

Hanson, R.K. & D. Thornton, *Notes on the Development of Static-2002* (User Report No. 2003-01) (Ottawa: Department of the Solicitor General of Canada, Public Works and Government Services Canada, 2002)

Hanson, R.K., *The Validity of Static-99 with Older Sexual Offenders* (Report No. 2005-01) (Ottawa: Minister of Public Safety and Emergency Preparedness of Canada, 2005)

Hare, R.D., *The Hare Psychopathy Checklist — Revised* (Toronto: Multi-Health Systems Inc., 1991)

Harris G.T. *et al.*, "Psychopathy and Violent Recidivism" (1991) 15 Law and Human Behaviour 625

Hart, S.D., "Complexity, Uncertainty, and the Reconceptualization of Violence Risk Assessment" (forthcoming)

Hart, S.D. *et al.*, *The Risk for Sexual Violence Protocol* (Burnaby, BC: Mental Health, Law, and Policy Institute, Simon Fraser University, 2003)

Hart, S.D. *et al.*, *The Hare Psychopathy Checklist: Screening Version* (Toronto: Multi-Health Systems Inc., 1995)

Heaton, R.K. *et al.*, *Wisconsin Card Sorting Test* (Lutz, FL: Psychological Assessment Resouces, Inc., 1993)

Heller, M.S. *et al.*, "Intelligence, Psychosis and Competency to Stand Trial" (1981) 9 Bulletin of the American Academy of Psychiatry and the Law 267

Hooper, H.E., *Hooper Visual Organization Test* (Los Angeles: Western Psychological Services, 1983)

Hucker, S., "The Current State of Knowledge of Sexual Anomalies and Their Treatment" in J.M. Cleghorn, ed., *Understanding and Treating Mental Illness: The Strengths and Limits of Modern Psychiatry* (Toronto: Hans Huber, 1991)

Hucker, S., *Psychiatric Aspects of Risk Assessment* (1993), online: www.forensicpsychiatry.ca

Hühner, M., *Disorders of The Sexual Function in the Male and Female* (Philadelphia: F.A. Davis Company Publishers, 1922)

Keiter, M., "Just Say No Excuse: The Rise and Fall of the Intoxication Defense" (1997) 87 Journal of Criminal Law and Criminology 482

Knight, R.A. & R.A. Prentky, "Classifying Sexual Offenders: The Development on Corroboration of Taxonomic Models" in W.L. Marshall, D.R. Laws, & H.E. Barbaree, eds., *Handbook of Sexual Assault: Issues, Theories, and Treatment of the Offenders* (New York, Plenum Press, 1990)

KOREN, G. & I. NULMAN, *The Motherisk Guide to Diagnosing Fetal Alcohol Spectrum Disorder* (Toronto: The Hospital for Sick Children, 1992)

KOZOL, H.L. *et al.*, "The Diagnosis and Treatment of Dangerousness" (1972) 18 Crime and Delinquency 371

KRAFFT-EBING, R.V., *Psychopathia Sexualis* (1886), 12th ed. (New York: Rebman Company, 1912)

KROPP, P.R. *et al.*, *Manual for the Spousal Assault Assessment Guide* (Toronto: Multi-Health Systems, Inc., 1999)

KROPP, P.R. & S.D. HART, "The Spousal Assault Risk Assessment Guide: Reliability and Validity in Adult Male Offenders" (2000) 24 Law and Human Behavior 101

KROPP, P.R. *et al.*, *Spousal Assault Risk Assessment Guide*, 3d ed. (Toronto: Multi-Health Systems, 2003)

LANGEVIN, R., *Sexual Preference Testing: A Brief Guide* (Toronto: Juniper Press, 1989)

LÅNGSTRÖM, N. & K.J. ZUCKER, "Transvestic Fetishism in the General Population: Prudence and Correlates" (2005) 31 Journal of Sex and Marital Therapy 87

LAWS, D.R., "Penile Plethysmography: Will We Ever Get it Right?" in T. Ward, D.R. Laws, & S.M. Hudson, eds., *Sexual Deviance: Issues and Controversies* (Thousand Oaks, CA: Sage Publications, 2003)

LEVENE, K.S. *et al.*, *The Early Assessment Risk List for Girls (EARL-21G), Version 1, Consultation Edition* (Toronto: Earlscourt Child and Family Centre, 2001)

LINK, B.G. & A. STUEVE, "Psychotic Symptoms and the Violent Illegal Behaviour of Mental Patients Compared to Community Controls" in J. Monahan & H. Steadman, eds., *Violence and Mental Disorder* (Chicago, IL: University of Chicago Press, 1994)

MALETZKY, B.M., "The Diagnosis of Pathological Intoxication" (1976) 37 Journal of Studies on Alcohol 1215

MARKWARDT, JR., F.C., *Peabody Individual Achievement Test — Revised* (Circle Pines, MN: AGS Publishing, 1998)

MILLER, R.D. & E.J. GERMAIN, "Evaluation of Competency to Stand Trial in Defendants Who Do Not Want to be Defended against the Crime Charged" (1987) 15 Bulletin of American Academy of Psychiatry and Law 371

MILLON, T. *et al.*, *Millon Clinical Multiaxial Inventory-III* (Bloomington, MN: National Computer Systems, 1994)

MONEY, J., *Lovemaps* (New York: Irvington Publishers, Inc., 1986)

MONAHAN, J., *Predicting Violent Behaviour: An Assessment of Clinical Techniques* (Beverly Hills, CA: Sage Publications, 1981)

MONAHAN, J., "Foreword" in C.D. Webster & M.A. Jackson, eds., *Impulsivity: Theory, Assessment, and Treatment* (New York, NY: Guilford Press, 1997)

MONAHAN, J. & H.J. STEADMAN, eds., *Violence and Mental Disorder: Developments in Risk Assessment* (Chicago, IL: University of Chicago Press, 1994)

MONAHAN, J. et al., *Rethinking Risk Assessment: The MacArthur Study of Mental Disorder and Violence* (Oxford; NY: Oxford University Press, 2001)

MOREY, L.C., *Personality Assessment Inventory* (Lutz, FL: Psychological Assessment Resouces, Inc., 1991)

MOSS, H.P. & R.E. TARTER, "Substance Abuse, Aggression, and Violence" (1993) 2 American Journal on Addictions 149

MOSSMAN, D., "Understanding Prediction Instruments" in R.I. Simon & L.H. Gold, eds., *Textbook of Forensic Psychiatry* (Washington, DC: American Psychiatric Publishing, Inc., 2004)

MURPHY, W.D. & H.E. BARBAREE, *Assessment of Sex Offenders by Measures of Erectile Response: Psychometric Properties and Decision Making* (Brandon, VT: Safer Society Press, 1994)

MURPHY, W.D. & J.M. PETERS, "Profiling Child Sexual Abusers: Psychological Considerations" (1992) 19 Criminal Justice and Behavior 24

NESTOR, P.G., "Mental Disorder and Violence: Personality Dimensions and Clinical Features" (2002) 159 American Journal of Psychiatry 1973

NICHOLS, H.R. & I. MOLINDER, *The Multiphasic Sex Inventory Manual* (Tacoma, WA: Nichols & Molinder, 1984)

NOVACO, R.W., *The Novaco Anger Scale and Provocation Inventory* (Los Angeles: Western Psychological Services, 2003)

OGLOFF, J.R.P. & K.E. WHITTEMORE, "Fitness to Stand Trial and Criminal Responsibility in Canada" in R.A. Schuller & J.R.P. Ogloff, eds., *Introduction to Psychology and Law: Canadian Perspectives* (Toronto: University of Toronto Press, 2001) 283

PAITICH, D. et al., "The Clarke SHQ: A Clinical Sex History Questionnaire for Males" (1977) 6 Archives of Sexual Behavior 421

PAULHUS, D.L., "Two-Component Models of Socially Desirable Responding" (1984) 46 Journal of Personality and Social Psychology 598

PERNANEN, K. et al., *Proportion of Crimes Associated with Alcohol and Other Drugs in Canada* (Ottawa: Canadian Centre on Substance Abuse, 2002)

PRICE, M. et al., "Telephone Scatalogia: Comorbidity with Other Paraphilias and Paraphilia-Related Disorders" (2002) 25 International Journal of Law and Psychiatry 37

QUINSEY, V.L. et al., *Violent Offenders: Appraising and Managing Risk* (Washington, DC: American Psychological Association, 1998)

ROESCH, R. et al., "Evaluating Fitness to Stand Trial: A Comparative Analysis of Fit and Unfit Defendants" (1981) 4 International Journal of Law and Psychiatry 145

ROESCH, R. & S.L. GOLDING, *Competency to Stand Trial* (Urbana: University of Illinois Press, 1980)

ROGERS, R. *et al.*, *Structured Interview of Reported Symptoms* (Lutz, FL: Psychological Assessment Resources, Inc., 1992)

SCHNEIDER, R.D. & H. BLOOM, "*R. v. Taylor*: A Decision Not in the Best Interests of Some Mentally Ill Accused" (1985) 38 Criminal Law Quarterly 183

SCHNEIDER, R.D., *Fitness to be Sentenced* (1998) 41 Criminal Law Quarterly 261

SCHNEIDER, R.D., "Sentencing Mentally Ill Offenders" in J.V. Roberts & D.P. Cole, eds., *Making Sense of Sentencing* (Toronto: University of Toronto Press, 1999)

SCHNEIDER, R.D., *Statistical Survey of Provincial and Territorial Review Board* (Ottawa: Department of Justice, 2000)

SELZER, M.L., "The Michigan Alcoholism Screening Test: The Quest for a New Diagnostic Instrument" (1971) 127 American Journal of Psychiatry 1653

SELZER, M.L. *et al.*, "A Self Administered Short Michigan Alcoholism Screening Test: A Review" (1975) 36 Journal of Studies on Alcohol 117

SETO M.C. *et al.*, "Child Pornographic Offenses are a Valid Diagnostic Indicator of Pedophilia" Journal of Abnormal Psychology (forthcoming)

SETO M.C. & A.W. ELKE, "The Criminal Histories and Later Offending of Child Pornography Offenders" (2005) 17 Sexual Abuse: A Journal of Research and Treatment 201

SHAH, S., "Dangerousness: A Paradigm for Exploring Some Issues in Law and Psychology" (1978) 33 American Psychologist 224

SHIPLEY, W.C. & R.A. ZACHARY, *Shipley Institute of Living Scale: Revised Manual* (Los Angeles: Western Psychological Services, 1988)

SIMON, W.T. & P.G.W. SCHOUTEN, "Plethysmography in the Assessment and Treatment of Sexual Deviance: An Overview" (1991) 20 Archives of Sexual Behavior 75

SKINNER, H.A., *Drug Abuse Screening Test* (Toronto: Centre for Addiction and Mental Health, 1982)

SKINNER, H.A. & J.L. HORN, *Alcohol Dependence Scale* (Toronto: Centre for Addiction and Mental Health, 1984)

SOLICITOR GENERAL OF CANADA, *High Risk Offenders: A Handbook for Criminal Justice Professionals* (Ottawa: Solicitor General of Canada, 2001)

SPIELBERGER, C.D., *State-Trait Anger Expression Inventory-2* (Lutz, FL: Psychological Assessment Resources, Inc., 1999)

STARK, C. *et al.*, (2004). "Newspaper Coverage of a Violent Assault by a Mentally Ill Person" (2004) 11 Journal of Psychiatric and Mental Health Nursing 635

STEADMAN, H.J. *et al.*, "Violence by People Discharged from Acute Psychiatric Inpatient Facilities and by Others in the Same Neighbourhoods" (1998) 55 Archives of General Psychiatry 393

STEIN D.J. *et al.*, "Hypersexual Disorder and Preoccupation with Internet Pornography" (2001) 158 American Journal of Psychiatry 1590

SWANSON, J.W. *et al.*, "Violence and Psychiatric Disorder in the Community: Evidence from the Epidemiological Catchment Area Surveys" (1990) 41 Hospital and Community Psychiatry 761

SWARTZ, M. *et al.*, "Violence and Severe Mental Illness: The Effects of Substance Abuse and Non-Adherence to Medication" (1998) 155 American Journal of Psychiatry 226

TARDIFF, K. *et al.*, "A Prospective Study of Violence by Psychiatric Patients after Hospital Discharge" (1997) 48 Psychiatric Services 678

TAYLOR, P.J. *et al.*, "Mental Disorder and Violence: A Special (High Security) Hospital Study" (1998) 172 British Journal of Psychiatry 218

TIFFANY, L.P. & M. TIFFANY, "Nosologic Objections to the Criminal Defense of Pathological Intoxication: What do the Doubters Doubt?" (1990) 13 International Journal of Law and Psychiatry 49

TOMBAUGH, T.N., *Test of Memory Malingering* (Toronto: Multi-Health Systems, 1996)

TULLY, B. & D. CAHILL, *Police Interviewing of the Mentally Handicapped: An Experimental Study* (London, UK: The Police Foundation, 1984)

WEBSTER, C.D., "Assessing Violence Risk in Mentally and Personality Disorder Individuals" in C.R. Hollin, ed., *The Essential Handbook of Offender Assessment and Treatment* (Toronto: John Wiley and Sons Ltd., 2004)

WEBSTER, C.D. & C. DASSINGER, "The Systematic Assessment of Risk for Aggressive and Violent Behaviour against Others" in H. Bloom, R.D. Schneider, & S.J. Hucker, eds., *Handbook of Psychiatry and the Law* (Toronto: Centre for Addiction and Mental Health and Irwin Law, forthcoming)

WEBSTER, C.D. *et al.*, *The HCR-20: Assessing the Risk for Violence Version 2* (Burnaby, BC: Mental Health, Law, and Policy Institute, Simon Fraser University, 1997)

WEBSTER, C.D. *et al.*, *The HCR-20 Scheme: The Assessment of Dangerousness and Risk* (Vancouver: Simon Fraser University and Forensic Psychiatric Services Commission of British Columbia, 1995)

WEBSTER, C.D. *et al.*, *The Violence Prediction Scheme: Assessing Dangerousness in High Risk Men* (Toronto: Centre of Criminology, 1994)

WEBSTER, C.D. *et al.*, *Clinical Assessment before Trial: Legal Issues and Mental Disorder* (Toronto: Butterworths, 1982)

WEBSTER, C.D. & S.J. HUCKER, *Release Decision Making* (Hamilton: Forensic Service, St. Joseph's Healthcare Hamilton, 2003)

WEBSTER, C.D. *et al.*, "Transcending the Actuarial versus Clinical Polemic in Assessing Risk for Violence" (2002) 29 Criminal Justice and Behavior 659

WECHSLER, D., *Wechsler Adult Intelligence Scale — Revised* (San Antonio, TX: PsychCorp., 1981)

WECHSLER, D., *Wechsler Intelligence Scale for Children — Revised*, 3d ed. (San Antonio, TX: PsychCorp., 1991)

WECHSLER, D., *Wechsler Memory Scale III* (San Antonio, TX: PsychCorp., 1997)

WHURR, R., *Aphasia Screening Test*, 2d ed. (London: Whurr Publishing, 1996)

WILKINSON, G.S., *Wide Range Achievement Test 3* (Wilmington, DE: Wide Range, Inc., 1993)

ZONANA, H. et al., Dangerous Sexual Offenders: A Task Force Report of the American Psychiatric Association (Washington, DC: America Psychiatric Association, 1999)

ZUSMAN, M.D. *et al.*, "Differences in Repeated Psychiatric Examinations of Litigants to a Lawsuit" (1983) 140 American Journal of Psychiatry 1300

Table of Cases

Index

About the Authors

Hy Bloom, LL.B., M.D., F.R.C.P.(C.) is a forensic psychiatrist and lawyer who assesses individuals who have mental illnesses and outstanding criminal charges. He is an Associate of the Central Branch of the PSILEX Group, Consultants in Behavioural Sciences and the Law. He is also a part-time staff member of the Law and Mental Health Program at the Clarke Branch of the Centre for Addiction and Mental Health, an Assistant Professor in the Department of Medicine at the University of Toronto, and an Assistant Clinical Professor in the Department of Psychiatry and Behavioural Neurosciences at McMaster University. Dr. Bloom is both an Alternate Chairperson and psychiatric member of the Ontario Review Board. He was called to the Bar of Ontario in 1980. He has published on a number of topics in psychiatry and the law.

Hon. Richard D. Schneider, Ph.D. LL.M., C.Psych. is a justice of the Ontario Court of Justice, where he presides at Toronto's Mental Health Court, and Alternate Chair of the Ontario and Nunavut Review Boards. He is also an Assistant Professor in the Department of Psychiatry, Faculty of Medicine, at the University of Toronto, and an Adjunct Lecturer in the Faculty of Law, University of Toronto. Prior to his appointment to the bench, Justice Schneider was a criminal defence lawyer, a clinical psychologist, and counsel to the Ontario Review Board. He was recently appointed Honorary President of the Canadian Psychological Association. He has published extensively in the area of mental disorder and the law.